# The Simple Ninja Dual Zone Air Fryer Cookbook

## 500 Quick and Delicious Recipes with

## 5 Ingredients to Air Fry, Dehydrate, Roast, and More for Beginners and Advanced Users

Carla Hollman

# CONTENTS

## Chapter 5. Beef,pork & Lamb Recipes....................53

## Chapter 6. Fish And Seafood Recipes.....................67

## Chapter 7. Vegetarians Recipes.................................................80

# Chapter 8. Vegetable Side Dishes Recipes......91

# Chapter 9. Desserts And Sweets......104

# Introduction

The Ninja Foodi Dual Zone Air Fryer has revolutionized kitchen technology to the point where users can now enjoy fresh, crispy food in no time. It's a dual-zone air fryer that combines six culinary functions: Air Broil, Air Fry, Roast, Bake, Dehydrate, and Reheat into one device. This equipment is ideal for those who enjoy baking and cooking crispy foods. The air fryer comes with two fryer baskets labelled "1" and "2," which should be inserted into their corresponding parts.

The Ninja Foodi Dual Zone Air Fryer is an advanced and multifunctional air fryer from the Ninja Foodi family. The beautiful dark grey stainless steel air fryer comes with an 8-quart cooking capacity, which is enough for the whole family. The cooking basket comes with non-stick ceramic coatings and long handles for easy hold. Ninja Foodi invented this unique air fryer with two separate cooking baskets to work both the cooking zones independently.

The Ninja Foodi Dual Zone Air Fryer works on dual-zone technology. It allows you to cook multiple dishes at the same time in two different cooking baskets. It also allows you to customize the time and temperature for both cooking zones as per your need. The cooking zones have their separate temperature controller unit and cyclonic fan to distribute heat evenly into the cooking basket. The smart finish feature ensures that both zones complete their cooking at the same time. The Ninja Foodi Dual Zone Air Fryer cooks your favourite fried food using 75 to 80% less fat and oil than the traditional method. It makes your food crispy without changing the taste and texture.

The Ninja Foodi Dual Zone Air Fryer comes with 6 customizable program settings. These functions include air fry, air broil, roast, bake, reheat and dehydrate. The air fryer works on 1690 watt power to cook your food rapidly. It allows you to cook your main meal with a side meal simultaneously between a temperature range of 105 °F to 450 °F. The air fryer comes with a non-stick interior for effortless cleaning.

This cookbook first introduces the features and functions of this revolutionary appliance, helping you unleash its full potential. Apart from that, this cookbook contains healthy and delicious recipes with 5 ingredients from different categories like appetizers and snacks, bread and breakfast, poultry recipes, beef, pork & lamb recipes, fish and seafood recipes, vegetarians recipes, vegetable side dishes, and desserts and sweets recipes. The recipes written in this cookbook start with their cooking time, followed by step-by-step instructions. I hope you love and enjoy all the Ninja Foodi Dual Zone Air Fryer recipes written in this cookbook.

# Chapter 1. Prepare for Your Ninja Foodi Dual Zone Air Fryer Journey

## What the Ninja Foodi Dual Zone Air Fryer is

The Ninja Foodi Dual Zone Air Fryer is the next revolutionary appliance coming from the awesome folks working at Ninja Kitchen! No matter how unbelievable the concept might sound, Ninja Kitchen has put on countless hours of engineering into crafting this meticulously designed appliance that takes the Air Frying game to a whole different level.

At its heart, the Ninja Foodi Dual Zone Air Fryer is a simple and exceedingly effective Air Fryer that gives you all the basic functions that you would expect from an Air Fryer. With this appliance, you can Air Frye, Bake, Broil, Dehydrate, Air Crisp, and more! You know, the usual Air Fryer stuffs.

However, what makes this unique is the super cool "Dual Zone" technology that completely flips the game in the Air Frying market.

If you are looking to cut down your cooking to half, or you want to make two different meals at the same time. The same appliance, then the Ninja Foodi Dual Zone Air Fryer is exactly what you need!

Simply put, the Dual Zone technology allows the appliance to be put on either single cook mode or multi cook mode. Single cook mode works as usual; you cook using just a single basket. However, with the Dual Cook mode, you can seamlessly set the different timer, mode, and temperature for both of the zones individually and cook the meals you require. Alternatively, you may give the same settings to both of the zones and cook the same meal in a doubled portion without spending any more time than you would need when making just a single portion.

While handling two Air Fryer baskets might sound a little bit complicated at first, the way how Ninja Kitchen has engineered this appliance has made it extremely accessible and easy to handle.

## The Smart Features of the Ninja Foodi Dual Zone Air Fryers

The Ninja Foodi Dual Zone Air Fryer is one of the innovative product designs manufactured. If you are looking for a perfect air fryer for your family, then the Ninja Foodi Dual Zone Air Fryer is one of the best options available for you. Some of the important features of the Ninja Foodi Dual Zone Air Fryer are mentioned as follows.

1.    **Large Capacity**

The Ninja Foodi Dual Zone Air Fryer has a total of 8-qt capacity, which is divided into two 4-qt cooking zones-Zone 1 and Zone 2. The number of the zone is given on the crisper plate so you could easily detect them. Each zone has a portion in the display, and it shows their respective settings. You can use the respective keys to set the time and temperature for each zone.

2.    **Multifunctional Air Fryer**

The Ninja Foodi Dual Zone Air Fryer comes with 6 preset functions. These easily customizable functions include max crisp, air fry, roast, bake, reheat and dehydrate. You never need to buy separate appliances for a single cooking function.

3.    **Smart Finish Technology**

The smart finish function can help you cook different things in each cooking zone at different temperatures and times. When you press the SYNC button, you can sync the cook times for both zones to finish at the same time. These functions will allow both of the cooking zones to complete their cooking simultaneously, even if both of the zones have completely different cook settings.

4.    **Match Cook**

This feature allows you to cook meals in both of drawers at the same temperature and for the same time duration. If you want to cook a large amount of the same food, or you want to cook two different foods at the same time, you can then use the MATCH button. Select the cooking mode, temperature, and time for Zone 1. Then press the MATCH button to copy these settings for zone 2. Now both zones will have the same settings. After pressing the START/STOP button, they will start cooking the food in their respective chambers.

# The Functions and Buttons of the Ninja Foodi Dual Zone Air Fryers

The Ninja Foodi Dual Zone Air Fryer comes with 6 in 1 cooking functions and different operating buttons which are mentioned as follows.

**Functions**

1.    **Max Crisp:** This function is ideal for frozen food like chicken nuggets and French fries. Using this function, you can add extra crispiness and crunch into your food.

2.    **Air Fry:** This function allows you to air fry your favourite food using minimal fats and oil compared with the traditional cooking method. Air frying makes your food crunchy, crisper from the outside and juicy tender from the inside. Using the air fry function, you can air fry your favourite food without changing the taste and texture of deep-fried food.

3. **Roast:** Using this function, you can convert your air fryer into a roaster oven which helps to tender your favourite meat, vegetables and more. It is one of the dry cooking methods that gives a nice brown texture to the food and enhances the flavor of your food.

4. **Reheat:** This function is ideal for reheating your leftover food. It makes your food warm and also makes it crispier as it was yesterday.

5. **Dehydrate:** This function is used to reduce the moisture content of food and is ideal for dehydrating your favourite vegetables, fruits, and meat slices. Using this method can also preserve your favourite food for a long time.

6. **Bake:** This function converts your air fryer into a convection oven. It is ideal for baking your favourite cakes, cookies, and desserts.

**Operation Buttons**

1. **Time Arrow Buttons:** Using up and down arrow keys, you can easily adjust the time settings as per your recipe needs.

2. **Temp Arrow Buttons:** Using up and down arrow keys, you can easily change the temperature settings as per your recipe needs.

3. **Sync Button:** This function is used to sync the cooking time automatically and ensures that both the cooking zones finish their cooking simultaneously, even if there is a difference between their cooking times.

4. **Match Button:** This function is used to match the cooking zone 2 settings with cooking zone 1 setting on a large quantity of the same food or different food cooking at the same function, temperature, and time.

5. **Start/Stop Button:** Use this button to start the cooking process after selecting the time and temperature settings as per your recipe needs.

6. **Standby Mode:** This equipment goes into standby mode when it is powered on but not in use for more than 10 minutes.

7. **Hold Mode:** When the time setting for both zones doesn't match but you want both zones to finish cooking at the same time, the zone with the lesser time will be on hold but when the time becomes equal the hold mode will disappear and the zone on hold will start cooking. This will also show during SYNC mode if the other zone takes too long to synchronize with the rest of the zone.

# Maintaining and Cleaning the Appliance

The interior parts of the Ninja Foodi Dual Zone Air Fryer are made of non-stick coating, so you can easily clean it. Here is how to clean and maintain your Ninja Foodi Dual Zone Air Fryer after cooking:

1.       Unplug your appliance before cleaning it and allow it to cool completely.

2.       Remove the air fryer baskets from the unit and let them cool.

3.       When cooled, remove their crispier plates and wash them in the dishwasher.

4.       Clean the baskets with soapy water and but don't use hard scrubbing; otherwise, it will damage the surface.

5.       Wipe the main unit with a clean piece of cloth or damp cloth.

6.       When all parts of the air fryer dried, return to the unit.

7.       Now, you can use it again for cooking

## Hearty Tips for Using the Appliance

Since this is a relatively new appliance to hit the market, people are still beginning to grasp this amazing appliance's full potential. They are exploring how to properly use this product. The following tips will greatly enhance your cooking experience with this appliance and make everything a breeze.

1.       It's always suggested that you collect all of the ingredients you require before starting your cooking session. If you are unable to find a specific ingredient, then make sure to find an alternative beforehand. The recipes in this book already have the best ingredients chosen to provide the best flavor. Still, since different people have different taste buds, you might consider altering a few if you feel like it.

2.       Make sure to read the recipes thoroughly before you start cooking; if you find any step confusing, then do a simple google search to properly understand the steps.

3.       Before starting your cooking session, make sure that your appliance to clean and free from any dirt or debris. Follow the steps provided in the section above if you are confused about how to do it.

4.       The air fryer location is extremely important if you want your meals to cook evenly since it relies heavily on the airflow. Therefore, make sure to keep it in a space where it has enough space to "Breath" in Air and cook the meals properly.

5.       If you are using frozen food, you should consider thawing them before putting them in your air fryer basket.

6.       Since the air fryer relies on Superheated Air to do the cooking, make sure to never overcrowd the cooking baskets. Always keep space in between heavy ingredients. Now that you have two zones to work with, this shouldn't be a problem at all!

7.       When cooking with the air fryer, it is always advised that you opt for organic ingredients. Try to find the freshest ones possible as they will give you the best flavors.

8.       When choosing a baking tray for your air fryer, try to go for lighter color trays/dishes. Dark colors such as black ones would absorb more heat that might result in uneven cooking.

It's about time that you give this appliance a try and do some cooking!

# Chapter 2. Appetizers And Snacks

## Bacon Butter

Servings:5
Cooking Time: 2 Minutes
**Ingredients:**
- ½ cup butter
- 3 oz bacon, chopped

**Directions:**
1. Preheat the air fryer to 400°F and put the bacon inside. Cook it for 8 minutes. Stir the bacon every 2 minutes. Meanwhile, soften the butter in the oven and put it in the butter mold. Add cooked bacon and churn the butter. Refrigerate the butter for 30 minutes.

## Cheddar Cheese Lumpia Rolls

Servings: 5
Cooking Time: 20 Minutes
**Ingredients:**
- 5 ounces mature cheddar cheese, cut into 15 sticks
- 15 pieces spring roll lumpia wrappers
- 2 tablespoons sesame oil

**Directions:**
1. Wrap the cheese sticks in the lumpia wrappers. Transfer to the Air Fryer basket. Brush with sesame oil.
2. Bake in the preheated Air Fryer at 395°F for 10 minutes or until the lumpia wrappers turn golden brown. Work in batches.
3. Shake the Air Fryer basket occasionally to ensure even cooking. Bon appétit!

## Cauliflower Buns

Servings:8
Cooking Time: 12 Minutes
**Ingredients:**
- 1 steamer bag cauliflower, cooked according to package instructions
- ½ cup shredded mozzarella cheese
- ¼ cup shredded mild Cheddar cheese
- ¼ cup blanched finely ground almond flour
- 1 large egg
- ½ teaspoon salt

**Directions:**
1. Let cooked cauliflower cool about 10 minutes. Use a kitchen towel to wring out excess moisture, then place cauliflower in a food processor.
2. Add mozzarella, Cheddar, flour, egg, and salt to the food processor and pulse twenty times until mixture is combined. It will resemble a soft, wet dough.
3. Divide mixture into eight piles. Wet your hands with water to prevent sticking, then press each pile into a flat bun shape, about ½" thick.

4. Cut a sheet of parchment to fit air fryer basket. Working in batches if needed, place the formed dough onto ungreased parchment in air fryer basket. Adjust the temperature to 350°F and set the timer for 12 minutes, turning buns halfway through cooking.
5. Let buns cool 10 minutes before serving. Serve warm.

## Skinny Fries

Servings: 2
Cooking Time: 15 Minutes
**Ingredients:**
- 2 to 3 russet potatoes, peeled and cut into ¼-inch sticks
- 2 to 3 teaspoons olive or vegetable oil
- salt

**Directions:**
1. Cut the potatoes into ¼-inch strips. Rinse the potatoes with cold water several times and let them soak in cold water for at least 10 minutes or as long as overnight.
2. Preheat the air fryer to 380°F.
3. Drain and dry the potato sticks really well, using a clean kitchen towel. Toss the fries with the oil in a bowl and then air-fry the fries in two batches at 380°F for 15 minutes, shaking the basket a couple of times while they cook.
4. Add the first batch of French fries back into the air fryer basket with the finishing batch and let everything warm through for a few minutes. As soon as the fries are done, season them with salt and transfer to a plate or basket. Serve them warm with ketchup or your favorite dip.

## Mozzarella Sticks

Servings: 4
Cooking Time: 5 Minutes
**Ingredients:**
- 1 egg
- 1 tablespoon water
- 8 eggroll wraps
- 8 mozzarella string cheese "sticks"
- sauce for dipping

**Directions:**
1. Beat together egg and water in a small bowl.
2. Lay out egg roll wraps and moisten edges with egg wash.
3. Place one piece of string cheese on each wrap near one end.
4. Fold in sides of egg roll wrap over ends of cheese, and then roll up.
5. Brush outside of wrap with egg wash and press gently to seal well.
6. Place in air fryer basket in single layer and cook 390°F for 5 minutes. Cook an additional 1 or 2minutes, if necessary, until they are golden brown and crispy.
7. Serve with your favorite dipping sauce.

# Tomato & Garlic Roasted Potatoes

Servings: 4
Cooking Time: 25 Minutes
**Ingredients:**

- 16 cherry tomatoes, halved
- 6 red potatoes, cubed
- 3 garlic cloves, minced
- Salt and pepper to taste
- 1 tsp chopped chives
- 1 tbsp extra-virgin olive oil

**Directions:**
1. Preheat air fryer to 370°F. Combine cherry potatoes, garlic, salt, pepper, chives and olive oil in a resealable plastic bag. Seal and shake the bag. Put the potatoes in the greased frying basket and Roast for 10 minutes. Shake the basket, place the cherry tomatoes in, and cook for 10 more minutes. Allow to cool slightly and serve.

# Cheese Rounds

Servings:4
Cooking Time: 6 Minutes
**Ingredients:**

- 1 cup Cheddar cheese, shredded

**Directions:**
1. Preheat the air fryer to 400°F. Then line the air fryer basket with baking paper. Sprinkle the cheese on the baking paper in the shape of small rounds. Cook them for 6 minutes or until the cheese is melted and starts to be crispy.

# Crunchy Tortellini Bites

Servings: 5
Cooking Time: 10 Minutes
**Ingredients:**

- 10 ounces Cheese tortellini
- ⅓ cup Yellow cornmeal
- ⅓ cup Seasoned Italian-style dried bread crumbs
- ⅓ cup Finely grated Parmesan cheese
- 1 Large egg
- Olive oil spray

**Directions:**
1. Bring a large pot of water to a boil over high heat. Add the tortellini and cook for 3 minutes. Drain in a colander set in the sink, then spread out the tortellini on a large baking sheet and cool for 15 minutes.
2. Preheat the air fryer to 400°F.
3. Mix the cornmeal, bread crumbs, and cheese in a large zip-closed plastic bag.
4. Whisk the egg in a medium bowl until uniform. Add the tortellini and toss well to coat, even along the inside curve of the pasta. Use a slotted spoon or kitchen tongs to transfer 5 or 6 tortellini to the plastic bag, seal, and shake gently to coat thoroughly and evenly. Set the coated tortellini aside on a cutting board and continue coating the rest in the same way.

5. Generously coat the tortellini on all sides with the olive oil spray, then set them in one layer in the basket. Air-fry undisturbed for 10 minutes, gently tossing the basket and rearranging the tortellini at the 4- and 7-minute marks, until brown and crisp.
6. Pour the contents of the basket onto a wire rack. Cool for 5 minutes before serving.

# Tortilla Chips

Servings: 4
Cooking Time: 5 Minutes
**Ingredients:**

- 8 white corn tortillas
- ¼ cup olive oil
- 2 tablespoons lime juice
- ½ teaspoon salt

**Directions:**
1. Preheat the air fryer to 350°F.
2. Cut each tortilla into fourths and brush lightly with oil.
3. Place chips in a single layer in the air fryer basket, working in batches as necessary. Cook 5 minutes, shaking the basket halfway through cooking time.
4. Sprinkle with lime juice and salt. Serve warm.

# Garlic Parmesan Kale Chips

Servings: 2
Cooking Time: 6 Minutes
**Ingredients:**

- 16 large kale leaves, washed and thick stems removed
- 1 tablespoon avocado oil
- ½ teaspoon garlic powder
- 1 teaspoon soy sauce or tamari
- ¼ cup grated Parmesan cheese

**Directions:**
1. Preheat the air fryer to 370°F.
2. Make a stack of kale leaves and cut them into 4 pieces.
3. Place the kale pieces into a large bowl. Drizzle the avocado oil onto the kale and rub to coat. Add the garlic powder, soy sauce or tamari, and cheese, tossing to coat.
4. Pour the chips into the air fryer basket and cook for 3 minutes, shake the basket, and cook another 3 minutes, checking for crispness every minute. When done cooking, pour the kale chips onto paper towels and cool at least 5 minutes before serving.

# Homemade French Fries

Servings: 2
Cooking Time: 25 Minutes
**Ingredients:**

- 2 to 3 russet potatoes, peeled and cut into ½-inch sticks
- 2 to 3 teaspoons olive or vegetable oil
- salt

**Directions:**
1. Bring a large saucepan of salted water to a boil on the stovetop while you peel and cut the potatoes. Blanch the

potatoes in the boiling salted water for 4 minutes while you Preheat the air fryer to 400°F. Strain the potatoes and rinse them with cold water. Dry them well with a clean kitchen towel.

2. Toss the dried potato sticks gently with the oil and place them in the air fryer basket. Air-fry for 25 minutes, shaking the basket a few times while the fries cook to help them brown evenly. Season the fries with salt mid-way through cooking and serve them warm with tomato ketchup, Sriracha mayonnaise or a mix of lemon zest, Parmesan cheese and parsley.

## Easy Crispy Prawns

Servings:4
Cooking Time:10 Minutes
**Ingredients:**
- 1 egg
- ½ pound nacho chips, crushed
- 18 prawns, peeled and deveined
- Salt and black pepper, to taste

**Directions:**
1. Preheat the Air fryer to 355°F and grease an Air fryer basket.
2. Crack egg in a shallow dish and beat well.
3. Place the crushed nacho chips in another shallow dish.
4. Coat prawns into egg and then roll into nacho chips.
5. Place the coated prawns into the Air fryer basket and cook for about 10 minutes.
6. Dish out and serve warm.

## Thick-crust Pepperoni Pizza

Servings: 2
Cooking Time: 10 Minutes
**Ingredients:**
- 10 ounces Purchased fresh pizza dough (not a prebaked crust)
- Olive oil spray
- ¼ cup Purchased pizza sauce
- 10 slices Sliced pepperoni
- ⅓ cup Purchased shredded Italian 3- or 4-cheese blend

**Directions:**
1. Preheat the air fryer to 400°F.
2. Generously coat the inside of a 6-inch round cake pan for a small air fryer, a 7-inch round cake pan for a medium air fryer, or an 8-inch round cake pan for a large model with olive oil spray.
3. Set the dough in the pan and press it to fill the bottom in an even, thick layer. Spread the sauce over the dough, then top with the pepperoni and cheese.
4. When the machine is at temperature, set the pan in the basket and air-fry undisturbed for 10 minutes, or until puffed, brown, and bubbling.
5. Use kitchen tongs to transfer the cake pan to a wire rack. Cool for only a minute or so. Use a spatula to loosen the pizza from the pan and lift it out and onto the rack. Continue

cooling for a few minutes before cutting into wedges to serve.

## Basil Pork Bites

Servings: 6
Cooking Time: 25 Minutes
**Ingredients:**
- 2 pounds pork belly, cut into strips
- 2 tablespoons olive oil
- 2 teaspoons fennel seeds
- A pinch of salt and black pepper
- A pinch of basil, dried

**Directions:**
1. In a bowl, mix all the ingredients, toss and put the pork strips in your air fryer's basket and cook at 425°F for 25 minutes. Divide into bowls and serve as a snack.

## Air Fry Bacon

Servings:11
Cooking Time: 10 Minutes
**Ingredients:**
- 11 bacon slices

**Directions:**
1. Place half bacon slices in air fryer basket.
2. Cook at 400°F for 10 minutes.
3. Cook remaining half bacon slices using same steps.
4. Serve and enjoy.

## Mini Greek Meatballs

Servings:36
Cooking Time: 10 Minutes
**Ingredients:**
- 1 cup fresh spinach leaves
- ¼ cup peeled and diced red onion
- ½ cup crumbled feta cheese
- 1 pound 85/15 ground turkey
- ½ teaspoon salt
- ½ teaspoon ground cumin
- ¼ teaspoon ground black pepper

**Directions:**
1. Place spinach, onion, and feta in a food processor, and pulse ten times until spinach is chopped. Scoop into a large bowl.
2. Add turkey to bowl and sprinkle with salt, cumin, and pepper. Mix until fully combined. Roll mixture into thirty-six meatballs.
3. Place meatballs into ungreased air fryer basket, working in batches if needed. Adjust the temperature to 350°F and set the timer for 10 minutes, shaking basket twice during cooking. Meatballs will be browned and have an internal temperature of at least 165°F when done. Serve warm.

# Roasted Chickpeas

Servings: 1
Cooking Time: 15 Minutes
**Ingredients:**
- 1 15-ounce can chickpeas, drained
- 2 teaspoons curry powder
- ¼ teaspoon salt
- 1 tablespoon olive oil

**Directions:**
1. Drain chickpeas thoroughly and spread in a single layer on paper towels. Cover with another paper towel and press gently to remove extra moisture. Don't press too hard or you'll crush the chickpeas.
2. Mix curry powder and salt together.
3. Place chickpeas in a medium bowl and sprinkle with seasonings. Stir well to coat.
4. Add olive oil and stir again to distribute oil.
5. Cook at 390°F for 15 minutes, stopping to shake basket about halfway through cooking time.
6. Cool completely and store in airtight container.

# Grilled Cheese Sandwich Deluxe

Servings: 4
Cooking Time: 6 Minutes
**Ingredients:**
- 8 ounces Brie
- 8 slices oat nut bread
- 1 large ripe pear, cored and cut into ½-inch-thick slices
- 2 tablespoons butter, melted

**Directions:**
1. Spread a quarter of the Brie on each of four slices of bread.
2. Top Brie with thick slices of pear, then the remaining 4 slices of bread.
3. Lightly brush both sides of each sandwich with melted butter.
4. Cooking 2 at a time, place sandwiches in air fryer basket and cook at 360°F for 6 minutes or until cheese melts and outside looks golden brown.

# Sugar-glazed Walnuts

Servings: 6
Cooking Time: 5 Minutes
**Ingredients:**
- 1 Large egg white(s)
- 2 tablespoons Granulated white sugar
- ⅛ teaspoon Table salt
- 2 cups Walnut halves

**Directions:**
1. Preheat the air fryer to 400°F.
2. Use a whisk to beat the egg white(s) in a large bowl until quite foamy, more so than just well combined but certainly not yet a meringue.

3. If you're working with the quantities for a small batch, remove half of the foamy egg white.
4. If you're working with the quantities for a large batch, remove a quarter of it. It's fine to eyeball the amounts.
5. You can store the removed egg white in a sealed container to save for another use.
6. Stir in the sugar and salt. Add the walnut halves and toss to coat evenly and well, including the nuts' crevasses.
7. When the machine is at temperature, use a slotted spoon to transfer the walnut halves to the basket, taking care not to dislodge any coating. Gently spread the nuts into as close to one layer as you can. Air-fry undisturbed for 2 minutes.
8. Break up any clumps, toss the walnuts gently but well, and air-fry for 3 minutes more, tossing after 1 minute, then every 30 seconds thereafter, until the nuts are browned in spots and very aromatic. Watch carefully so they don't burn.
9. Gently dump the nuts onto a lipped baking sheet and spread them into one layer. Cool for at least 10 minutes before serving, separating any that stick together. The walnuts can be stored in a sealed container at room temperature for up to 5 days.

# Green Olive And Mushroom Tapenade

Servings: 1
Cooking Time: 10 Minutes
**Ingredients:**
- ¾ pound Brown or Baby Bella mushrooms, sliced
- 1½ cups (about ½ pound) Pitted green olives
- 3 tablespoons Olive oil
- 1½ tablespoons Fresh oregano leaves, loosely packed
- ¼ teaspoon Ground black pepper

**Directions:**
1. Preheat the air fryer to 400°F.
2. When the machine is at temperature, arrange the mushroom slices in as close to an even layer as possible in the basket. They will overlap and even stack on top of each other.
3. Air-fry for 10 minutes, tossing the basket and rearranging the mushrooms every 2 minutes, until shriveled but with still-noticeable moisture.
4. Pour the mushrooms into a food processor. Add the olives, olive oil, oregano leaves, and pepper. Cover and process until grainy, not too much, just not fully smooth for better texture, stopping the machine at least once to scrape down the inside of the canister. Scrape the tapenade into a bowl and serve warm, or cover and refrigerate for up to 4 days.

# Garlic–cream Cheese Wontons

Servings: 4
Cooking Time: 8 Minutes
**Ingredients:**
- 6 ounces full-fat cream cheese, softened
- 1 teaspoon garlic powder
- 12 wonton wrappers
- ¼ cup water

**Directions:**
1. Preheat the air fryer to 375°F.
2. In a medium bowl, mix cream cheese and garlic powder until smooth.
3. For each wonton, place 1 tablespoon cream cheese mixture in center of a wonton wrapper.
4. Brush edges of wonton with water to help it seal. Fold wonton to form a triangle. Spritz both sides with cooking spray. Repeat with remaining wontons and cream cheese mixture.
5. Place wontons in the air fryer basket. Cook 8 minutes, turning halfway through cooking time, until golden brown and crispy. Serve warm.

# Sweet Potato Chips

Servings: 4
Cooking Time: 10 Minutes
**Ingredients:**
- 2 medium sweet potatoes, washed
- 2 cups filtered water
- 1 tablespoon avocado oil
- 2 teaspoons brown sugar
- ½ teaspoon salt

**Directions:**
1. Using a mandolin, slice the potatoes into ⅛-inch pieces.
2. Add the water to a large bowl. Place the potatoes in the bowl, and soak for at least 30 minutes.
3. Preheat the air fryer to 350°F.
4. Drain the water and pat the chips dry with a paper towel or kitchen cloth. Toss the chips with the avocado oil, brown sugar, and salt. Liberally spray the air fryer basket with olive oil mist.
5. Set the chips inside the air fryer, separating them so they're not on top of each other. Cook for 5 minutes, shake the basket, and cook another 5 minutes, or until browned.
6. Remove and let cool a few minutes prior to serving. Repeat until all the chips are cooked.

# Eggplant Fries

Servings: 18
Cooking Time: 10 Minutes
**Ingredients:**
- ¾ cup All-purpose flour or tapioca flour
- 1 Large egg(s), well beaten
- 1 cup Seasoned Italian-style dried bread crumbs (gluten-free, if a concern)
- 3 tablespoons (about ½ ounce) Finely grated Asiago or Parmesan cheese
- 3 Peeled ½-inch-thick eggplant slices
- Olive oil spray

**Directions:**
1. Preheat the air fryer to 375°F.
2. Set up and fill three shallow soup plates or small pie plates on your counter: one for the flour, one for the egg(s), and one for the bread crumbs mixed with the cheese until well combined.
3. Cut each eggplant slice into six ½-inch-wide strips or sticks. Dip one strip in the flour, coating it well on all sides. Gently shake off the excess flour, then dip the strip in the beaten egg(s) to coat it without losing the flour. Let any excess egg slip back into the rest, then roll the strip in the bread-crumb mixture to coat evenly on all sides, even the ends. Set the strips aside on a cutting board and continue dipping and coating the remaining strips as you did the first one.
4. Generously coat the strips with olive oil spray on all sides. Set them in the basket in one layer and air-fry undisturbed for 10 minutes, or until golden brown and crisp. If the machine is at 390°F, the strips may be done in 8 minutes.
5. Remove the basket from the machine and cool for a couple of minutes. Then use kitchen tongs to transfer the eggplant fries to a wire rack to cool for only a minute or two more before serving.

# Bacon-wrapped Mozzarella Sticks

Servings:6
Cooking Time: 12 Minutes
**Ingredients:**
- 6 sticks mozzarella string cheese
- 6 slices sugar-free bacon

**Directions:**
1. Place mozzarella sticks on a medium plate, cover, and place into freezer 1 hour until frozen solid.
2. Wrap each mozzarella stick in 1 piece of bacon and secure with a toothpick. Place into ungreased air fryer basket. Adjust the temperature to 400°F and set the timer for 12 minutes, turning sticks once during cooking. Bacon will be crispy when done. Serve warm.

# Roasted Peanuts

Servings:10
Cooking Time: 14 Minutes
**Ingredients:**
- 2½ cups raw peanuts
- 1 tablespoon olive oil
- Salt, as required

**Directions:**
1. Set the temperature of Air Fryer to 320°F.
2. Add the peanuts in an Air Fryer basket in a single layer.
3. Air Fry for about 9 minutes, tossing twice.

4. Remove the peanuts from Air Fryer basket and transfer into a bowl.
5. Add the oil, and salt and toss to coat well.
6. Return the nuts mixture into Air Fryer basket.
7. Air Fry for about 5 minutes.
8. Once done, transfer the hot nuts in a glass or steel bowl and serve.

# Greek Street Tacos

Servings: 8
Cooking Time: 3 Minutes
**Ingredients:**
- 8 small flour tortillas
- 8 tablespoons hummus
- 4 tablespoons crumbled feta cheese
- 4 tablespoons chopped kalamata or other olives (optional)
- olive oil for misting

**Directions:**
1. Place 1 tablespoon of hummus or tapenade in the center of each tortilla. Top with 1 teaspoon of feta crumbles and 1 teaspoon of chopped olives, if using.
2. Using your finger or a small spoon, moisten the edges of the tortilla all around with water.
3. Fold tortilla over to make a half-moon shape. Press center gently. Then press the edges firmly to seal in the filling.
4. Mist both sides with olive oil.
5. Place in air fryer basket very close but try not to overlap.
6. Cook at 390°F for 3minutes, just until lightly browned and crispy.

# Cinnamon Pita Chips

Servings: 4
Cooking Time: 6 Minutes
**Ingredients:**
- 2 tablespoons sugar
- 2 teaspoons cinnamon
- 2 whole 6-inch pitas, whole grain or white
- oil for misting or cooking spray

**Directions:**
1. Mix sugar and cinnamon together.
2. Cut each pita in half and each half into 4 wedges. Break apart each wedge at the fold.
3. Mist one side of pita wedges with oil or cooking spray. Sprinkle them all with half of the cinnamon sugar.
4. Turn the wedges over, mist the other side with oil or cooking spray, and sprinkle with the remaining cinnamon sugar.
5. Place pita wedges in air fryer basket and cook at 330°F for 2minutes.
6. Shake basket and cook 2 more minutes. Shake again, and if needed cook 2 more minutes, until crisp. Watch carefully because at this point they will cook very quickly.

# Chili Kale Chips

Servings:4
Cooking Time: 5 Minutes
**Ingredients:**
- 1 teaspoon nutritional yeast
- 1 teaspoon salt
- 2 cups kale, chopped
- ½ teaspoon chili flakes
- 1 teaspoon sesame oil

**Directions:**
1. Mix up kale leaves with nutritional yeast, salt, chili flakes, and sesame oil. Shake the greens well. Preheat the air fryer to 400°F and put the kale leaves in the air fryer basket. Cook them for 3 minutes and then give a good shake. Cook the kale leaves for 2 minutes more.

# Cheese Arancini

Servings: 8
Cooking Time: 12 Minutes
**Ingredients:**
- 1 cup Water
- ½ cup Raw white Arborio rice
- 1½ teaspoons Butter
- ¼ teaspoon Table salt
- 8 ¾-inch semi-firm mozzarella cubes (not fresh mozzarella)
- 2 Large egg(s), well beaten
- 1 cup Seasoned Italian-style dried bread crumbs (gluten-free, if a concern)
- Olive oil spray

**Directions:**
1. Combine the water, rice, butter, and salt in a small saucepan. Bring to a boil over medium-high heat, stirring occasionally. Cover, reduce the heat to very low, and simmer very slowly for 20 minutes.
2. Take the saucepan off the heat and let it stand, covered, for 10 minutes. Uncover it and fluff the rice. Cool for 20 minutes.
3. Preheat the air fryer to 375°F .
4. Set up and fill two shallow soup plates or small bowls on your counter: one with the beaten egg(s) and one with the bread crumbs.
5. With clean but wet hands, scoop up about 2 tablespoons of the cooked rice and form it into a ball. Push a cube of mozzarella into the middle of the ball and seal the cheese inside. Dip the ball in the egg(s) to coat completely, letting any excess egg slip back into the rest. Roll the ball in the bread crumbs to coat evenly but lightly. Set aside and continue making more rice balls.
6. Generously spray the balls with olive oil spray, then set them in the basket in one layer. They must not touch. Air-fry undisturbed for 10 minutes, or until crunchy and golden brown. If the machine is at 360°F, you may need to add 2 minutes to the cooking time.

7. Use a nonstick-safe spatula, and maybe a flatware spoon for balance, to gently transfer the balls to a wire rack. Cool for at least 5 minutes or up to 20 minutes before serving.

## Spicy Sweet Potato Tater-tots

Servings: 6
Cooking Time: 10 Minutes
**Ingredients:**
- 6 cups filtered water
- 2 medium sweet potatoes, peeled and cut in half
- 1 teaspoon garlic powder
- ½ teaspoon black pepper, divided
- ½ teaspoon salt, divided
- 1 cup panko breadcrumbs
- 1 teaspoon blackened seasoning

**Directions:**
1. In a large stovetop pot, bring the water to a boil. Add the sweet potatoes and let boil about 10 minutes, until a metal fork prong can be inserted but the potatoes still have a slight give.
2. Carefully remove the potatoes from the pot and let cool.
3. When you're able to touch them, grate the potatoes into a large bowl. Mix the garlic powder, ¼ teaspoon of the black pepper, and ¼ teaspoon of the salt into the potatoes. Place the mixture in the refrigerator and let set at least 45 minutes.
4. Before assembling, mix the breadcrumbs and blackened seasoning in a small bowl.
5. Remove the sweet potatoes from the refrigerator and preheat the air fryer to 400°F.
6. Assemble the tater-tots by using a teaspoon to portion batter evenly and form into a tater-tot shape. Roll each tater-tot in the breadcrumb mixture. Then carefully place the tater-tots in the air fryer basket. Be sure that you've liberally sprayed the air fryer basket with an olive oil mist. Repeat until tater-tots fill the basket without touching one another. You'll need to do multiple batches, depending on the size of your air fryer.
7. Cook the tater-tots for 3 to 6 minutes, flip, and cook another 3 to 6 minutes.
8. Remove from the air fryer carefully and keep warm until ready to serve.

## Bacon-wrapped Jalapeño Poppers

Servings:4
Cooking Time: 12 Minutes
**Ingredients:**
- 3 ounces full-fat cream cheese
- ½ cup shredded sharp Cheddar cheese
- ¼ teaspoon garlic powder
- 6 jalapeño peppers, trimmed and halved lengthwise, seeded and membranes removed
- 12 slices bacon

**Directions:**
1. Preheat the air fryer to 400°F.

2. In a large microwave-safe bowl, place cream cheese, Cheddar, and garlic powder. Microwave 20 seconds until softened and stir. Spoon cheese mixture into hollow jalapeño halves.
3. Wrap a bacon slice around each jalapeño half, completely covering pepper.
4. Place in the air fryer basket and cook 12 minutes, turning halfway through cooking time. Serve warm.

## Beet Chips

Servings: 4
Cooking Time: 20 Minutes
**Ingredients:**
- 2 large red beets, washed and skinned
- 1 tablespoon avocado oil
- ¼ teaspoon salt

**Directions:**
1. Preheat the air fryer to 330°F.
2. Using a mandolin or sharp knife, slice the beets in ⅛-inch slices. Place them in a bowl of water and let them soak for 30 minutes. Drain the water and pat the beets dry with a paper towel or kitchen cloth.
3. In a medium bowl, toss the beets with avocado oil and sprinkle them with salt.
4. Lightly spray the air fryer basket with olive oil mist and place the beet chips into the basket. To allow for even cooking, don't overlap the beets; cook in batches if necessary.
5. Cook the beet chips 15 to 20 minutes, shaking the basket every 5 minutes, until the outer edges of the beets begin to flip up like a chip. Remove from the basket and serve warm. Repeat with the remaining chips until they're all cooked.

## Thyme Sweet Potato Chips

Servings: 2
Cooking Time: 20 Minutes
**Ingredients:**
- 1 tbsp olive oil
- 1 sweet potato, sliced
- ¼ tsp dried thyme
- Salt to taste

**Directions:**
1. Preheat air fryer to 390°F. Spread the sweet potato slices in the greased basket and brush with olive oil. Air Fry for 6 minutes. Remove the basket, shake, and sprinkle with thyme and salt. Cook for 6 more minutes or until lightly browned. Serve warm and enjoy!

# Corn Dog Bites

Servings: 3
Cooking Time: 12 Minutes
**Ingredients:**
- 3 cups Purchased cornbread stuffing mix
- ⅓ cup All-purpose flour
- 2 Large egg(s), well beaten
- 3 Hot dogs, cut into 2-inch pieces (vegetarian hot dogs, if preferred)
- Vegetable oil spray

**Directions:**
1. Preheat the air fryer to 375°F .
2. Put the cornbread stuffing mix in a food processor. Cover and pulse to grind into a mixture like fine bread crumbs.
3. Set up and fill three shallow soup plates or small pie plates on your counter: one for the flour, one for the egg(s), and one for the stuffing mix crumbs.
4. Dip a hot dog piece in the flour to coat it completely, then gently shake off any excess. Dip the hot dog piece into the egg(s) and gently roll it around to coat all surfaces, then pick it up and allow any excess egg to slip back into the rest. Set the hot dog piece in the stuffing mix crumbs and roll it gently to coat it evenly and well on all sides, even the ends. Set it aside on a cutting board and continue dipping and coating the remaining hot dog pieces.
5. Give the coated hot dog pieces a generous coating of vegetable oil spray on all sides, then set them in the basket in one layer with some space between them. Air-fry undisturbed for 10 minutes, or until golden brown and crunchy.
6. Use a nonstick-safe spatula, and perhaps a flatware fork for balance, to transfer the corn dog bites to a wire rack. Cool for 5 minutes before serving.

# Korean-style Wings

Servings: 4
Cooking Time: 10 Minutes
**Ingredients:**
- 1 pound chicken wings, drums and flats separated
- ½ teaspoon salt
- ¼ teaspoon ground black pepper
- ¼ cup gochujang sauce
- 2 tablespoons soy sauce
- 1 teaspoon ground ginger
- ¼ cup mayonnaise

**Directions:**
1. Preheat the air fryer to 350°F.
2. Sprinkle wings with salt and pepper. Place wings in the air fryer basket and cook 15 minutes, turning halfway through cooking time.
3. In a medium bowl, mix gochujang sauce, soy sauce, ginger, and mayonnaise.

4. Toss wings in sauce mixture and adjust the air fryer temperature to 400°F.
5. Place wings back in the air fryer basket and cook an additional 5 minutes until the internal temperature reaches at least 165°F. Serve warm.

# Roasted Peppers

Servings: 4
Cooking Time: 40 Minutes
**Ingredients:**
- 12 medium bell peppers
- 1 sweet onion, small
- 1 tbsp. Maggi sauce
- 1 tbsp. extra virgin olive oil

**Directions:**
1. Warm up the olive oil and Maggi sauce in Air Fryer at 320°F.
2. Peel the onion, slice it into 1-inch pieces, and add it to the Air Fryer.
3. Wash and de-stem the peppers. Slice them into 1-inch pieces and remove all the seeds, with water if necessary.
4. Place the peppers in the Air Fryer.
5. Cook for about 25 minutes, or longer if desired. Serve hot.

# Sweet Chili Peanuts

Servings: 6
Cooking Time: 5 Minutes
**Ingredients:**
- 2 cups Shelled raw peanuts
- 2 tablespoons Granulated white sugar
- 2 teaspoons Hot red pepper sauce, such as Cholula or Tabasco (gluten-free, if a concern)

**Directions:**
1. Preheat the air fryer to 400°F.
2. Toss the peanuts, sugar, and hot pepper sauce in a bowl until the peanuts are well coated.
3. When the machine is at temperature, pour the peanuts into the basket, spreading them into one layer as much as you can. Air-fry undisturbed for 3 minutes.
4. Shake the basket to rearrange the peanuts. Continue air-frying for 2 minutes more, shaking and stirring the peanuts every 30 seconds, until golden brown.
5. Pour the peanuts onto a large lipped baking sheet. Spread them into one layer and cool for 5 minutes before serving.

# Rumaki

Servings: 24
Cooking Time: 12 Minutes
**Ingredients:**
- 10 ounces raw chicken livers
- 1 can sliced water chestnuts, drained
- ¼ cup low-sodium teriyaki sauce
- 12 slices turkey bacon

- toothpicks

**Directions:**
1. Cut livers into 1½-inch pieces, trimming out tough veins as you slice.
2. Place livers, water chestnuts, and teriyaki sauce in small container with lid. If needed, add another tablespoon of teriyaki sauce to make sure livers are covered. Refrigerate for 1 hour.
3. When ready to cook, cut bacon slices in half crosswise.
4. Wrap 1 piece of liver and 1 slice of water chestnut in each bacon strip. Secure with toothpick.
5. When you have wrapped half of the livers, place them in the air fryer basket in a single layer.
6. Cook at 390°F for 12 minutes, until liver is done and bacon is crispy.
7. While first batch cooks, wrap the remaining livers. Repeat step 6 to cook your second batch.

# Onion Rings

Servings: 4
Cooking Time: 12 Minutes
**Ingredients:**
- 1 cup all-purpose flour
- 1 tablespoon seasoned salt
- 1 cup whole milk
- 1 large egg
- 1 cup panko bread crumbs
- 1 large Vidalia onion, peeled and sliced into ¼"-thick rings

**Directions:**
1. Preheat the air fryer to 350°F.
2. In a large bowl, whisk together flour and seasoned salt.
3. In a medium bowl, whisk together milk and egg. Place bread crumbs in a separate large bowl.
4. Dip onion rings into flour mixture to coat and set them aside. Pour milk mixture into the bowl of flour and stir to combine.
5. Dip onion rings into wet mixture and then press into bread crumbs to coat.
6. Place onion rings in the air fryer basket and spritz with cooking spray. Cook 12 minutes until the edges are crispy and golden. Serve warm.

# Sweet And Spicy Beef Jerky

Servings:6
Cooking Time: 4 Hours
**Ingredients:**
- 1 pound eye of round beef, fat trimmed, sliced into ¼"-thick strips
- ¼ cup soy sauce
- 2 tablespoons sriracha hot chili sauce
- ½ teaspoon ground black pepper
- 2 tablespoons granular brown erythritol

**Directions:**

1. Place beef in a large sealable bowl or bag. Pour soy sauce and sriracha into bowl or bag, then sprinkle in pepper and erythritol. Shake or stir to combine ingredients and coat steak. Cover and place in refrigerator to marinate at least 2 hours up to overnight.
2. Once marinated, remove strips from marinade and pat dry. Place into ungreased air fryer basket in a single layer, working in batches if needed. Adjust the temperature to 180°F and set the timer for 4 hours. Jerky will be chewy and dark brown when done. Store in airtight container in a cool, dry place up to 2 weeks.

# Carrot Chips

Servings: 4
Cooking Time: 10 Minutes
**Ingredients:**
- 1 pound carrots, thinly sliced
- 2 tablespoons extra-virgin olive oil
- ¼ teaspoon garlic powder
- ¼ teaspoon black pepper
- ½ teaspoon salt

**Directions:**
1. Preheat the air fryer to 390°F.
2. In a medium bowl, toss the carrot slices with the olive oil, garlic powder, pepper, and salt.
3. Liberally spray the air fryer basket with olive oil mist.
4. Place the carrot slices in the air fryer basket. To allow for even cooking, don't overlap the carrots; cook in batches if necessary.
5. Cook for 5 minutes, shake the basket, and cook another 5 minutes.
6. Remove from the basket and serve warm. Repeat with the remaining carrot slices until they're all cooked.

# Blistered Shishito Peppers

Servings: 3
Cooking Time: 5 Minutes
**Ingredients:**
- 6 ounces Shishito peppers
- Vegetable oil spray
- For garnishing Coarse sea or kosher salt and lemon wedges

**Directions:**
1. Preheat the air fryer to 400°F.
2. Put the peppers in a bowl and lightly coat them with vegetable oil spray. Toss gently, spray again, and toss until the peppers are glistening but not drenched.
3. Pour the peppers into the basket, spread them into as close to one layer as you can, and air-fry for 5 minutes, tossing and rearranging the peppers at the 2- and 4-minute marks, until the peppers are blistered and even blackened in spots.
4. Pour the peppers into a bowl, add salt to taste, and toss gently. Serve the peppers with lemon wedges to squeeze over them.

# Cheese Wafers

Servings: 4
Cooking Time: 6 Minutes Per Batch
**Ingredients:**
- 4 ounces sharp Cheddar cheese, grated
- ¼ cup butter
- ½ cup flour
- ¼ teaspoon salt
- ½ cup crisp rice cereal
- oil for misting or cooking spray

**Directions:**
1. Cream the butter and grated cheese together. You can do it by hand, but using a stand mixer is faster and easier.
2. Sift flour and salt together. Add it to the cheese mixture and mix until well blended.
3. Stir in cereal.
4. Place dough on wax paper and shape into a long roll about 1 inch in diameter. Wrap well with the wax paper and chill for at least 4 hours.
5. When ready to cook, preheat air fryer to 360°F.
6. Cut cheese roll into ¼-inch slices.
7. Spray air fryer basket with oil or cooking spray and place slices in a single layer, close but not touching.
8. Cook for 6minutes or until golden brown. When done, place them on paper towels to cool.
9. Repeat previous step to cook remaining cheese bites.

# Grilled Cheese Sandwich

Servings: 2
Cooking Time: 5 Minutes
**Ingredients:**
- 4 slices bread
- 4 ounces Cheddar cheese slices
- 2 teaspoons butter or oil

**Directions:**
1. Lay the four cheese slices on two of the bread slices and top with the remaining two slices of bread.
2. Brush both sides with butter or oil and cut the sandwiches in rectangular halves.
3. Place in air fryer basket and cook at 390°F for 5minutes until the outside is crisp and the cheese melts.

# Bbq Chicken Wings

Servings: 4
Cooking Time: 15 Minutes
**Ingredients:**
- 1 lb chicken wings
- 1/2 cup BBQ sauce, sugar-free
- 1/4 tsp garlic powder
- Pepper

**Directions:**
1. Preheat the air fryer to 400 F.
2. Season chicken wings with garlic powder and pepper and place into the air fryer basket.
3. Cook chicken wings for 15 minutes. Shake basket 3-4 times while cooking.
4. Transfer cooked chicken wings in a large mixing bowl. Pour BBQ sauce over chicken wings and toss to coat.
5. Serve and enjoy.

# Cheese Crackers

Servings:4
Cooking Time: 10 Minutes Per Batch
**Ingredients:**
- 4 ounces sharp Cheddar cheese, shredded
- ½ cup all-purpose flour
- 2 tablespoons salted butter, cubed
- ½ teaspoon salt
- 2 tablespoons cold water

**Directions:**
1. In a large bowl, using an electric hand mixer, mix all ingredients until dough forms. Pack dough together into a ball and wrap tightly in plastic wrap. Chill in the freezer 15 minutes.
2. Preheat the air fryer to 375°F. Cut parchment paper to fit the air fryer basket.
3. Spread a separate large sheet of parchment paper on a work surface. Remove dough from the freezer and roll out ¼" thick on parchment paper. Use a pizza cutter to cut dough into 1" squares.
4. Place crackers on precut parchment in the air fryer basket and cook 10 minutes, working in batches as necessary.
5. Allow crackers to cool at least 10 minutes before serving.

# Crispy & Healthy Kale Chips

Servings: 2
Cooking Time: 5 Minutes
**Ingredients:**
- 1 bunch of kale, remove stem and cut into pieces
- 1/2 tsp garlic powder
- 1 tsp olive oil
- 1/2 tsp salt

**Directions:**
1. Preheat the air fryer to 370°F.
2. Add all ingredients into the large bowl and toss well.
3. Transfer kale mixture into the air fryer basket and cook for 3 minutes.
4. Shake basket well and cook for 2 minutes more.
5. Serve and enjoy.

# Buffalo Chicken Dip

Servings: 6
Cooking Time: 25 Minutes
**Ingredients:**
- 4 ounces full-fat cream cheese, softened
- ½ teaspoon garlic powder
- ½ cup buffalo sauce

- 1 cup shredded Cheddar cheese, divided
- 2 cups cooked and shredded chicken breast

**Directions:**

1. Preheat the air fryer to 350°F.
2. In a large bowl, mix cream cheese, garlic powder, buffalo sauce, and ½ cup Cheddar until well combined. Fold in chicken until well coated.
3. Scrape mixture into a 6" round baking dish and top with remaining ½ cup Cheddar.
4. Place dish in the air fryer basket and cook 10 minutes until top is brown and edges are bubbling. Serve warm.

## Honey Tater Tots With Bacon

Servings: 4
Cooking Time: 25 Minutes

**Ingredients:**

- 24 frozen tater tots
- 6 bacon slices
- 1 tbsp honey
- 1 cup grated cheddar

**Directions:**

1. Preheat air fryer to 400°F. Air Fry the tater tots for 10 minutes, shaking the basket once halfway through cooking. Cut the bacon into pieces. When the tater tots are done, remove them from the fryer to a baking pan. Top them with bacon and drizzle with honey. Air Fry for 5 minutes to crisp up the bacon. Top the tater tots with cheese and cook for 2 minutes to melt the cheese. Serve.

## Sausage-stuffed Mushrooms

Servings:6
Cooking Time: 20 Minutes

**Ingredients:**

- ½ pound ground pork sausage
- ¼ teaspoon salt
- ¼ teaspoon garlic powder
- 2 medium scallions, trimmed and chopped
- ½ ounce plain pork rinds, finely crushed
- 1 pound cremini mushrooms, stems removed

**Directions:**

1. In a large bowl, mix sausage, salt, garlic powder, scallions, and pork rinds. Scoop 1 tablespoon mixture into center of each mushroom cap.
2. Place mushrooms into ungreased air fryer basket. Adjust the temperature to 375°F and set the timer for 20 minutes. Pork will be fully cooked to at least 145°F in the center and browned when done. Serve warm.

## Italian Bruschetta With Mushrooms & Cheese

Servings: 4
Cooking Time: 25 Minutes

**Ingredients:**

- ½ cup button mushrooms, chopped

- ½ baguette, sliced
- 1 garlic clove, minced
- 3 oz sliced Parmesan cheese
- 1 tbsp extra virgin olive oil
- Salt and pepper to taste

**Directions:**

1. Preheat air fryer to 350°F. Add the mushrooms, olive oil, salt, pepper, and garlic to a mixing bowl and stir thoroughly to combine. Divide the mushroom mixture between the bread slices, drizzling all over the surface with olive oil, then cover with Parmesan slices. Place the covered bread slices in the greased frying basket and Bake for 15 minutes. Serve and enjoy!

## Roasted Red Pepper Dip

Servings: 2
Cooking Time: 15 Minutes

**Ingredients:**

- 2 Medium-size red bell pepper(s)
- 1¾ cups Canned white beans, drained and rinsed
- 1 tablespoon Fresh oregano leaves, packed
- 3 tablespoons Olive oil
- 1 tablespoon Lemon juice
- ½ teaspoon Table salt
- ½ teaspoon Ground black pepper

**Directions:**

1. Preheat the air fryer to 400°F.
2. Set the pepper(s) in the basket and air-fry undisturbed for 15 minutes, until blistered and even blackened.
3. Use kitchen tongs to transfer the pepper(s) to a zip-closed plastic bag or small bowl. Seal the bag or cover the bowl with plastic wrap. Set aside for 20 minutes.
4. Peel each pepper, then stem it, cut it in half, and remove all its seeds and their white membranes.
5. Set the pieces of the pepper in a food processor. Add the beans, oregano, olive oil, lemon juice, salt, and pepper. Cover and process until smooth, stopping the machine at least once to scrape down the inside of the canister. Scrape the dip into a bowl and serve warm, or cover and refrigerate for up to 3 days.

## Broccoli And Carrot Bites

Servings:20
Cooking Time: 12 Minutes

**Ingredients:**

- 1 steamer bag broccoli, cooked according to package instructions
- ½ cup shredded sharp Cheddar cheese
- 2 tablespoons peeled and grated carrot
- ½ cup blanched finely ground almond flour
- 1 large egg, whisked
- ¼ teaspoon salt
- ¼ teaspoon ground black pepper

**Directions:**

1. Let cooked broccoli cool 5 minutes, then wring out excess moisture with a kitchen towel. In a large bowl, mix broccoli with Cheddar, carrot, flour, egg, salt, and pepper. Scoop 2 tablespoons of the mixture into a ball, then roll into a bite-sized piece. Repeat with remaining mixture to form twenty bites.

2. Cut a piece of parchment to fit into the bottom of air fryer basket. Place bites into a single layer on ungreased parchment. Adjust the temperature to 320°F and set the timer for 12 minutes, turning bites halfway through cooking. Bites will be golden brown when done. Serve warm.

## Baba Ghanouj

Servings: 2
Cooking Time: 40 Minutes
**Ingredients:**
- 2 Small purple Italian eggplant(s)
- ¼ cup Olive oil
- ¼ cup Tahini
- ½ teaspoon Ground black pepper
- ¼ teaspoon Onion powder
- ¼ teaspoon Mild smoked paprika (optional)
- Up to 1 teaspoon Table salt

**Directions:**
1. Preheat the air fryer to 400°F.
2. Prick the eggplant(s) on all sides with a fork. When the machine is at temperature, set the eggplant(s) in the basket in one layer. Air-fry undisturbed for 40 minutes, or until blackened and soft.
3. Remove the basket from the machine. Cool the eggplant(s) in the basket for 20 minutes.
4. Use a nonstick-safe spatula, and perhaps a flatware tablespoon for balance, to gently transfer the eggplant(s) to a bowl. The juices will run out. Make sure the bowl is close to the basket. Split the eggplant(s) open.
5. Scrape the soft insides of half an eggplant into a food processor. Repeat with the remaining piece(s). Add any juices from the bowl to the eggplant in the food processor, but discard the skins and stems.
6. Add the olive oil, tahini, pepper, onion powder, and smoked paprika. Add about half the salt, then cover and process until smooth, stopping the machine at least once to scrape down the inside of the canister. Check the spread for salt and add more as needed. Scrape the baba ghanouj into a bowl and serve warm, or set aside at room temperature for up to 2 hours, or cover and store in the refrigerator for up to 4 days.

## Buffalo Bites

Servings: 16
Cooking Time: 12 Minutes
**Ingredients:**
- 1 pound ground chicken
- 8 tablespoons buffalo wing sauce
- 2 ounces Gruyère cheese, cut into 16 cubes
- 1 tablespoon maple syrup

**Directions:**
1. Mix 4 tablespoons buffalo wing sauce into all the ground chicken.
2. Shape chicken into a log and divide into 16 equal portions.
3. With slightly damp hands, mold each chicken portion around a cube of cheese and shape into a firm ball. When you have shaped 8 meatballs, place them in air fryer basket.
4. Cook at 390°F for approximately 5minutes. Shake basket, reduce temperature to 360°F, and cook for 5 minutes longer.
5. While the first batch is cooking, shape remaining chicken and cheese into 8 more meatballs.
6. Repeat step 4 to cook second batch of meatballs.
7. In a medium bowl, mix the remaining 4 tablespoons of buffalo wing sauce with the maple syrup. Add all the cooked meatballs and toss to coat.
8. Place meatballs back into air fryer basket and cook at 390°F for 2 minutes to set the glaze. Skewer each with a toothpick and serve.

## Plantain Chips

Servings: 2
Cooking Time: 14 Minutes
**Ingredients:**
- 1 large green plantain
- 2½ cups filtered water, divided
- 2 teaspoons sea salt, divided
- Cooking spray

**Directions:**
1. Slice the plantain into 1-inch pieces. Place the plantains into a large bowl, cover with 2 cups water and 1 teaspoon salt. Soak the plantains for 30 minutes; then remove and pat dry.
2. Preheat the air fryer to 390°F.
3. Place the plantain pieces into the air fryer basket, leaving space between the plantain rounds. Cook the plantains for 5 minutes, and carefully remove them from the air fryer basket.
4. Add the remaining water to a small bowl.
5. Using a small drinking glass, dip the bottom of the glass into the water and mash the warm plantains until they're ¼-inch thick. Return the plantains to the air fryer basket, sprinkle with the remaining sea salt, and spray lightly with cooking spray.
6. Cook for another 6 to 8 minutes, or until lightly golden brown edges appear.

# Potato Skins

Servings: 4
Cooking Time: 35 Minutes Per Batch
**Ingredients:**
- 4 large russet potatoes
- ½ cup shredded sharp Cheddar cheese
- 1 teaspoon salt
- ½ teaspoon ground black pepper
- ½ cup sour cream
- 1 medium green onion, sliced

**Directions:**
1. Preheat the air fryer to 400°F.
2. Using a fork, poke several holes in potatoes. Place potatoes in the air fryer basket and cook 30 minutes until fork tender.
3. Once potatoes are cool enough to handle, slice them in half lengthwise and scoop out the insides, being careful to maintain the structural integrity of the potato skins. Reserve potato flesh for another use.
4. Sprinkle insides of potato skins with Cheddar, salt, and pepper. Working in batches if needed, place back in the air fryer basket and cook 5 minutes until cheese is melted and bubbling.
5. Let cool 5 minutes, then top with sour cream and green onion. Serve.

# Fiery Bacon-wrapped Dates

Servings: 16
Cooking Time: 6 Minutes
**Ingredients:**
- 8 Thin-cut bacon strips, halved widthwise (gluten-free, if a concern)
- 16 Medium or large Medjool dates, pitted
- 3 tablespoons (about ¾ ounce) Shredded semi-firm mozzarella
- 32 Pickled jalapeño rings

**Directions:**
1. Preheat the air fryer to 400°F.
2. Lay a bacon strip half on a clean, dry work surface. Split one date lengthwise without cutting through it, so that it opens like a pocket. Set it on one end of the bacon strip and open it a bit. Place 1 teaspoon of the shredded cheese and 2 pickled jalapeño rings in the date, then gently squeeze it together without fully closing it. Roll up the date in the bacon strip and set it bacon seam side down on a cutting board. Repeat this process with the remaining bacon strip halves, dates, cheese, and jalapeño rings.
3. Place the bacon-wrapped dates bacon seam side down in the basket. Air-fry undisturbed for 6 minutes, or until crisp and brown.
4. Use kitchen tongs to gently transfer the wrapped dates to a wire rack or serving platter. Cool for a few minutes before serving.

# Bacon-wrapped Onion Rings

Servings: 8
Cooking Time: 10 Minutes
**Ingredients:**
- 1 large white onion, peeled and cut into 16 (¼"-thick) slices
- 8 slices sugar-free bacon

**Directions:**
1. Stack 2 slices onion and wrap with 1 slice bacon. Secure with a toothpick. Repeat with remaining onion slices and bacon.
2. Place onion rings into ungreased air fryer basket. Adjust the temperature to 350°F and set the timer for 10 minutes, turning rings halfway through cooking. Bacon will be crispy when done. Serve warm.

# Roasted Red Salsa

Servings: 4
Cooking Time: 10 Minutes
**Ingredients:**
- 10 medium Roma tomatoes, quartered
- 1 medium white onion, peeled and sliced
- 2 medium cloves garlic, peeled
- 2 tablespoons olive oil
- ¼ cup chopped fresh cilantro
- ½ teaspoon salt

**Directions:**
1. Preheat the air fryer to 340°F.
2. Place tomatoes, onion, and garlic into a 6" round baking dish. Drizzle with oil and toss to coat.
3. Place in the air fryer basket and cook 10 minutes, stirring twice during cooking, until vegetables start to turn dark brown and caramelize.
4. In a food processor, add roasted vegetables, cilantro, and salt. Pulse five times until vegetables are mostly broken down. Serve immediately.

# Charred Shishito Peppers

Servings: 4
Cooking Time: 5 Minutes
**Ingredients:**
- 20 shishito peppers
- 1 teaspoon vegetable oil
- coarse sea salt
- 1 lemon

**Directions:**
1. Preheat the air fryer to 390°F.
2. Toss the shishito peppers with the oil and salt. You can do this in a bowl or directly in the air fryer basket.
3. Air-fry at 390°F for 5 minutes, shaking the basket once or twice while they cook.
4. Turn the charred peppers out into a bowl. Squeeze some lemon juice over the top and season with coarse sea salt.

These should be served as finger foods – pick the pepper up by the stem and eat the whole pepper, seeds and all.

## Spicy Cheese-stuffed Mushrooms

Servings:20
Cooking Time: 8 Minutes
**Ingredients:**
- 4 ounces cream cheese, softened
- 6 tablespoons shredded pepper jack cheese
- 2 tablespoons chopped pickled jalapeños
- 20 medium button mushrooms, stems removed
- 2 tablespoons olive oil
- ¼ teaspoon salt
- ⅛ teaspoon ground black pepper

**Directions:**
1. In a large bowl, mix cream cheese, pepper jack, and jalapeños together.
2. Drizzle mushrooms with olive oil, then sprinkle with salt and pepper. Spoon 2 tablespoons cheese mixture into each mushroom and place in a single layer into ungreased air fryer basket. Adjust the temperature to 370°F and set the timer for 8 minutes, checking halfway through cooking to ensure even cooking, rearranging if some are darker than others. When they're golden and cheese is bubbling, mushrooms will be done. Serve warm.

## Croutons

Servings:4
Cooking Time: 5 Minutes
**Ingredients:**
- 4 slices sourdough bread, diced into small cubes
- 2 tablespoons salted butter, melted
- 1 teaspoon chopped fresh parsley
- 2 tablespoons grated Parmesan cheese

**Directions:**
1. Preheat the air fryer to 400°F.
2. Place bread cubes in a large bowl.
3. Pour butter over bread cubes. Add parsley and Parmesan. Toss bread cubes until evenly coated.
4. Place bread cubes in the air fryer basket in a single layer. Cook 5 minutes until well toasted. Serve cooled for maximum crunch.

## Grilled Cheese Sandwiches

Servings:2
Cooking Time:5 Minutes
**Ingredients:**
- 4 white bread slices
- ½ cup melted butter, softened
- ½ cup sharp cheddar cheese, grated
- 1 tablespoon mayonnaise

**Directions:**
1. Preheat the Air fryer to 355°F and grease an Air fryer basket.
2. Spread the mayonnaise and melted butter over one side of each bread slice.
3. Sprinkle the cheddar cheese over the buttered side of the 2 slices.
4. Cover with the remaining slices of bread and transfer into the Air fryer basket.
5. Cook for about 5 minutes and dish out to serve warm.

## Buttered Corn On The Cob

Servings:2
Cooking Time:20 Minutes
**Ingredients:**
- 2 corn on the cob
- 2 tablespoons butter, softened and divided
- Salt and black pepper, to taste

**Directions:**
1. Preheat the Air fryer to 320°F and grease an Air fryer basket.
2. Season the cobs evenly with salt and black pepper and rub with 1 tablespoon butter.
3. Wrap the cobs in foil paper and arrange in the Air fryer basket.
4. Cook for about 20 minutes and top with remaining butter.
5. Dish out and serve warm.

## Sweet-and-salty Pretzels

Servings: 4
Cooking Time: 5 Minutes
**Ingredients:**
- 2 cups Plain pretzel nuggets
- 1 tablespoon Worcestershire sauce
- 2 teaspoons Granulated white sugar
- 1 teaspoon Mild smoked paprika
- ½ teaspoon Garlic or onion powder

**Directions:**
1. Preheat the air fryer to 350°F .
2. Put the pretzel nuggets, Worcestershire sauce, sugar, smoked paprika, and garlic or onion powder in a large bowl. Toss gently until the nuggets are well coated.
3. When the machine is at temperature, pour the nuggets into the basket, spreading them into as close to a single layer as possible. Air-fry, shaking the basket three or four times to rearrange the nuggets, for 5 minutes, or until the nuggets are toasted and aromatic. Although the coating will darken, don't let it burn, especially if the machine's temperature is 360°F.
4. Pour the nuggets onto a wire rack and gently spread them into one layer. Cool for 5 minutes before serving.

# Chapter 3. Bread And Breakfast

## Goat Cheese, Beet, And Kale Frittata

Servings: 6
Cooking Time: 20 Minutes
**Ingredients:**
- 6 large eggs
- ½ teaspoon garlic powder
- ¼ teaspoon black pepper
- ¼ teaspoon salt
- 1 cup chopped kale
- 1 cup cooked and chopped red beets
- ⅓ cup crumbled goat cheese

**Directions:**
1. Preheat the air fryer to 320°F.
2. In a medium bowl, whisk the eggs with the garlic powder, pepper, and salt. Mix in the kale, beets, and goat cheese.
3. Spray an oven-safe 7-inch springform pan with cooking spray. Pour the egg mixture into the pan and place it in the air fryer basket.
4. Cook for 20 minutes, or until the internal temperature reaches 145°F.
5. When the frittata is cooked, let it set for 5 minutes before removing from the pan.
6. Slice and serve immediately.

## Chicken Saltimbocca Sandwiches

Servings: 3
Cooking Time: 11 Minutes
**Ingredients:**
- 3 5- to 6-ounce boneless skinless chicken breasts
- 6 Thin prosciutto slices
- 6 Provolone cheese slices
- 3 Long soft rolls, such as hero, hoagie, or Italian sub rolls (gluten-free, if a concern), split open lengthwise
- 3 tablespoons Pesto, purchased or homemade

**Directions:**
1. Preheat the air fryer to 400°F.
2. Wrap each chicken breast with 2 prosciutto slices, spiraling the prosciutto around the breast and overlapping the slices a bit to cover the breast. The prosciutto will stick to the chicken more readily than bacon does.
3. When the machine is at temperature, set the wrapped chicken breasts in the basket and air-fry undisturbed for 10 minutes, or until the prosciutto is frizzled and the chicken is cooked through.
4. Overlap 2 cheese slices on each breast. Air-fry undisturbed for 1 minute, or until melted. Take the basket out of the machine.
5. Smear the insides of the rolls with the pesto, then use kitchen tongs to put a wrapped and cheesy chicken breast in each roll.

## Eggs Salad

Servings: 4
Cooking Time: 10 Minutes
**Ingredients:**
- 1 tablespoon lime juice
- 4 eggs, hard boiled, peeled and sliced
- 2 cups baby spinach
- Salt and black pepper to the taste
- 3 tablespoons heavy cream
- 2 tablespoons olive oil

**Directions:**
1. In your Air Fryer, mix the spinach with cream, eggs, salt and pepper, cover and cook at 360°F for 6 minutes. Transfer this to a bowl, add the lime juice and oil, toss and serve for breakfast.

## Scrambled Eggs

Servings: 2
Cooking Time: 6 Minutes
**Ingredients:**
- 4 eggs
- 1/4 tsp garlic powder
- 1/4 tsp onion powder
- 1 tbsp parmesan cheese
- Pepper
- Salt

**Directions:**
1. Whisk eggs with garlic powder, onion powder, parmesan cheese, pepper, and salt.
2. Pour egg mixture into the air fryer baking dish.
3. Place dish in the air fryer and cook at 360°F for 2 minutes. Stir quickly and cook for 3-4 minutes more.
4. Stir well and serve.

## Breakfast Quiche

Servings:4
Cooking Time: 18 Minutes
**Ingredients:**
- 1 refrigerated piecrust
- 2 large eggs
- ¼ cup heavy cream
- ½ teaspoon salt
- ¼ teaspoon ground black pepper
- ½ cup shredded Cheddar cheese
- 2 slices bacon, cooked and crumbled

**Directions:**
1. Preheat the air fryer to 325°F. Spray a 6" pie pan with cooking spray. Trim piecrust to fit the pan.
2. In a medium bowl, whisk together eggs, cream, salt, and pepper. Stir in Cheddar and bacon.

3. Pour egg mixture into crust and cook 18 minutes until firm, brown, and a knife inserted into the center comes out clean. Serve warm.

## Buttery Scallops

Servings: 2
Cooking Time: 8 Minutes
**Ingredients:**
- 1 lb jumbo scallops
- 1 tbsp fresh lemon juice
- 2 tbsp butter, melted

**Directions:**
1. Preheat the air fryer to 400°F.
2. In a small bowl, mix together lemon juice and butter.
3. Brush scallops with lemon juice and butter mixture and place into the air fryer basket.
4. Cook scallops for 4 minutes. Turn halfway through.
5. Again brush scallops with lemon butter mixture and cook for 4 minutes more. Turn halfway through.
6. Serve and enjoy.

## Tri-color Frittata

Servings: 4
Cooking Time: 30 Minutes
**Ingredients:**
- 8 eggs, beaten
- 1 red bell pepper, diced
- Salt and pepper to taste
- 1 garlic clove, minced
- ½ tsp dried oregano
- ½ cup ricotta

**Directions:**
1. Preheat air fryer to 360°F. Place the beaten eggs, bell pepper, oregano, salt, black pepper, and garlic and mix well. Fold in ¼ cup half of ricotta cheese.
2. Pour the egg mixture into a greased cake pan and top with the remaining ricotta. Place into the air fryer and Bake for 18-20 minutes or until the eggs are set in the center. Let the frittata cool for 5 minutes. Serve sliced.

## Fry Bread

Servings: 4
Cooking Time: 5 Minutes
**Ingredients:**
- 1 cup flour
- 2 teaspoons baking powder
- ¼ teaspoon salt
- ¼ cup lukewarm milk
- 1 teaspoon oil
- 2–3 tablespoons water
- oil for misting or cooking spray

**Directions:**
1. Stir together flour, baking powder, and salt. Gently mix in the milk and oil. Stir in 1 tablespoon water. If needed, add more water 1 tablespoon at a time until stiff dough forms. Dough shouldn't be sticky, so use only as much as you need.
2. Divide dough into 4 portions and shape into balls. Cover with a towel and let rest for 10minutes.
3. Preheat air fryer to 390°F.
4. Shape dough as desired:
5. a. Pat into 3-inch circles. This will make a thicker bread to eat plain or with a sprinkle of cinnamon or honey butter. You can cook all 4 at once.
6. b. Pat thinner into rectangles about 3 x 6 inches. This will create a thinner bread to serve as a base for dishes such as Indian tacos. The circular shape is more traditional, but rectangles allow you to cook 2 at a time in your air fryer basket.
7. Spray both sides of dough pieces with oil or cooking spray.
8. Place the 4 circles or 2 of the dough rectangles in the air fryer basket and cook at 390°F for 3minutes. Spray tops, turn, spray other side, and cook for 2 more minutes. If necessary, repeat to cook remaining bread.
9. Serve piping hot as is or allow to cool slightly and add toppings to create your own Native American tacos.

## Sausage Bacon Fandango

Servings:4
Cooking Time:20 Minutes
**Ingredients:**
- 8 bacon slices
- 8 chicken sausages
- 4 eggs
- Salt and black pepper, to taste

**Directions:**
1. Preheat the Air fryer to 320°F and grease 4 ramekins lightly.
2. Place bacon slices and sausages in the Air fryer basket.
3. Cook for about 10 minutes and crack 1 egg in each prepared ramekin.
4. Season with salt and black pepper and cook for about 10 more minutes.
5. Divide bacon slices and sausages in serving plates.
6. Place 1 egg in each plate and serve warm.

## Strawberry Pastry

Servings:8
Cooking Time: 15 Minutes Per Batch
**Ingredients:**
- 1 package refrigerated piecrust
- 1 cup strawberry jam
- 1 large egg, whisked
- ½ cup confectioners' sugar
- 2 tablespoons whole milk
- ½ teaspoon vanilla extract

**Directions:**
1. Preheat the air fryer to 320°F. Cut parchment paper to fit the air fryer basket.

2. On a lightly floured surface, lay piecrusts out flat. Cut each piecrust round into six 4" × 3" rectangles, reserving excess dough.

3. Form remaining dough into a ball, then roll out and cut four additional 4" × 3" rectangles, bringing the total to sixteen.

4. For each pastry, spread 2 tablespoons jam on a pastry rectangle, leaving a 1" border around the edges. Top with a second pastry rectangle and use a fork to gently press all four edges together. Repeat with remaining jam and pastry.

5. Brush tops of each pastry with egg and cut an X in the center of each to prevent excess steam from building up.

6. Place pastries on parchment in the air fryer basket, working in batches as necessary. Cook 12 minutes, then carefully flip and cook an additional 3 minutes until each side is golden brown. Let cool 10 minutes.

7. In a small bowl, whisk confectioners' sugar, milk, and vanilla. Brush each pastry with glaze, then place in the refrigerator 5 minutes to set before serving.

# Sausage Solo

Servings:4
Cooking Time:22 Minutes
**Ingredients:**
- 6 eggs
- 4 cooked sausages, sliced
- 2 bread slices, cut into sticks
- ½ cup mozzarella cheese, grated
- ½ cup cream

**Directions:**
1. Preheat the Air fryer to 355°F and grease 4 ramekins lightly.
2. Whisk together eggs and cream in a bowl and beat well.
3. Transfer the egg mixture into ramekins and arrange the bread sticks and sausage slices around the edges.
4. Top with mozzarella cheese evenly and place the ramekins in Air fryer basket.
5. Cook for about 22 minutes and dish out to serve warm.

# Spice Muffins

Servings:6
Cooking Time: 15 Minutes
**Ingredients:**
- 1 cup blanched finely ground almond flour
- ¼ cup granular erythritol
- 2 tablespoons salted butter, melted
- 1 large egg, whisked
- 2 teaspoons baking powder
- 1 teaspoon ground allspice

**Directions:**
1. In a large bowl, combine all ingredients. Evenly pour batter into six silicone muffin cups greased with cooking spray.

2. Place muffin cups into air fryer basket. Adjust the temperature to 320°F and set the timer for 15 minutes. Cooked muffins should be golden brown.

3. Let muffins cool in cups 15 minutes to avoid crumbling. Serve warm.

# Spinach Omelet

Servings:2
Cooking Time: 12 Minutes
**Ingredients:**
- 4 large eggs
- 1½ cups chopped fresh spinach leaves
- 2 tablespoons peeled and chopped yellow onion
- 2 tablespoons salted butter, melted
- ½ cup shredded mild Cheddar cheese
- ¼ teaspoon salt

**Directions:**
1. In an ungreased 6" round nonstick baking dish, whisk eggs. Stir in spinach, onion, butter, Cheddar, and salt.

2. Place dish into air fryer basket. Adjust the temperature to 320°F and set the timer for 12 minutes. Omelet will be done when browned on the top and firm in the middle.

3. Slice in half and serve warm on two medium plates.

# Crispy Bacon

Servings: 6
Cooking Time: 20 Minutes
**Ingredients:**
- 12 ounces bacon

**Directions:**
1. Preheat the air fryer to 350°F for 3 minutes.
2. Lay out the bacon in a single layer, slightly overlapping the strips of bacon.
3. Air fry for 10 minutes or until desired crispness.
4. Repeat until all the bacon has been cooked.

# Garlic-cheese Biscuits

Servings: 8
Cooking Time: 8 Minutes
**Ingredients:**
- 1 cup self-rising flour
- 1 teaspoon garlic powder
- 2 tablespoons butter, diced
- 2 ounces sharp Cheddar cheese, grated
- ½ cup milk
- cooking spray

**Directions:**
1. Preheat air fryer to 330°F.
2. Combine flour and garlic in a medium bowl and stir together.
3. Using a pastry blender or knives, cut butter into dry ingredients.
4. Stir in cheese.
5. Add milk and stir until stiff dough forms.

6. If dough is too sticky to handle, stir in 1 or 2 more tablespoons of self-rising flour before shaping. Biscuits should be firm enough to hold their shape. Otherwise, they'll stick to the air fryer basket.

7. Divide dough into 8 portions and shape into 2-inch biscuits about ¾-inch thick.

8. Spray air fryer basket with nonstick cooking spray.

9. Place all 8 biscuits in basket and cook at 330°F for 8 minutes.

## Scones

Servings: 9
Cooking Time: 8 Minutes Per Batch
**Ingredients:**
- 2 cups self-rising flour, plus ¼ cup for kneading
- ⅓ cup granulated sugar
- ¼ cup butter, cold
- 1 cup milk

**Directions:**
1. Preheat air fryer at 360°F.
2. In large bowl, stir together flour and sugar.
3. Cut cold butter into tiny cubes, and stir into flour mixture with fork.
4. Stir in milk until soft dough forms.
5. Sprinkle ¼ cup of flour onto wax paper and place dough on top. Knead lightly by folding and turning the dough about 6 to 8 times.
6. Pat dough into a 6 x 6-inch square.
7. Cut into 9 equal squares.
8. Place all squares in air fryer basket or as many as will fit in a single layer, close together but not touching.
9. Cook at 360°F for 8minutes. When done, scones will be lightly browned on top and will spring back when pressed gently with a dull knife.
10. Repeat steps 8 and 9 to cook remaining scones.

## Country Gravy

Servings: 2
Cooking Time: 7 Minutes
**Ingredients:**
- ¼ pound pork sausage, casings removed
- 1 tablespoon butter
- 2 tablespoons flour
- 2 cups whole milk
- ½ teaspoon salt
- freshly ground black pepper
- 1 teaspoon fresh thyme leaves

**Directions:**
1. Preheat a saucepan over medium heat. Add and brown the sausage, crumbling it into small pieces as it cooks. Add the butter and flour, stirring well to combine. Continue to cook for 2 minutes, stirring constantly.
2. Slowly pour in the milk, whisking as you do, and bring the mixture to a boil to thicken. Season with salt and freshly ground black pepper, lower the heat and simmer until the sauce has thickened to your desired consistency – about 5 minutes. Stir in the fresh thyme, season to taste and serve hot.

## Chocolate Chip Muffins

Servings:6
Cooking Time: 15 Minutes
**Ingredients:**
- 1½ cups blanched finely ground almond flour
- ⅓ cup granular brown erythritol
- 4 tablespoons salted butter, melted
- 2 large eggs, whisked
- 1 tablespoon baking powder
- ½ cup low-carb chocolate chips

**Directions:**
1. In a large bowl, combine all ingredients. Evenly pour batter into six silicone muffin cups greased with cooking spray.
2. Place muffin cups into air fryer basket. Adjust the temperature to 320°F and set the timer for 15 minutes. Muffins will be golden brown when done.
3. Let muffins cool in cups 15 minutes to avoid crumbling. Serve warm.

## Eggplant Parmesan Subs

Servings: 2
Cooking Time: 13 Minutes
**Ingredients:**
- 4 Peeled eggplant slices
- Olive oil spray
- 2 tablespoons plus 2 teaspoons Jarred pizza sauce, any variety except creamy
- ¼ cup (about ⅔ ounce) Finely grated Parmesan cheese
- 2 Small, long soft rolls, such as hero, hoagie, or Italian sub rolls (gluten-free, if a concern), split open lengthwise

**Directions:**
1. Preheat the air fryer to 350°F .
2. When the machine is at temperature, coat both sides of the eggplant slices with olive oil spray. Set them in the basket in one layer and air-fry undisturbed for 10 minutes, until lightly browned and softened.
3. Increase the machine's temperature to 375°F. Top each eggplant slice with 2 teaspoons pizza sauce, then 1 tablespoon cheese. Air-fry undisturbed for 2 minutes, or until the cheese has melted.
4. Use a nonstick-safe spatula, and perhaps a flatware fork for balance, to transfer the eggplant slices cheese side up to a cutting board. Set the roll(s) cut side down in the basket in one layer and air-fry undisturbed for 1 minute, to toast the rolls a bit and warm them up. Set 2 eggplant slices in each warm roll.

# Very Berry Breakfast Puffs

Servings:3
Cooking Time: 20 Minutes
**Ingredients:**
- 2 tbsp mashed strawberries
- 2 tbsp mashed raspberries
- ¼ tsp vanilla extract
- 2 cups cream cheese
- 1 tbsp honey

**Directions:**
1. Preheat the air fryer to 375°F. Divide the cream cheese between the dough sheets and spread it evenly. In a small bowl, combine the berries, honey and vanilla.
2. Divide the mixture between the pastry sheets. Pinch the ends of the sheets, to form puff. Place the puffs on a lined baking dish. Place the dish in the air fryer and cook for 15 minutes.

# Tomatoes Frittata

Servings: 4
Cooking Time: 20 Minutes
**Ingredients:**
- 4 eggs, whisked
- 1 pound cherry tomatoes, halved
- 1 tablespoon parsley, chopped
- Cooking spray
- 1 tablespoon cheddar, grated
- Salt and black pepper to the taste

**Directions:**
1. Put the tomatoes in the air fryer's basket, cook at 360°F for 5 minutes and transfer them to the baking pan that fits the machine greased with cooking spray. In a bowl, mix the eggs with the remaining ingredients, whisk, pour over the tomatoes an cook at 360°F for 15 minutes. Serve right away for breakfast.

# Almond Oatmeal

Servings: 4
Cooking Time: 15 Minutes
**Ingredients:**
- 2 cups almond milk
- 1 cup coconut, shredded
- 2 teaspoons stevia
- 2 teaspoons vanilla extract

**Directions:**
1. In a pan that fits your air fryer, mix all the ingredients, stir well, introduce the pan in the machine and cook at 360°F for 15 minutes. Divide into bowls and serve for breakfast.

# Pancake For Two

Servings:2
Cooking Time: 30 Minutes
**Ingredients:**
- 1 cup blanched finely ground almond flour
- 2 tablespoons granular erythritol
- 1 tablespoon salted butter, melted
- 1 large egg
- ⅓ cup unsweetened almond milk
- ½ teaspoon vanilla extract

**Directions:**
1. In a large bowl, mix all ingredients together, then pour half the batter into an ungreased 6" round nonstick baking dish.
2. Place dish into air fryer basket. Adjust the temperature to 320°F and set the timer for 15 minutes. The pancake will be golden brown on top and firm, and a toothpick inserted in the center will come out clean when done. Repeat with remaining batter.
3. Slice in half in dish and serve warm.

# Zucchini And Spring Onions Cakes

Servings: 4
Cooking Time: 8 Minutes
**Ingredients:**
- 8 ounces zucchinis, chopped
- 2 spring onions, chopped
- 2 eggs, whisked
- Salt and black pepper to the taste
- ¼ teaspoon sweet paprika, chopped
- Cooking spray

**Directions:**
1. In a bowl, mix all the ingredients except the cooking spray, stir well and shape medium fritters out of this mix. Put the basket in the Air Fryer, add the fritters inside, grease them with cooking spray and cook at 400°F for 8 minutes. Divide the fritters between plates and serve for breakfast.

# Jalapeño Egg Cups

Servings:4
Cooking Time: 14 Minutes
**Ingredients:**
- 4 large eggs
- ½ teaspoon salt
- ¼ teaspoon ground black pepper
- ¼ cup chopped pickled jalapeños
- 2 ounces cream cheese, softened
- ¼ teaspoon garlic powder
- ½ cup shredded sharp Cheddar cheese

**Directions:**
1. In a medium bowl, beat eggs together with salt and pepper, then pour evenly into four 4" ramekins greased with cooking spray.
2. In a separate large bowl, mix jalapeños, cream cheese, garlic powder, and Cheddar. Spoon ¼ of the mixture into the center of one ramekin. Repeat with remaining mixture and ramekins.

3. Place ramekins in air fryer basket. Adjust the temperature to 320°F and set the timer for 14 minutes. Eggs will be set when done. Serve warm.

# Banana-nut Muffins

Servings:12
Cooking Time: 15 Minutes
**Ingredients:**
- 1 ½ cups all-purpose flour
- ½ cup granulated sugar
- 1 teaspoon baking powder
- ½ cup salted butter, melted
- 1 large egg
- 2 medium bananas, peeled and mashed
- ½ cup chopped pecans

**Directions:**
1. Preheat the air fryer to 300°F.
2. In a large bowl, whisk together flour, sugar, and baking powder.
3. Add butter, egg, and bananas to dry mixture. Stir until well combined. Batter will be thick.
4. Gently fold in pecans. Divide batter evenly among twelve silicone or aluminum muffin cups, filling cups about halfway full.
5. Place cups in the air fryer basket, working in batches as necessary. Cook 15 minutes until muffin edges are brown and a toothpick inserted into the center comes out clean. Let cool 5 minutes before serving.

# Coconut Pudding

Servings: 4
Cooking Time: 20 Minutes
**Ingredients:**
- 1 cup cauliflower rice
- ½ cup coconut, shredded
- 3 cups coconut milk
- 2 tablespoons stevia

**Directions:**
1. In a pan that fits the air fryer, combine all the ingredients and whisk well. Introduce the in your air fryer and cook at 360°F for 20 minutes. Divide into bowls and serve for breakfast.

# Grilled Bbq Sausages

Servings:3
Cooking Time: 30 Minutes
**Ingredients:**
- 6 sausage links
- ½ cup prepared BBQ sauce

**Directions:**
1. Preheat the air fryer at 390°F.
2. Place the grill pan accessory in the air fryer.
3. Place the sausage links and grill for 30 minutes.
4. Flip halfway through the cooking time.
5. Before serving brush with prepared BBQ sauce.

# Egg In A Hole

Servings: 4
Cooking Time: 10 Minutes
**Ingredients:**
- 4 slices white sandwich bread
- 4 large eggs
- ½ teaspoon salt
- ¼ teaspoon ground black pepper

**Directions:**
1. Preheat the air fryer to 350°F. Spray a 6" round cake pan with cooking spray.
2. Place as many pieces of bread as will fit in one layer in prepared pan, working in batches as necessary.
3. Using a small cup or cookie cutter, cut a circle out of the center of each bread slice. Crack an egg directly into each cutout and sprinkle eggs with salt and pepper.
4. Cook 5 minutes, then carefully turn and cook an additional 5 minutes or less, depending on your preference. Serve warm.

# English Breakfast

Servings: 2
Cooking Time: 30 Minutes
**Ingredients:**
- 6 bacon strips
- 1 cup cooked white beans
- 1 tbsp melted butter
- ½ tbsp flour
- Salt and pepper to taste
- 2 eggs

**Directions:**
1. Preheat air fryer to 360°F. In a second bowl, combine the beans, butter, flour, salt, and pepper. Mix well. Put the bacon in the frying basket and Air Fry for 10 minutes, flipping once. Remove the bacon and stir in the beans. Crack the eggs on top and cook for 10-12 minutes until the eggs are set. Serve with bacon.

# Tuna And Arugula Salad

Servings: 4
Cooking Time: 15 Minutes
**Ingredients:**
- ½ pound smoked tuna, flaked
- 1 cup arugula
- 2 spring onions, chopped
- 1 tablespoon olive oil
- A pinch of salt and black pepper

**Directions:**
1. In a bowl, all the ingredients except the oil and the arugula and whisk. Preheat the Air Fryer over 360°F, add the oil and grease it. Pour the tuna mix, stir well, and cook for 15 minutes. In a salad bowl, combine the arugula with the tuna mix, toss and serve for breakfast.

# Cheese Eggs And Leeks

Servings: 2
Cooking Time: 7 Minutes
**Ingredients:**
- 2 leeks, chopped
- 4 eggs, whisked
- ¼ cup Cheddar cheese, shredded
- ½ cup Mozzarella cheese, shredded
- 1 teaspoon avocado oil

**Directions:**
1. Preheat the air fryer to 400°F. Then brush the air fryer basket with avocado oil and combine the eggs with the rest of the ingredients inside. Cook for 7 minutes and serve.

# Greek-style Frittata

Servings:2
Cooking Time: 10 Minutes
**Ingredients:**
- 2 tbsp heavy cream
- 2 cups spinach, chopped
- 1 cup chopped mushrooms
- 3 oz feta cheese, crumbled
- A handful of fresh parsley, chopped
- Salt and black pepper

**Directions:**
1. Spray your air fryer basket with cooking spray. In a bowl, whisk eggs and until combined. Stir in spinach, mushrooms, feta, parsley, salt, and black pepper.
2. Pour into the basket and cook for 6 minutes at 350°F. Serve immediately with a touch of tomato relish.

# Bacon & Hot Dogs Omelet

Servings:2
Cooking Time: 10 Minutes
**Ingredients:**
- 4 eggs
- 1 bacon slice, chopped
- 2 hot dogs, chopped
- 2 small onions, chopped

**Directions:**
1. Set the temperature of Air Fryer to 320°F.
2. In an Air Fryer baking pan, crack the eggs and beat them well.
3. Now, add in the remaining ingredients and gently, stir to combine.
4. Air Fry for about 10 minutes.
5. Serve hot.

# Whole-grain Cornbread

Servings: 6
Cooking Time: 25 Minutes
**Ingredients:**
- 1 cup stoneground cornmeal
- ½ cup brown rice flour

- 1 teaspoon sugar
- 2 teaspoons baking powder
- ¼ teaspoon salt
- 1 cup milk
- 2 tablespoons oil
- 2 eggs
- cooking spray

**Directions:**
1. Preheat the air fryer to 360°F.
2. In a medium mixing bowl, mix cornmeal, brown rice flour, sugar, baking powder, and salt together.
3. Add the remaining ingredients and beat with a spoon until batter is smooth.
4. Spray air fryer baking pan with nonstick cooking spray and add the cornbread batter.
5. Bake at 360°F for 25 minutes, until center is done.

# French Toast Sticks

Servings:4
Cooking Time: 8 Minutes
**Ingredients:**
- 4 slices Texas toast, or other thick-sliced bread
- 2 large eggs
- ¼ cup heavy cream
- 4 tablespoons salted butter, melted
- ½ cup granulated sugar
- 1 ½ tablespoons ground cinnamon

**Directions:**
1. Preheat the air fryer to 350°F. Cut parchment paper to fit the air fryer basket.
2. Slice each piece of bread into four even sticks.
3. In a medium bowl, whisk together eggs and cream. Dip each bread stick into mixture and place on parchment in the air fryer basket.
4. Cook 5 minutes, then carefully turn over and cook an additional 3 minutes until golden brown on both sides.
5. Drizzle sticks with butter and toss to ensure they're covered on all sides.
6. In a medium bowl, mix sugar and cinnamon. Dip both sides of each stick into the mixture and shake off excess. Serve warm.

# Puffed Egg Tarts

Servings:4
Cooking Time:42 Minutes
**Ingredients:**
- 1 sheet frozen puff pastry half, thawed and cut into 4 squares
- ¾ cup Monterey Jack cheese, shredded and divided
- 4 large eggs
- 1 tablespoon fresh parsley, minced
- 1 tablespoon olive oil

**Directions:**
1. Preheat the Air fryer to 390°F

2. Place 2 pastry squares in the air fryer basket and cook for about 10 minutes.

3. Remove Air fryer basket from the Air fryer and press each square gently with a metal tablespoon to form an indentation.

4. Place 3 tablespoons of cheese in each hole and top with 1 egg each.

5. Return Air fryer basket to Air fryer and cook for about 11 minutes.

6. Remove tarts from the Air fryer basket and sprinkle with half the parsley.

7. Repeat with remaining pastry squares, cheese and eggs.

8. Dish out and serve warm.

# Quiche Cups

Servings: 10
Cooking Time: 16 Minutes

**Ingredients:**
- ¼ pound all-natural ground pork sausage
- 3 eggs
- ¾ cup milk
- 20 foil muffin cups
- cooking spray
- 4 ounces sharp Cheddar cheese, grated

**Directions:**
1. Divide sausage into 3 portions and shape each into a thin patty.

2. Place patties in air fryer basket and cook 390°F for 6minutes.

3. While sausage is cooking, prepare the egg mixture. A large measuring cup or bowl with a pouring lip works best. Combine the eggs and milk and whisk until well blended. Set aside.

4. When sausage has cooked fully, remove patties from basket, drain well, and use a fork to crumble the meat into small pieces.

5. Double the foil cups into 10 sets. Remove paper liners from the top muffin cups and spray the foil cups lightly with cooking spray.

6. Divide crumbled sausage among the 10 muffin cup sets.

7. Top each with grated cheese, divided evenly among the cups.

8. Place 5 cups in air fryer basket.

9. Pour egg mixture into each cup, filling until each cup is at least ⅔ full.

10. Cook for 8 minutes and test for doneness. A knife inserted into the center shouldn't have any raw egg on it when removed.

11. If needed, cook 2 more minutes, until egg completely sets.

12. Repeat steps 8 through 11 for the remaining quiches.

# Baked Eggs

Servings: 4
Cooking Time: 6 Minutes

**Ingredients:**
- 4 large eggs
- ⅛ teaspoon black pepper
- ⅛ teaspoon salt

**Directions:**
1. Preheat the air fryer to 330°F. Place 4 silicone muffin liners into the air fryer basket.

2. Crack 1 egg at a time into each silicone muffin liner. Sprinkle with black pepper and salt.

3. Bake for 6 minutes. Remove and let cool 2 minutes prior to serving.

# English Muffin Sandwiches

Servings: 4
Cooking Time: 15 Minutes

**Ingredients:**
- 4 English muffins
- 8 pepperoni slices
- 4 cheddar cheese slices
- 1 tomato, sliced

**Directions:**
1. Preheat air fryer to 370°F. Split open the English muffins along the crease. On the bottom half of the muffin, layer 2 slices of pepperoni and one slice of the cheese and tomato. Place the top half of the English muffin to finish the sandwich. Lightly spray with cooking oil. Place the muffin sandwiches in the air fryer. Bake for 8 minutes, flipping once. Let cool slightly before serving.

# Pigs In A Blanket

Servings: 10
Cooking Time: 8 Minutes

**Ingredients:**
- 1 cup all-purpose flour, plus more for rolling
- 1 teaspoon baking powder
- ¼ cup salted butter, cut into small pieces
- ½ cup buttermilk
- 10 fully cooked breakfast sausage links

**Directions:**
1. In a large mixing bowl, whisk together the flour and baking powder. Using your fingers or a pastry blender, cut in the butter until you have small pea-size crumbles.

2. Using a rubber spatula, make a well in the center of the flour mixture. Pour the buttermilk into the well, and fold the mixture together until you form a dough ball.

3. Place the sticky dough onto a floured surface and, using a floured rolling pin, roll out until ½-inch thick. Using a round biscuit cutter, cut out 10 rounds, reshaping the dough and rolling out, as needed.

4. Place 1 fully cooked breakfast sausage link on the left edge of each biscuit and roll up, leaving the ends slightly exposed.

5. Using a pastry brush, brush the biscuits with the whisked eggs, and spray them with cooking spray.

6. Place the pigs in a blanket into the air fryer basket with at least 1 inch between each biscuit. Set the air fryer to 340°F and cook for 8 minutes.

# Cheesy Bell Pepper Eggs

Servings:4
Cooking Time: 15 Minutes
**Ingredients:**
- 4 medium green bell peppers, tops removed, seeded
- 1 tablespoon coconut oil
- 3 ounces chopped cooked no-sugar-added ham
- ¼ cup peeled and chopped white onion
- 4 large eggs
- ½ teaspoon salt
- 1 cup shredded mild Cheddar cheese

**Directions:**
1. Place peppers upright into ungreased air fryer basket. Drizzle each pepper with coconut oil. Divide ham and onion evenly among peppers.
2. In a medium bowl, whisk eggs, then sprinkle with salt. Pour mixture evenly into each pepper. Top each with ¼ cup Cheddar.
3. Adjust the temperature to 320°F and set the timer for 15 minutes. Peppers will be tender and eggs will be firm when done.
4. Serve warm on four medium plates.

# Flaky Cinnamon Rolls

Servings:8
Cooking Time: 12 Minutes Per Batch
**Ingredients:**
- 1 sheet frozen puff pastry, thawed
- 6 tablespoons unsalted butter, melted
- ¾ cup granulated sugar
- 2 tablespoons ground cinnamon
- ½ cup confectioners' sugar
- 2 tablespoons heavy cream

**Directions:**
1. Preheat the air fryer to 320°F. Cut parchment paper to fit the air fryer basket.
2. Unroll puff pastry into a large rectangle. Brush with butter, then evenly sprinkle sugar and cinnamon around dough, coating as evenly as possible.
3. Starting at one of the long sides, roll dough into a log, then use a little water on your fingers to seal the edge.
4. Slice dough into eight rounds. Place on parchment in the air fryer basket, working in batches as necessary, and cook 12 minutes until golden brown and flaky. Let cool 5 minutes.
5. In a small bowl, whisk confectioners' sugar and cream together until smooth. Drizzle over cinnamon rolls and serve.

# Simple Egg Soufflé

Servings: 2
Cooking Time: 8 Minutes
**Ingredients:**
- 2 eggs
- 1/4 tsp chili pepper
- 2 tbsp heavy cream
- 1/4 tsp pepper
- 1 tbsp parsley, chopped
- Salt

**Directions:**
1. In a bowl, whisk eggs with remaining gradients.
2. Spray two ramekins with cooking spray.
3. Pour egg mixture into the prepared ramekins and place into the air fryer basket.
4. Cook soufflé at 390°F for 8 minutes.
5. Serve and enjoy.

# Bacon And Cheese Quiche

Servings:2
Cooking Time: 12 Minutes
**Ingredients:**
- 3 large eggs
- 2 tablespoons heavy whipping cream
- ¼ teaspoon salt
- 4 slices cooked sugar-free bacon, crumbled
- ½ cup shredded mild Cheddar cheese

**Directions:**
1. In a large bowl, whisk eggs, cream, and salt together until combined. Mix in bacon and Cheddar.
2. Pour mixture evenly into two ungreased 4" ramekins. Place into air fryer basket. Adjust the temperature to 320°F and set the timer for 12 minutes. Quiche will be fluffy and set in the middle when done.
3. Let quiche cool in ramekins 5 minutes. Serve warm.

# Onion Marinated Skirt Steak

Servings:3
Cooking Time: 45 Minutes
**Ingredients:**
- 1 large red onion, grated or pureed
- 2 tablespoons brown sugar
- 1 tablespoon vinegar
- 1 ½ pounds skirt steak
- Salt and pepper to taste

**Directions:**
1. Place all ingredients in a Ziploc bag and allow to marinate in the fridge for at least 2 hours.
2. Preheat the air fryer at 390°F.
3. Place the grill pan accessory in the air fryer.
4. Grill for 15 minutes per batch.
5. Flip every 8 minutes for even grilling.

## Sausage Egg Muffins

Servings: 4
Cooking Time: 30 Minutes
**Ingredients:**
- 6 oz Italian sausage
- 6 eggs
- 1/8 cup heavy cream
- 3 oz cheese

**Directions:**
1. Preheat the fryer to 350°F.
2. Grease a muffin pan.
3. Slice the sausage links and place them two to a tin.
4. Beat the eggs with the cream and season with salt and pepper.
5. Pour over the sausages in the tin.
6. Sprinkle with cheese and the remaining egg mixture.
7. Cook for 20 minutes or until the eggs are done and serve!

## Spinach Spread

Servings: 4
Cooking Time: 10 Minutes
**Ingredients:**
- 2 tablespoons coconut cream
- 3 cups spinach leaves
- 2 tablespoons cilantro
- 2 tablespoons bacon, cooked and crumbled
- Salt and black pepper to the taste

**Directions:**
1. In a pan that fits the air fryer, combine all the ingredients except the bacon, put the pan in the machine and cook at 360°F for 10 minutes. Transfer to a blender, pulse well, divide into bowls and serve with bacon sprinkled on top.

## White Wheat Walnut Bread

Servings: 8
Cooking Time: 25 Minutes
**Ingredients:**
- 1 cup lukewarm water
- 1 packet RapidRise yeast
- 1 tablespoon light brown sugar
- 2 cups whole-grain white wheat flour
- 1 egg, room temperature, beaten with a fork
- 2 teaspoons olive oil
- ½ teaspoon salt
- ½ cup chopped walnuts
- cooking spray

**Directions:**
1. In a small bowl, mix the water, yeast, and brown sugar.
2. Pour yeast mixture over flour and mix until smooth.
3. Add the egg, olive oil, and salt and beat with a wooden spoon for 2minutes.
4. Stir in chopped walnuts. You will have very thick batter rather than stiff bread dough.

5. Spray air fryer baking pan with cooking spray and pour in batter, smoothing the top.
6. Let batter rise for 15minutes.
7. Preheat air fryer to 360°F.
8. Cook bread for 25 minutes, until toothpick pushed into center comes out with crumbs clinging. Let bread rest for 10minutes before removing from pan.

## Smoked Fried Tofu

Servings: 2
Cooking Time:22 Minutes
**Ingredients:**
- 1 tofu block; pressed and cubed
- 1 tbsp. smoked paprika
- 1/4 cup cornstarch
- Salt and black pepper to the taste
- Cooking spray

**Directions:**
1. Grease your air fryer's basket with cooking spray and heat the fryer at 370°F.
2. In a bowl; mix tofu with salt, pepper, smoked paprika and cornstarch and toss well.
3. Add tofu to you air fryer's basket and cook for 12 minutes shaking the fryer every 4 minutes. Divide into bowls and serve for breakfast.

## Hashbrown Potatoes Lyonnaise

Servings: 4
Cooking Time: 33 Minutes
**Ingredients:**
- 1 Vidalia (or other sweet) onion, sliced
- 1 teaspoon butter, melted
- 1 teaspoon brown sugar
- 2 large russet potatoes, sliced ½-inch thick
- 1 tablespoon vegetable oil
- salt and freshly ground black pepper

**Directions:**
1. Preheat the air fryer to 370°F.
2. Toss the sliced onions, melted butter and brown sugar together in the air fryer basket. Air-fry for 8 minutes, shaking the basket occasionally to help the onions cook evenly.
3. While the onions are cooking, bring a 3-quart saucepan of salted water to a boil on the stovetop. Par-cook the potatoes in boiling water for 3 minutes. Drain the potatoes and pat them dry with a clean kitchen towel.
4. Add the potatoes to the onions in the air fryer basket and drizzle with vegetable oil. Toss to coat the potatoes with the oil and season with salt and freshly ground black pepper.
5. Increase the air fryer temperature to 400°F and air-fry for 22 minutes tossing the vegetables a few times during the cooking time to help the potatoes brown evenly. Season to taste again with salt and freshly ground black pepper and serve warm.

# Taj Tofu

Servings: 4
Cooking Time: 40 Minutes
**Ingredients:**
- 1 block firm tofu, pressed and cut into 1-inch thick cubes
- 2 tbsp. soy sauce
- 2 tsp. sesame seeds, toasted
- 1 tsp. rice vinegar
- 1 tbsp. cornstarch

**Directions:**
1. Set your Air Fryer at 400°F to warm.
2. Add the tofu, soy sauce, sesame seeds and rice vinegar in a bowl together and mix well to coat the tofu cubes. Then cover the tofu in cornstarch and put it in the basket of your fryer.
3. Cook for 25 minutes, giving the basket a shake at five-minute intervals to ensure the tofu cooks evenly.

# Chives Omelet

Servings: 4
Cooking Time: 20 Minutes
**Ingredients:**
- 6 eggs, whisked
- 1 cup chives, chopped
- Cooking spray
- 1 cup mozzarella, shredded
- Salt and black pepper to the taste

**Directions:**
1. In a bowl, mix all the ingredients except the cooking spray and whisk well. Grease a pan that fits your air fryer with the cooking spray, pour the eggs mix, spread, put the pan into the machine and cook at 350°F for 20 minutes. Divide the omelet between plates and serve for breakfast.

# Parmesan Breakfast Casserole

Servings: 3
Cooking Time: 20 Minutes
**Ingredients:**
- 5 eggs
- 2 tbsp heavy cream
- 3 tbsp chunky tomato sauce
- 2 tbsp parmesan cheese, grated

**Directions:**
1. Preheat the air fryer to 325°F.
2. In mixing bowl, combine together cream and eggs.
3. Add cheese and tomato sauce and mix well.
4. Spray air fryer baking dish with cooking spray.
5. Pour mixture into baking dish and place in the air fryer basket.
6. Cook for 20 minutes.
7. Serve and enjoy.

# Mini Bacon Egg Quiches

Servings:6
Cooking Time: 30 Minutes
**Ingredients:**
- 3 eggs
- 2 tbsp heavy cream
- ¼ tsp Dijon mustard
- Salt and pepper to taste
- 3 oz cooked bacon, crumbled
- ¼ cup grated cheddar

**Directions:**
1. Preheat air fryer to 350°F. Beat the eggs with salt and pepper in a bowl until fluffy. Stir in heavy cream, mustard, cooked bacon, and cheese. Divide the mixture between 6 greased muffin cups and place them in the frying basket. Bake for 8-10 minutes. Let cool slightly before serving.

# Coconut Eggs Mix

Servings: 4
Cooking Time: 8 Minutes
**Ingredients:**
- 1 tablespoon olive oil
- 1 and ½ cup coconut cream
- 8 eggs, whisked
- ½ cup mint, chopped
- Salt and black pepper to the taste

**Directions:**
1. In a bowl, mix the cream with salt, pepper, eggs and mint, whisk, pour into the air fryer greased with the oil, spread, cook at 350°F for 8 minutes, divide between plates and serve.

# Parmesan Garlic Naan

Servings: 6
Cooking Time: 4 Minutes
**Ingredients:**
- 1 cup bread flour
- 1 teaspoon baking powder
- ⅛ teaspoon salt
- 1 teaspoon garlic p⌐
- 2 tablespoon shre⌐
- 1 cup plain 2% f⌐
- 1 tablespoon e⌐

**Directions:**
1. Preheat the ⌐
2. In a medi⌐ garlic powde⌐ using your ⌐
3. On a ⌐ into 6 e⌐ circle.
4. Lig⌐ place one ⌐ minutes. Ren⌐

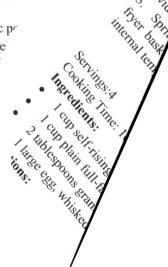

Servings:4
Cooking Time: ⌐
**Ingredients:**
- 1 cup self-rising⌐
- 1 cup plain full-f⌐
- 2 tablespoons gran⌐
- 1 large egg, whisked⌐

**⌐ions:**

5. Serve warm.

# Breakfast Bake

Servings:4
Cooking Time: 15 Minutes
**Ingredients:**
- 6 large eggs
- 2 tablespoons heavy cream
- ½ teaspoon salt
- ¼ teaspoon ground black pepper
- ⅓ pound ground pork breakfast sausage, cooked and drained
- ½ cup shredded Cheddar cheese

**Directions:**
1. Preheat the air fryer to 320°F. Spray a 6" round cake pan with cooking spray.
2. In a large bowl, whisk eggs, cream, salt, and pepper until fully combined.
3. Arrange cooked sausage in the bottom of prepared pan. Pour egg mixture into pan on top of sausage. Sprinkle Cheddar on top.
4. Place in the air fryer basket and cook 15 minutes until the top begins to brown and the center is set. Let cool 5 minutes before serving. Serve warm.

# Sweet And Spicy Breakfast Sausage

Servings:6
Cooking Time: 10 Minutes
**Ingredients:**
- 1 pound 84% lean ground pork
- 2 tablespoons brown sugar
- 1 teaspoon salt
- ½ teaspoon ground black pepper
- ½ teaspoon garlic powder
- ½ teaspoon dried fennel
- ½ teaspoon crushed red pepper flakes

**Directions:**
1. Preheat the air fryer to 400°F.
2. In a large bowl, mix all ingredients until well combined. Divide mixture into eight portions and form into patties.
3. Spray patties with cooking spray and place in the air fryer basket. Cook 10 minutes until patties are brown and temperature reaches at least 145°F. Serve warm.

# Bagels

Servings: 4
Cooking Time: 10 Minutes
**Ingredients:**
- 1 cup all-purpose flour
- 1 cup nonfat Greek yogurt
- 1 teaspoon granulated sugar
- 1 large egg

**Directions:**
1. Preheat the air fryer to 320°F.
2. In a large bowl, mix flour, yogurt, and sugar together until a ball of dough forms.
3. Turn dough out onto a lightly floured surface. Knead dough for 3 minutes, then form into a smooth ball. Cut dough into four sections. Roll each piece into an 8" rope, then shape into a circular bagel shape. Brush top and bottom of each bagel with egg.
4. Place in the air fryer basket and cook 10 minutes, turning halfway through cooking time to ensure even browning. Let cool 5 minutes before serving.

# Blueberry Muffins

Servings:12
Cooking Time:15 Minutes
**Ingredients:**
- 1 cup all-purpose flour
- ½ cup granulated sugar
- 1 teaspoon baking powder
- ¼ cup salted butter, melted
- 1 large egg
- ½ cup whole milk
- 1 cup fresh blueberries

**Directions:**
1. Preheat the air fryer to 300°F.
2. In a large bowl, whisk together flour, sugar, and baking powder.
3. Add butter, egg, and milk to dry mixture. Stir until well combined.
4. Gently fold in blueberries. Divide batter evenly among twelve silicone or aluminum muffin cups, filling cups about halfway full.
5. Place cups in the air fryer basket, working in batches as necessary. Cook 15 minutes until muffins are brown at the edges and a toothpick inserted in the center comes out clean. Serve warm.

# Crust-less Quiche

Servings:2
Cooking Time:30 Minutes
**Ingredients:**
- 4 eggs
- ¼ cup onion, chopped
- ½ cup tomatoes, chopped
- ½ cup milk
- 1 cup Gouda cheese, shredded
- Salt, to taste

**Directions:**
1. Preheat the Air fryer to 340°F and grease 2 ramekins lightly.
2. Mix together all the ingredients in a ramekin until well combined.
3. Place in the Air fryer and cook for about 30 minutes.
4. Dish out and serve.

# Chapter 4. Poultry Recipes

## Peppery Lemon-chicken Breast

Servings:1
Cooking Time:
**Ingredients:**
- 1 chicken breast
- 1 teaspoon minced garlic
- 2 lemons, rinds and juice reserved
- Salt and pepper to taste

**Directions:**
1. Preheat the air fryer.
2. Place all ingredients in a baking dish that will fit in the air fryer.
3. Place in the air fryer basket.
4. Close and cook for 20 minutes at 400°F.

## Yummy Stuffed Chicken Breast

Servings:4
Cooking Time:15 Minutes
**Ingredients:**
- 2 chicken fillets, skinless and boneless, each cut into 2 pieces
- 4 brie cheese slices
- 1 tablespoon chive, minced
- 4 cured ham slices
- Salt and black pepper, to taste

**Directions:**
1. Preheat the Air fryer to 355°F and grease an Air fryer basket.
2. Make a slit in each chicken piece horizontally and season with the salt and black pepper.
3. Insert cheese slice in the slits and sprinkle with chives.
4. Wrap each chicken piece with one ham slice and transfer into the Air fryer basket.
5. Cook for about 15 minutes and dish out to serve warm.

## Tuscan Stuffed Chicken

Servings: 4
Cooking Time: 30 Minutes
**Ingredients:**
- 1/3 cup ricotta cheese
- 1 cup Tuscan kale, chopped
- 4 chicken breasts
- 1 tbsp chicken seasoning
- Salt and pepper to taste
- 1 tsp paprika

**Directions:**
1. Preheat air fryer to 370°F. Soften the ricotta cheese in a microwave-safe bowl for 15 seconds. Combine in a bowl along with Tuscan kale. Set aside. Cut 4-5 slits in the top of each chicken breast about ¾ of the way down. Season with chicken seasoning, salt, and pepper.
2. Place the chicken with the slits facing up in the greased frying basket. Lightly spray the chicken with oil. Bake for 6-8 minutes. Slide-out and stuff the cream cheese mixture into the chicken slits. Sprinkle ½ tsp of paprika and cook for another 3 minutes. Serve and enjoy!

## Family Chicken Fingers

Servings: 4
Cooking Time: 30 Minutes
**Ingredients:**
- 1 lb chicken breast fingers
- 1 tbsp chicken seasoning
- ½ tsp mustard powder
- Salt and pepper to taste
- 2 eggs
- 1 cup bread crumbs

**Directions:**
1. Preheat air fryer to 400°F. Add the chicken fingers to a large bowl along with chicken seasoning, mustard, salt, and pepper; mix well. Set up two small bowls. In one bowl, beat the eggs. In the second bowl, add the bread crumbs. Dip the chicken in the egg, then dredge in breadcrumbs. Place the nuggets in the air fryer. Lightly spray with cooking oil, then Air Fry for 8 minutes, shaking the basket once until crispy and cooked through. Serve warm.

## Hasselback Alfredo Chicken

Servings:4
Cooking Time: 20 Minutes
**Ingredients:**
- 4 boneless, skinless chicken breasts
- 4 teaspoons coconut oil
- ½ teaspoon salt
- ¼ teaspoon ground black pepper
- 4 strips cooked sugar-free bacon, broken into 24 pieces
- ½ cup Alfredo sauce
- 1 cup shredded mozzarella cheese
- ¼ teaspoon crushed red pepper flakes

**Directions:**
1. Cut six horizontal slits in the top of each chicken breast. Drizzle with coconut oil and sprinkle with salt and black pepper. Place into an ungreased 6" round nonstick baking dish.
2. Place 1 bacon piece in each slit in chicken breasts. Pour Alfredo sauce over chicken and sprinkle with mozzarella and red pepper flakes.
3. Place dish into air fryer basket. Adjust the temperature to 370°F and set the timer for 20 minutes. Chicken will be

done when internal temperature is at least 165°F and cheese is browned. Serve warm.

## Pulled Turkey Quesadillas

Servings: 4
Cooking Time: 15 Minutes
**Ingredients:**
- ¾ cup pulled cooked turkey breast
- 6 tortilla wraps
- 1/3 cup grated Swiss cheese
- 1 small red onion, sliced
- 2 tbsp Mexican chili sauce

**Directions:**
1. Preheat air fryer to 400°F. Lay 3 tortilla wraps on a clean workspace, then spoon equal amounts of Swiss cheese, turkey, Mexican chili sauce, and red onion on the tortillas. Spritz the exterior of the tortillas with cooking spray. Air Fry the quesadillas, one at a time, for 5-8 minutes. The cheese should be melted and the outsides crispy. Serve.

## Surprisingly Tasty Chicken

Servings:4
Cooking Time:1 Hour
**Ingredients:**
- 1 whole chicken
- 1 pound small potatoes
- Salt and black pepper, to taste
- 1 tablespoon olive oil, scrubbed

**Directions:**
1. Preheat the Air fryer to 390°F and grease an Air fryer basket.
2. Season the chicken with salt and black pepper and transfer into the Air fryer.
3. Cook for about 40 minutes and dish out in a plate, covering with a foil paper.
4. Mix potato, oil, salt and black pepper in a bowl and toss to coat well
5. Arrange the potatoes into the Air fryer basket and cook for 20 minutes.
6. Dish out and serve warm.

## Barbecue Chicken Enchiladas

Servings:4
Cooking Time: 15 Minutes Per Batch
**Ingredients:**
- 1 ½ cups barbecue sauce, divided
- 3 cups shredded cooked chicken
- 8 flour tortillas
- 1 ½ cups shredded Mexican-blend cheese, divided
- ⅓ cup diced red onion

**Directions:**
1. Preheat the air fryer to 350°F.
2. In a large bowl, mix 1 cup barbecue sauce and shredded chicken.

3. Place ¼ cup chicken onto each tortilla and top with 2 tablespoons cheese.
4. Roll each tortilla and place seam side down into two 6" round baking dishes. Brush tortillas with remaining sauce, top with remaining cheese, and sprinkle with onion.
5. Working in batches, place in the air fryer basket and cook 15 minutes until the sauce is bubbling and cheese is melted. Serve warm.

## Balsamic Duck And Cranberry Sauce

Servings: 4
Cooking Time: 25 Minutes
**Ingredients:**
- 4 duck breasts, boneless, skin-on and scored
- A pinch of salt and black pepper
- 1 tablespoon olive oil
- ¼ cup balsamic vinegar
- ½ cup dried cranberries

**Directions:**
1. Heat up a pan that fits your air fryer with the oil over medium-high heat, add the duck breasts skin side down and cook for 5 minutes. Add the rest of the ingredients, toss, put the pan in the fryer and cook at 380°F for 20 minutes. Divide between plates and serve.

## Simple Salsa Chicken Thighs

Servings:2
Cooking Time: 35 Minutes
**Ingredients:**
- 1 lb boneless, skinless chicken thighs
- 1 cup mild chunky salsa
- ½ tsp taco seasoning
- 2 lime wedges for serving

**Directions:**
1. Preheat air fryer to 350ºF. Add chicken thighs into a baking pan and pour salsa and taco seasoning over. Place the pan in the frying basket and Air Fry for 30 minutes until golden brown. Serve with lime wedges.

## Chicken Nuggets

Servings:4
Cooking Time: 10 Minutes
**Ingredients:**
- 1 pound ground chicken breast
- 1 ½ teaspoons salt, divided
- ¾ teaspoon ground black pepper, divided
- 1 ½ cups plain bread crumbs, divided
- 2 large eggs

**Directions:**
1. Preheat the air fryer to 400°F.
2. In a large bowl, mix chicken, 1 teaspoon salt, ½ teaspoon pepper, and ½ cup bread crumbs.

3. In a small bowl, whisk eggs. In a separate medium bowl, mix remaining 1 cup bread crumbs with remaining ½ teaspoon salt and ¼ teaspoon pepper.

4. Scoop 1 tablespoon chicken mixture and flatten it into a nugget shape.

5. Dip into eggs, shaking off excess before rolling in bread crumb mixture. Repeat with remaining chicken mixture to make twenty nuggets.

6. Place nuggets in the air fryer basket and spritz with cooking spray. Cook 10 minutes, turning halfway through cooking time, until internal temperature reaches 165°F. Serve warm.

## Mustardy Chicken Bites

Servings: 4
Cooking Time: 20 Minutes + Chilling Time
**Ingredients:**
- 2 tbsp horseradish mustard
- 1 tbsp mayonnaise
- 1 tbsp olive oil
- 2 chicken breasts, cubes
- 1 tbsp parsley

**Directions:**
1. Combine all ingredients, excluding parsley, in a bowl. Let marinate covered in the fridge for 30 minutes. Preheat air fryer at 350°F. Place chicken cubes in the greased frying basket and Air Fry for 9 minutes, tossing once. Serve immediately sprinkled with parsley.

## Herb Seasoned Turkey Breast

Servings: 4
Cooking Time: 35 Minutes
**Ingredients:**
- 2 lbs turkey breast
- 1 tsp fresh sage, chopped
- 1 tsp fresh rosemary, chopped
- 1 tsp fresh thyme, chopped
- Pepper
- Salt

**Directions:**
1. Spray air fryer basket with cooking spray.

2. In a small bowl, mix together sage, rosemary, and thyme.

3. Season turkey breast with pepper and salt and rub with herb mixture.

4. Place turkey breast in air fryer basket and cook at 390°F for 30-35 minutes.

5. Slice and serve.

## Chipotle Drumsticks

Servings:4
Cooking Time: 25 Minutes
**Ingredients:**
- 1 tablespoon tomato paste
- ½ teaspoon chipotle powder
- ¼ teaspoon apple cider vinegar
- ¼ teaspoon garlic powder
- 8 chicken drumsticks
- ½ teaspoon salt
- ⅛ teaspoon ground black pepper

**Directions:**
1. In a small bowl, combine tomato paste, chipotle powder, vinegar, and garlic powder.

2. Sprinkle drumsticks with salt and pepper, then place into a large bowl and pour in tomato paste mixture. Toss or stir to evenly coat all drumsticks in mixture.

3. Place drumsticks into ungreased air fryer basket. Adjust the temperature to 400°F and set the timer for 25 minutes, turning drumsticks halfway through cooking. Drumsticks will be dark red with an internal temperature of at least 165°F when done. Serve warm.

## Cheesy Chicken Nuggets

Servings:4
Cooking Time: 15 Minutes
**Ingredients:**
- 1 pound ground chicken thighs
- ½ cup shredded mozzarella cheese
- 1 large egg, whisked
- ½ teaspoon salt
- ¼ teaspoon dried oregano
- ¼ teaspoon garlic powder

**Directions:**
1. In a large bowl, combine all ingredients. Form mixture into twenty nugget shapes, about 2 tablespoons each.

2. Place nuggets into ungreased air fryer basket, working in batches if needed. Adjust the temperature to 375°F and set the timer for 15 minutes, turning nuggets halfway through cooking. Let cool 5 minutes before serving.

## Buttermilk-fried Chicken Thighs

Servings:4
Cooking Time: 1 Hour
**Ingredients:**
- 1 cup buttermilk
- 2 tablespoons seasoned salt, divided
- 1 pound bone-in, skin-on chicken thighs
- 1 cup all-purpose flour
- ¼ cup cornstarch

**Directions:**
1. In a large bowl, combine buttermilk and 1 tablespoon seasoned salt. Add chicken. Cover and let marinate in refrigerator 30 minutes.

2. Preheat the air fryer to 375°F.

3. In a separate bowl, mix flour, cornstarch, and remaining seasoned salt. Dredge chicken thighs, one at a time, in flour mixture, covering completely.

4. Spray chicken generously with cooking spray, being sure that no dry spots remain. Place chicken in the air fryer

basket and cook 30 minutes, turning halfway through cooking time and spraying any dry spots, until chicken is dark golden brown and crispy and internal temperature reaches at least 165°F.

5.  Serve warm.

## Chicken Gruyere

Servings:4
Cooking Time: 20 Minutes
**Ingredients:**
- ¼ cup Gruyere cheese, grated
- 1 pound chicken breasts, boneless, skinless
- ½ cup flour
- 2 eggs, beaten
- Sea salt and black pepper to taste
- 4 lemon slices
- Cooking spray

**Directions:**
1.  Preheat your Air Fryer to 370°F. Spray the air fryer basket with cooking spray.
2.  Mix the breadcrumbs with Gruyere cheese in a bowl, pour the eggs in another bowl, and the flour in a third bowl. Toss the chicken in the flour, then in the eggs, and then in the breadcrumb mixture. Place in the fryer basket, close and cook for 12 minutes. At the 6-minute mark, turn the chicken over. Once golden brown, remove onto a serving plate and serve topped with lemon slices.

## Crispy 'n Salted Chicken Meatballs

Servings:6
Cooking Time: 20 Minutes
**Ingredients:**
- ½ cup almond flour
- ¾ pound skinless boneless chicken breasts, ground
- 1 ½ teaspoon herbs de Provence
- 1 tablespoon coconut milk
- 2 eggs, beaten
- Salt and pepper to taste

**Directions:**
1.  Mix all ingredient in a bowl.
2.  Form small balls using the palms of your hands.
3.  Place in the fridge to set for at least 2 hours.
4.  Preheat the air fryer for 5 minutes.
5.  Place the chicken balls in the fryer basket.
6.  Cook for 20 minutes at 325°F.
7.  Halfway through the cooking time, give the fryer basket a shake to cook evenly on all sides.

## Cajun-breaded Chicken Bites

Servings:4
Cooking Time: 12 Minutes
**Ingredients:**
- 1 pound boneless, skinless chicken breasts, cut into 1" cubes

- ½ cup heavy whipping cream
- ½ teaspoon salt
- ¼ teaspoon ground black pepper
- 1 ounce plain pork rinds, finely crushed
- ¼ cup unflavored whey protein powder
- ½ teaspoon Cajun seasoning

**Directions:**
1.  Place chicken in a medium bowl and pour in cream. Stir to coat. Sprinkle with salt and pepper.
2.  In a separate large bowl, combine pork rinds, protein powder, and Cajun seasoning. Remove chicken from cream, shaking off any excess, and toss in dry mix until fully coated.
3.  Place bites into ungreased air fryer basket. Adjust the temperature to 400°F and set the timer for 12 minutes, shaking the basket twice during cooking. Bites will be done when golden brown and have an internal temperature of at least 165°F. Serve warm.

## Jerk Chicken Wings

Servings:4
Cooking Time: 1 Hour 20 Minutes
**Ingredients:**
- ¼ cup Jamaican jerk marinade
- 1 teaspoon onion powder
- 1 teaspoon garlic powder
- 1 teaspoon salt
- 2 pounds chicken wings, flats and drums separated

**Directions:**
1.  In a large bowl, combine jerk seasoning, onion powder, garlic powder, and salt. Add chicken wings and toss to coat well. Cover and let marinate in refrigerator at least 1 hour.
2.  Preheat the air fryer to 400°F.
3.  Place wings in the air fryer basket in a single layer, working in batches as necessary. Cook wings 20 minutes, turning halfway through cooking time, until internal temperature reaches at least 165°F. Cool 5 minutes before serving.

## Jerk Chicken Kebabs

Servings:4
Cooking Time: 14 Minutes
**Ingredients:**
- 8 ounces boneless, skinless chicken thighs, cut into 1" cubes
- 2 tablespoons jerk seasoning
- 2 tablespoons coconut oil
- ½ medium red bell pepper, seeded and cut into 1" pieces
- ¼ medium red onion, peeled and cut into 1" pieces
- ½ teaspoon salt

**Directions:**
1.  Place chicken in a medium bowl and sprinkle with jerk seasoning and coconut oil. Toss to coat on all sides.

2. Using eight 6" skewers, build skewers by alternating chicken, pepper, and onion pieces, about three repetitions per skewer.

3. Sprinkle salt over skewers and place into ungreased air fryer basket. Adjust the temperature to 370°F and set the timer for 14 minutes, turning skewers halfway through cooking. Chicken will be golden and have an internal temperature of at least 165°F when done. Serve warm.

## Chicken Chunks

Servings: 4
Cooking Time: 10 Minutes
**Ingredients:**
- 1 pound chicken tenders cut in large chunks, about 1½ inches
- salt and pepper
- ½ cup cornstarch
- 2 eggs, beaten
- 1 cup panko breadcrumbs
- oil for misting or cooking spray

**Directions:**
1. Season chicken chunks to your liking with salt and pepper.
2. Dip chicken chunks in cornstarch. Then dip in egg and shake off excess. Then roll in panko crumbs to coat well.
3. Spray all sides of chicken chunks with oil or cooking spray.
4. Place chicken in air fryer basket in single layer and cook at 390°F for 5minutes. Spray with oil, turn chunks over, and spray other side.
5. Cook for an additional 5minutes or until chicken juices run clear and outside is golden brown.
6. Repeat steps 4 and 5 to cook remaining chicken.

## Betty's Baked Chicken

Servings: 1
Cooking Time: 70 Minutes
**Ingredients:**
- ½ cup butter
- 1 tsp. pepper
- 3 tbsp. garlic, minced
- 1 whole chicken

**Directions:**
1. Pre-heat your fryer at 350°F.
2. Allow the butter to soften at room temperature, then mix well in a small bowl with the pepper and garlic.
3. Massage the butter into the chicken. Any remaining butter can go inside the chicken.
4. Cook the chicken in the fryer for half an hour. Flip, then cook on the other side for another thirty minutes.
5. Test the temperature of the chicken by sticking a meat thermometer into the fat of the thigh to make sure it has reached 165°F. Take care when removing the chicken from the fryer. Let sit for ten minutes before you carve it and serve.

## Gingered Chicken Drumsticks

Servings:3
Cooking Time:25 Minutes
**Ingredients:**
- ¼ cup full-fat coconut milk
- 3 chicken drumsticks
- 2 teaspoons fresh ginger, minced
- 2 teaspoons galangal, minced
- 2 teaspoons ground turmeric
- Salt, to taste

**Directions:**
1. Preheat the Air fryer to 375°F and grease an Air fryer basket.
2. Mix the coconut milk, galangal, ginger, and spices in a bowl.
3. Add the chicken drumsticks and coat generously with the marinade.
4. Refrigerate to marinate for at least 8 hours and transfer into the Air fryer basket.
5. Cook for about 25 minutes and dish out the chicken drumsticks onto a serving platter.

## Quick Chicken For Filling

Servings: 2
Cooking Time: 8 Minutes
**Ingredients:**
- 1 pound chicken tenders, skinless and boneless
- ½ teaspoon ground cumin
- ½ teaspoon garlic powder
- cooking spray

**Directions:**
1. Sprinkle raw chicken tenders with seasonings.
2. Spray air fryer basket lightly with cooking spray to prevent sticking.
3. Place chicken in air fryer basket in single layer.
4. Cook at 390°F for 4minutes, turn chicken strips over, and cook for an additional 4minutes.
5. Test for doneness. Thick tenders may require an additional minute or two.

## Lemon Sage Roast Chicken

Servings: 4
Cooking Time: 60 Minutes
**Ingredients:**
- 1 chicken
- 1 bunch sage, divided
- 1 lemon, zest and juice
- salt and freshly ground black pepper

**Directions:**
1. Preheat the air fryer to 350°F and pour a little water into the bottom of the air fryer drawer.
2. Run your fingers between the skin and flesh of the chicken breasts and thighs. Push a couple of sage leaves up

underneath the skin of the chicken on each breast and each thigh.

3. Push some of the lemon zest up under the skin of the chicken next to the sage. Sprinkle some of the zest inside the chicken cavity, and reserve any leftover zest. Squeeze the lemon juice all over the chicken and in the cavity as well.

4. Season the chicken, inside and out, with the salt and freshly ground black pepper. Set a few sage leaves aside for the final garnish. Crumple up the remaining sage leaves and push them into the cavity of the chicken, along with one of the squeezed lemon halves.

5. Place the chicken breast side up into the air fryer basket and air-fry for 20 minutes at 350°F. Flip the chicken over so that it is breast side down and continue to air-fry for another 20 minutes. Return the chicken to breast side up and finish air-frying for 20 more minutes. The internal temperature of the chicken should register 165°F in the thickest part of the thigh when fully cooked. Remove the chicken from the air fryer and let it rest on a cutting board for at least 5 minutes.

6. Cut the rested chicken into pieces, sprinkle with the reserved lemon zest and garnish with the reserved sage leaves.

## Air Fried Cheese Chicken

Servings:6
Cooking Time: 15 Minutes
**Ingredients:**

- 6 tbsp seasoned breadcrumbs
- 2 tbsp Parmesan cheese, grated
- 1 tbsp melted butter
- ½ cup mozzarella cheese, shredded
- 1 tbsp marinara sauce
- Cooking spray as needed

**Directions:**

1. Preheat your air fryer to 390°F. Grease the cooking basket with cooking spray. In a small bowl, mix breadcrumbs and Parmesan cheese. Brush the chicken pieces with butter and dredge into the breadcrumbs. Add chicken to the cooking basket and cook for 6 minutes. Turn over and top with marinara sauce and shredded mozzarella; cook for 3 more minutes.

## Tangy Mustard Wings

Servings:4
Cooking Time: 25 Minutes
**Ingredients:**

- 1 pound bone-in chicken wings, separated at joints
- ¼ cup yellow mustard
- ½ teaspoon salt
- ¼ teaspoon ground black pepper

**Directions:**

1. Place wings in a large bowl and toss with mustard to fully coat. Sprinkle with salt and pepper.

2. Place wings into ungreased air fryer basket. Adjust the temperature to 400°F and set the timer for 25 minutes,

shaking the basket three times during cooking. Wings will be done when browned and cooked to an internal temperature of at least 165°F. Serve warm.

## Sweet Nutty Chicken Breasts

Servings:4
Cooking Time: 30 Minutes
**Ingredients:**

- 2 chicken breasts, halved lengthwise
- ¼ cup honey mustard
- ¼ cup chopped pecans
- 1 tbsp olive oil
- 1 tbsp parsley, chopped

**Directions:**

1. Preheat air fryer to 350°F. Brush chicken breasts with honey mustard and olive oil on all sides. Place the pecans in a bowl. Add and coat the chicken breasts. Place the breasts in the greased frying basket and Air Fry for 25 minutes, turning once. Let chill onto a serving plate for 5 minutes. Sprinkle with parsley and serve.

## Spinach And Feta Stuffed Chicken Breasts

Servings: 4
Cooking Time: 27 Minutes
**Ingredients:**

- 1 package frozen spinach, thawed and drained well
- 1 cup feta cheese, crumbled
- ½ teaspoon freshly ground black pepper
- 4 boneless chicken breasts
- salt and freshly ground black pepper
- 1 tablespoon olive oil

**Directions:**

1. Prepare the filling. Squeeze out as much liquid as possible from the thawed spinach. Rough chop the spinach and transfer it to a mixing bowl with the feta cheese and the freshly ground black pepper.

2. Prepare the chicken breast. Place the chicken breast on a cutting board and press down on the chicken breast with one hand to keep it stabilized. Make an incision about 1-inch long in the fattest side of the breast. Move the knife up and down inside the chicken breast, without poking through either the top or the bottom, or the other side of the breast. The inside pocket should be about 3-inches long, but the opening should only be about 1-inch wide. If this is too difficult, you can make the incision longer, but you will have to be more careful when cooking the chicken breast since this will expose more of the stuffing.

3. Once you have prepared the chicken breasts, use your fingers to stuff the filling into each pocket, spreading the mixture down as far as you can.

4. Preheat the air fryer to 380°F.

5. Lightly brush or spray the air fryer basket and the chicken breasts with olive oil. Transfer two of the stuffed

chicken breasts to the air fryer. Air-fry for 12 minutes, turning the chicken breasts over halfway through the cooking time. Remove the chicken to a resting plate and air-fry the second two breasts for 12 minutes. Return the first batch of chicken to the air fryer with the second batch and air-fry for 3 more minutes. When the chicken is cooked, an instant read thermometer should register 165°F in the thickest part of the chicken, as well as in the stuffing.

6.  Remove the chicken breasts and let them rest on a cutting board for 2 to 3 minutes. Slice the chicken on the bias and serve with the slices fanned out.

## Turkey-hummus Wraps

Servings: 4
Cooking Time: 7 Minutes Per Batch
Ingredients:
*   4 large whole wheat wraps
*   ½ cup hummus
*   16 thin slices deli turkey
*   8 slices provolone cheese
*   1 cup fresh baby spinach (or more to taste)

Directions:
1.  To assemble, place 2 tablespoons of hummus on each wrap and spread to within about a half inch from edges. Top with 4 slices of turkey and 2 slices of provolone. Finish with ¼ cup of baby spinach—or pile on as much as you like.
2.  Roll up each wrap. You don't need to fold or seal the ends.
3.  Place 2 wraps in air fryer basket, seam side down.
4.  Cook at 360°F for 4minutes to warm filling and melt cheese. If you like, you can continue cooking for 3 more minutes, until the wrap is slightly crispy.
5.  Repeat step 4 to cook remaining wraps.

## Chicken Pesto Pizzas

Servings:4
Cooking Time: 12 Minutes
Ingredients:
*   1 pound ground chicken thighs
*   ¼ teaspoon salt
*   ⅛ teaspoon ground black pepper
*   ¼ cup basil pesto
*   1 cup shredded mozzarella cheese
*   4 grape tomatoes, sliced

Directions:
1.  Cut four squares of parchment paper to fit into your air fryer basket.
2.  Place ground chicken in a large bowl and mix with salt and pepper. Divide mixture into four equal sections.
3.  Wet your hands with water to prevent sticking, then press each section into a 6" circle onto a piece of ungreased parchment. Place each chicken crust into air fryer basket, working in batches if needed.
4.  Adjust the temperature to 350°F and set the timer for 10 minutes, turning crusts halfway through cooking.

5.  When the timer beeps, spread 1 tablespoon pesto across the top of each crust, then sprinkle with ¼ cup mozzarella and top with 1 sliced tomato. Continue cooking at 350°F for 2 minutes. Cheese will be melted and brown when done. Serve warm.

## Spicy Pork Rind Fried Chicken

Servings:4
Cooking Time: 20 Minutes
Ingredients:
*   ¼ cup buffalo sauce
*   4 boneless, skinless chicken breasts
*   ½ teaspoon paprika
*   ½ teaspoon garlic powder
*   ¼ teaspoon ground black pepper
*   2 ounces plain pork rinds, finely crushed

Directions:
1.  Pour buffalo sauce into a large sealable bowl or bag. Add chicken and toss to coat. Place sealed bowl or bag into refrigerator and let marinate at least 30 minutes up to overnight.
2.  Remove chicken from marinade but do not shake excess sauce off chicken. Sprinkle both sides of thighs with paprika, garlic powder, and pepper.
3.  Place pork rinds into a large bowl and press each chicken breast into pork rinds to coat evenly on both sides.
4.  Place chicken into ungreased air fryer basket. Adjust the temperature to 400°F and set the timer for 20 minutes, turning chicken halfway through cooking. Chicken will be golden and have an internal temperature of at least 165°F when done. Serve warm.

## Dill Pickle–ranch Wings

Servings:4
Cooking Time: 2 Hours 20 Minutes
Ingredients:
*   1 cup pickle juice
*   2 pounds chicken wings, flats and drums separated
*   ½ teaspoon salt
*   ½ teaspoon ground black pepper
*   2 teaspoons dry ranch seasoning

Directions:
1.  In a large bowl or resealable plastic bag, combine pickle juice and wings. Cover and let marinate in refrigerator 2 hours.
2.  Preheat the air fryer to 400°F.
3.  In a separate bowl, mix salt, pepper, and ranch seasoning. Remove wings from marinade and toss in dry seasoning.
4.  Place wings in the air fryer basket in a single layer, working in batches as necessary. Cook 20 minutes, turning halfway through cooking time, until wings reach an internal temperature of at least 165°F. Cool 5 minutes before serving.

# Shishito Pepper Rubbed Wings

Servings:6
Cooking Time: 30 Minutes
**Ingredients:**
- 1 ½ cups shishito peppers, pureed
- 2 tablespoons sesame oil
- 3 pounds chicken wings
- Salt and pepper to taste

**Directions:**
1. Place all Ingredients in a Ziploc bowl and allow to marinate for at least 2 hours in the fridge.
2. Preheat the air fryer to 390°F.
3. Place the grill pan accessory in the air fryer.
4. Grill for at least 30 minutes flipping the chicken every 5 minutes and basting with the remaining sauce.

# Italian Roasted Chicken Thighs

Servings: 6
Cooking Time: 14 Minutes
**Ingredients:**
- 6 boneless chicken thighs
- ½ teaspoon dried oregano
- ½ teaspoon garlic powder
- ½ teaspoon sea salt
- ½ teaspoon black pepper
- ¼ teaspoon crushed red pepper flakes

**Directions:**
1. Pat the chicken thighs with paper towel.
2. In a small bowl, mix the oregano, garlic powder, salt, pepper, and crushed red pepper flakes. Rub the spice mixture onto the chicken thighs.
3. Preheat the air fryer to 400°F.
4. Place the chicken thighs in the air fryer basket and spray with cooking spray. Cook for 10 minutes, turn over, and cook another 4 minutes. When cooking completes, the internal temperature should read 165°F.

# Hot Chicken Skin

Servings: 4
Cooking Time: 30 Minutes
**Ingredients:**
- ½ teaspoon chili paste
- 8 oz chicken skin
- 1 teaspoon sesame oil
- ½ teaspoon chili powder
- ½ teaspoon salt

**Directions:**
1. In the shallow bowl mix up chili paste, sesame oil, chili powder, and salt. Then brush the chicken skin with chili mixture well and leave for 10 minutes to marinate. Meanwhile, preheat the air fryer to 365°F. Put the marinated chicken skin in the air fryer and cook it for 20 minutes. When the time is finished, flip the chicken skin on another side and cook it for 10 minutes more or until the chicken skin is crunchy.

# 15-minute Chicken

Servings:4
Cooking Time: 15 Minutes
**Ingredients:**
- 4 boneless, skinless chicken breasts
- 2 tablespoons olive oil
- 1 teaspoon salt
- 1 teaspoon garlic powder
- 1 teaspoon paprika
- ½ teaspoon ground black pepper

**Directions:**
1. Preheat the air fryer to 375°F.
2. Carefully butterfly chicken breasts lengthwise, leaving the two halves connected. Drizzle chicken with oil, then sprinkle with salt, garlic powder, paprika, and pepper.
3. Place in the air fryer basket and cook 15 minutes, turning halfway through cooking time, until chicken is golden brown and the internal temperature reaches at least 165°F. Serve warm.

# Buffalo Chicken Meatballs

Servings:5
Cooking Time: 12 Minutes
**Ingredients:**
- 1 pound ground chicken breast
- 1 packet dry ranch seasoning
- ⅓ cup plain bread crumbs
- 3 tablespoons mayonnaise
- 5 tablespoons buffalo sauce, divided

**Directions:**
1. Preheat the air fryer to 370°F.
2. In a large bowl, mix chicken, ranch seasoning, bread crumbs, and mayonnaise. Pour in 2 tablespoons buffalo sauce and stir to combine.
3. Roll meat mixture into balls, about 2 tablespoons for each, to make twenty meatballs.
4. Place meatballs in the air fryer basket and cook 12 minutes, shaking the basket twice during cooking, until brown and internal temperature reaches at least 165°F.
5. Toss meatballs in remaining buffalo sauce and serve.

# Perfect Grill Chicken Breast

Servings: 2
Cooking Time: 12 Minutes
**Ingredients:**
- 2 chicken breast, skinless and boneless
- 2 tsp olive oil
- Pepper
- Salt

**Directions:**

1.  Remove air fryer basket and replace it with air fryer grill pan.
2.  Place chicken breast to the grill pan. Season chicken with pepper and salt. Drizzle with oil.
3.  Cook chicken for 375°F for 12 minutes.
4.  Serve and enjoy.

# Crunchy Chicken Strips

Servings: 4
Cooking Time: 40 Minutes
**Ingredients:**
*   1 chicken breast, sliced into strips
*   1 tbsp grated Parmesan cheese
*   1 cup breadcrumbs
*   1 tbsp chicken seasoning
*   2 eggs, beaten
*   Salt and pepper to taste
**Directions:**
1.  Preheat air fryer to 350°F. Mix the breadcrumbs, Parmesan cheese, chicken seasoning, salt, and pepper in a mixing bowl. Coat the chicken with the crumb mixture, then dip in the beaten eggs. Finally, coat again with the dry ingredients. Arrange the coated chicken pieces on the greased frying basket and Air Fry for 15 minutes. Turn over halfway through cooking and cook for another 15 minutes. Serve immediately.

# Easy & Crispy Chicken Wings

Servings: 8
Cooking Time: 20 Minutes
**Ingredients:**
*   1 1/2 lbs chicken wings
*   2 tbsp olive oil
*   Pepper
*   Salt
**Directions:**
1.  Toss chicken wings with oil and place in the air fryer basket.
2.  Cook chicken wings at 370°F for 15 minutes.
3.  Shake basket and cook at 400 F for 5 minutes more.
4.  Season chicken wings with pepper and salt.
5.  Serve and enjoy.

# Cheesy Chicken And Broccoli Casserole

Servings:4
Cooking Time: 30 Minutes
**Ingredients:**
*   1 pound boneless, skinless chicken breast, cubed
*   1 teaspoon salt
*   ½ teaspoon ground black pepper
*   1 cup uncooked instant long-grain white rice
*   1 cup chopped broccoli florets
*   1 cup chicken broth

*   1 cup shredded sharp Cheddar cheese
**Directions:**
1.  Preheat the air fryer to 400°F.
2.  In a 6" round baking dish, add chicken and sprinkle with salt and pepper.
3.  Place in the air fryer basket and cook 10 minutes, stirring twice during cooking.
4.  Add rice, broccoli, broth, and Cheddar. Stir until combined. Cover with foil, being sure to tuck foil under the bottom of the dish to ensure the air fryer fan does not blow it off.
5.  Place dish back in the air fryer basket and cook 20 minutes until rice is tender. Serve warm.

# Party Buffalo Chicken Drumettes

Servings: 6
Cooking Time: 30 Minutes
**Ingredients:**
*   16 chicken drumettes
*   1 tsp garlic powder
*   1 tbsp chicken seasoning
*   Black pepper to taste
*   ¼ cup Buffalo wings sauce
*   2 spring onions, sliced
*   Cooking spray
**Directions:**
1.  Preheat air fryer to 400°F. Sprinkle garlic, chicken seasoning, and black pepper on the drumettes. Place them in the fryer and spray with cooking oil. Air Fry for 10 minutes, shaking the basket once. Transfer the drumettes to a large bowl. Drizzle with Buffalo wing sauce and toss to coat. Place in the fryer and Fry for 7-8 minutes, until crispy. Allow to cool slightly. Top with spring onions and serve warm.

# Chicken Adobo

Servings: 6
Cooking Time: 12 Minutes
**Ingredients:**
*   6 boneless chicken thighs
*   ¼ cup soy sauce or tamari
*   ½ cup rice wine vinegar
*   4 cloves garlic, minced
*   ⅛ teaspoon crushed red pepper flakes
*   ½ teaspoon black pepper
**Directions:**
1.  Place the chicken thighs into a resealable plastic bag with the soy sauce or tamari, the rice wine vinegar, the garlic, and the crushed red pepper flakes. Seal the bag and let the chicken marinate at least 1 hour in the refrigerator.
2.  Preheat the air fryer to 400°F.
3.  Drain the chicken and pat dry with a paper towel. Season the chicken with black pepper and liberally spray with cooking spray.

4. Place the chicken in the air fryer basket and cook for 9 minutes, turn over at 9 minutes and check for an internal temperature of 165°F, and cook another 3 minutes.

# Butter And Bacon Chicken

Servings:6
Cooking Time: 65 Minutes
**Ingredients:**
- 1 whole chicken
- 2 tablespoons salted butter, softened
- 1 teaspoon dried thyme
- ½ teaspoon garlic powder
- 1 teaspoon salt
- ½ teaspoon ground black pepper
- 6 slices sugar-free bacon

**Directions:**
1. Pat chicken dry with a paper towel, then rub with butter on all sides. Sprinkle thyme, garlic powder, salt, and pepper over chicken.
2. Place chicken into ungreased air fryer basket, breast side up. Lay strips of bacon over chicken and secure with toothpicks.
3. Adjust the temperature to 350°F and set the timer for 65 minutes. Halfway through cooking, remove and set aside bacon and flip chicken over. Chicken will be done when the skin is golden and crispy and the internal temperature is at least 165°F. Serve warm with bacon.

# Pretzel-crusted Chicken

Servings:4
Cooking Time: 12 Minutes
**Ingredients:**
- 2 cups mini twist pretzels
- ½ cup mayonnaise
- 2 tablespoons honey
- 2 tablespoons yellow mustard
- 4 boneless, skinless chicken breasts, sliced in half lengthwise
- 1 teaspoon salt
- ½ teaspoon ground black pepper
- Cooking spray

**Directions:**
1. Preheat the air fryer to 375°F.
2. In a food processor, place pretzels and pulse ten times.
3. In a medium bowl, mix mayonnaise, honey, and mustard.
4. Sprinkle chicken with salt and pepper, then brush with sauce mixture until well coated.
5. Pour pretzel crumbs onto a shallow plate and press each piece of chicken into them until well coated.
6. Spritz chicken with cooking spray and place in the air fryer basket. Cook 12 minutes, turning halfway through cooking time, until edges are golden brown and the internal temperature reaches at least 165°F. Serve warm.

# Basic Chicken Breasts.

Servings:4
Cooking Time: 15 Minutes
**Ingredients:**
- 2 tsp olive oil
- 2 chicken breasts
- Salt and pepper to taste
- ½ tsp garlic powder
- ½ tsp rosemary

**Directions:**
1. Preheat air fryer to 350ºF. Rub the chicken breasts with olive oil over tops and bottom and sprinkle with garlic powder, rosemary, salt, and pepper. Place the chicken in the frying basket and Air Fry for 9 minutes, flipping once. Let rest onto a serving plate for 5 minutes before cutting into cubes. Serve and enjoy!

# Broccoli And Cheese–stuffed Chicken

Servings:4
Cooking Time: 20 Minutes
**Ingredients:**
- 2 ounces cream cheese, softened
- 1 cup chopped fresh broccoli, steamed
- ½ cup shredded sharp Cheddar cheese
- 4 boneless, skinless chicken breasts
- 2 tablespoons mayonnaise
- ¼ teaspoon salt
- ¼ teaspoon garlic powder
- ⅛ teaspoon ground black pepper

**Directions:**
1. In a medium bowl, combine cream cheese, broccoli, and Cheddar. Cut a 4" pocket into each chicken breast. Evenly divide mixture between chicken breasts; stuff the pocket of each chicken breast with the mixture.
2. Spread ¼ tablespoon mayonnaise per side of each chicken breast, then sprinkle both sides of breasts with salt, garlic powder, and pepper.
3. Place stuffed chicken breasts into ungreased air fryer basket so that the open seams face up. Adjust the temperature to 350°F and set the timer for 20 minutes, turning chicken halfway through cooking. When done, chicken will be golden and have an internal temperature of at least 165°F. Serve warm.

# Chicken Cordon Bleu

Servings:4
Cooking Time: 15 Minutes
**Ingredients:**
- 4 boneless, skinless chicken breasts
- ¾ teaspoon salt
- ½ teaspoon ground black pepper
- 8 slices deli Black Forest ham
- 8 slices Gruyère cheese
- 1 large egg, beaten
- 2 cups panko bread crumbs

**Directions:**
1. Preheat the air fryer to 375°F.
2. Cut each chicken breast in half lengthwise. Use a mallet to pound to ¼" thickness. Sprinkle salt and pepper on each side of chicken.
3. Place a slice of ham and a slice of cheese on each piece of chicken. Roll up chicken and secure with toothpicks.
4. In a medium bowl, add egg. In a separate medium bowl, add bread crumbs. Dip each chicken roll into egg, then into bread crumbs, pressing gently to adhere.
5. Spritz rolls with cooking spray and place in the air fryer basket. Cook 15 minutes, turning halfway through cooking time, until rolls are golden brown and internal temperature reaches at least 165°F. Serve warm.

# Chicken Wrapped In Bacon

Servings: 6
Cooking Time: 25 Minutes
**Ingredients:**
- 6 rashers unsmoked back bacon
- 1 small chicken breast
- 1 tbsp. garlic soft cheese

**Directions:**
1. Cut the chicken breast into six bite-sized pieces.
2. Spread the soft cheese across one side of each slice of bacon.
3. Put the chicken on top of the cheese and wrap the bacon around it, holding it in place with a toothpick.
4. Transfer the wrapped chicken pieces to the Air Fryer and cook for 15 minutes at 350°F.

# Fantasy Sweet Chili Chicken Strips

Servings: 2
Cooking Time: 20 Minutes
**Ingredients:**
- 1 lb chicken strips
- 1 cup sweet chili sauce
- ½ cup bread crumbs
- ½ cup cornmeal

**Directions:**
1. Preheat air fryer at 350°F. Combine chicken strips and sweet chili sauce in a bowl until fully coated. In another bowl, mix the remaining ingredients. Dredge strips in the mixture. Shake off any excess. Place chicken strips in the greased frying basket and Air Fry for 10 minutes, tossing once. Serve right away.

# Teriyaki Chicken Legs

Servings: 2
Cooking Time: 20 Minutes
**Ingredients:**
- 4 tablespoons teriyaki sauce
- 1 tablespoon orange juice
- 1 teaspoon smoked paprika
- 4 chicken legs
- cooking spray

**Directions:**
1. Mix together the teriyaki sauce, orange juice, and smoked paprika. Brush on all sides of chicken legs.
2. Spray air fryer basket with nonstick cooking spray and place chicken in basket.
3. Cook at 360°F for 6minutes. Turn and baste with sauce. Cook for 6 moreminutes, turn and baste. Cook for 8 minutes more, until juices run clear when chicken is pierced with a fork.

# Lemon Pepper Chicken Wings

Servings: 4
Cooking Time: 16 Minutes
**Ingredients:**
- 1 lb chicken wings
- 1 tsp lemon pepper
- 1 tbsp olive oil
- 1 tsp salt

**Directions:**
1. Add chicken wings into the large mixing bowl.
2. Add remaining ingredients over chicken and toss well to coat.
3. Place chicken wings in the air fryer basket.
4. Cook chicken wings for 8 minutes at 400°F.
5. Turn chicken wings to another side and cook for 8 minutes more.
6. Serve and enjoy.

# Jumbo Buffalo Chicken Meatballs

Servings:4
Cooking Time: 15 Minutes
**Ingredients:**
- 1 pound ground chicken thighs
- 1 large egg, whisked
- ½ cup hot sauce, divided
- ½ cup crumbled blue cheese
- 2 tablespoons dry ranch seasoning
- ¼ teaspoon salt
- ¼ teaspoon ground black pepper

**Directions:**

1. In a large bowl, combine ground chicken, egg, ¼ cup hot sauce, blue cheese, ranch seasoning, salt, and pepper.
2. Divide mixture into eight equal sections of about ¼ cup each and form each section into a ball. Place meatballs into ungreased air fryer basket. Adjust the temperature to 370°F and set the timer for 15 minutes. Meatballs will be done when golden and have an internal temperature of at least 165°F.
3. Transfer meatballs to a large serving dish and toss with remaining hot sauce. Serve warm.

## Quick 'n Easy Garlic Herb Wings

Servings:4
Cooking Time: 35 Minutes
**Ingredients:**
- ¼ cup chopped rosemary
- 2 pounds chicken wings
- 6 medium garlic cloves , grated
- Salt and pepper to taste

**Directions:**
1. Season the chicken with garlic, rosemary, salt and pepper.
2. Preheat the air fryer to 390°F.
3. Place the grill pan accessory in the air fryer.
4. Grill for 35 minutes and make sure to flip the chicken every 10 minutes.

## Chicken Thighs In Salsa Verde

Servings: 4
Cooking Time: 35 Minutes
**Ingredients:**
- 4 boneless, skinless chicken thighs
- 1 cup salsa verde
- 1 tsp mashed garlic

**Directions:**
1. Preheat air fryer at 350°F. Add chicken thighs to a cake pan and cover with salsa verde and mashed garlic. Place cake pan in the frying basket and Bake for 30 minutes. Let rest for 5 minutes before serving.

## Yummy Shredded Chicken

Servings: 2
Cooking Time: 15 Minutes
**Ingredients:**
- 2 large chicken breasts
- ¼ tsp Pepper
- 1 tsp garlic puree
- 1 tsp mustard
- Salt

**Directions:**
1. Add all ingredients to the bowl and toss well.
2. Transfer chicken into the air fryer basket and cook at 360°F for 15 minutes.
3. Remove chicken from air fryer and shred using a fork.
4. Serve and enjoy.

## Parmesan Chicken Tenders

Servings:4
Cooking Time: 12 Minutes
**Ingredients:**
- 1 pound boneless, skinless chicken breast tenderloins
- ½ cup mayonnaise
- 1 cup grated Parmesan cheese
- 1 cup panko bread crumbs
- ½ teaspoon garlic powder
- 1 teaspoon salt
- ½ teaspoon ground black pepper
- Cooking spray

**Directions:**
1. Preheat the air fryer to 400°F.
2. In a large bowl, add chicken and mayonnaise and toss to coat.
3. In a medium bowl, mix Parmesan, bread crumbs, garlic powder, salt, and pepper. Press chicken into bread crumb mixture to fully coat. Spritz with cooking spray and place in the air fryer basket.
4. Cook 12 minutes, turning halfway through cooking time, until tenders are golden and crisp on the edges and internal temperature reaches at least 165°F. Serve warm.

## Rosemary Partridge

Servings: 4
Cooking Time: 14 Minutes
**Ingredients:**
- 10 oz partridges
- 1 teaspoon dried rosemary
- 1 tablespoon butter, melted
- 1 teaspoon salt

**Directions:**
1. Cut the partridges into the halves and sprinkle with dried rosemary and salt. Then brush them with melted butter. Preheat the air fryer to 385°F. Put the partridge halves in the air fryer and cook them for 8 minutes. Then flip the poultry on another side and cook for 6 minutes more.

## Bacon-wrapped Chicken

Servings: 6
Cooking Time: 20 Minutes
**Ingredients:**
- 1 chicken breast, cut into 6 pieces
- 6 rashers back bacon
- 1 tbsp. soft cheese

**Directions:**
1. Put the bacon rashers on a flat surface and cover one side with the soft cheese.
2. Lay the chicken pieces on each bacon rasher. Wrap the bacon around the chicken and use a toothpick stick to hold each one in place. Put them in Air Fryer basket.
3. Air fry at 350°F for 15 minutes.

## Grilled Chicken Pesto

Servings:8
Cooking Time: 30 Minutes
**Ingredients:**
- 1 ¾ cup commercial pesto
- 8 chicken thighs
- Salt and pepper to taste

**Directions:**
1. Place all Ingredients in the Ziploc bag and allow to marinate in the fridge for at least 2 hours.
2. Preheat the air fryer to 390°F.
3. Place the grill pan accessory in the air fryer.
4. Grill the chicken for at least 30 minutes.
5. Make sure to flip the chicken every 10 minutes for even grilling.

# Chapter 5. Beef,pork & Lamb Recipes

## Air Fried Steak

Servings: 2
Cooking Time: 10 Minutes
**Ingredients:**
- 2 sirloin steaks
- 2 tsp olive oil
- 2 tbsp steak seasoning
- Pepper
- Salt

**Directions:**
1. Preheat the air fryer to 350°F.
2. Coat steak with olive oil and season with steak seasoning, pepper, and salt.
3. Spray air fryer basket with cooking spray and place steak in the air fryer basket.
4. Cook for 10 minutes. Turn halfway through.
5. Slice and serve.

## Ground Beef

Servings:4
Cooking Time: 9 Minutes
**Ingredients:**
- 1 pound 70/30 ground beef
- ¼ cup water
- 1 teaspoon salt
- ½ teaspoon ground black pepper
- 1 teaspoon garlic powder

**Directions:**
1. Preheat the air fryer to 400°F.
2. In a medium bowl, mix beef with remaining ingredients. Place beef in a 6" round cake pan and press into an even layer.
3. Place in the air fryer basket and set the timer to 10 minutes. After 5 minutes, open the air fryer and stir ground beef with a spatula. Return to the air fryer.
4. After 2 more minutes, open the air fryer, remove the pan and drain any excess fat from the ground beef. Return to the air fryer for and cook 2 more minutes until beef is brown and no pink remains.

## Easy & The Traditional Beef Roast Recipe

Servings:12
Cooking Time: 2 Hours
**Ingredients:**
- 1 cup organic beef broth
- 3 pounds beef round roast
- 4 tablespoons olive oil
- Salt and pepper to taste

**Directions:**
1. Place in a Ziploc bag all the ingredients and allow to marinate in the fridge for 2 hours.
2. Preheat the air fryer for 5 minutes.
3. Transfer all ingredients in a baking dish that will fit in the air fryer.
4. Place in the air fryer and cook for 2 hours for 400°F.

## Barbecue-style London Broil

Servings: 5
Cooking Time: 17 Minutes
**Ingredients:**
- ¾ teaspoon Mild smoked paprika
- ¾ teaspoon Dried oregano
- ¾ teaspoon Table salt
- ¾ teaspoon Ground black pepper
- ¼ teaspoon Garlic powder
- ¼ teaspoon Onion powder
- 1½ pounds Beef London broil (in one piece)
- Olive oil spray

**Directions:**
1. Preheat the air fryer to 400°F.
2. Mix the smoked paprika, oregano, salt, pepper, garlic powder, and onion powder in a small bowl until uniform.

3. Pat and rub this mixture across all surfaces of the beef. Lightly coat the beef on all sides with olive oil spray.

4. When the machine is at temperature, lay the London broil flat in the basket and air-fry undisturbed for 8 minutes for the small batch, 10 minutes for the medium batch, or 12 minutes for the large batch for medium-rare, until an instant-read meat thermometer inserted into the center of the meat registers 130°F. Add 1, 2, or 3 minutes, respectively for medium, until an instant-read meat thermometer registers 135°F. Or add 3, 4, or 5 minutes respectively for medium, until an instant-read meat thermometer registers 145°F.

5. Use kitchen tongs to transfer the London broil to a cutting board. Let the meat rest for 10 minutes. It needs a long time for the juices to be reincorporated into the meat's fibers. Carve it against the grain into very thin slices to serve.

## Maple'n Soy Marinated Beef

Servings:4
Cooking Time: 45 Minutes
**Ingredients:**
- 2 pounds sirloin flap steaks, pounded
- 3 tablespoons balsamic vinegar
- 3 tablespoons maple syrup
- 3 tablespoons soy sauce
- 4 cloves of garlic, minced

**Directions:**
1. Preheat the air fryer to 390°F.
2. Place the grill pan accessory in the air fryer.
3. On a deep dish, place the flap steaks and season with soy sauce, balsamic vinegar, and maple syrup, and garlic.
4. Place on the grill pan and cook for 15 minutes in batches.

## German-style Pork Patties

Servings: 6
Cooking Time: 35 Minutes
**Ingredients:**
- 1 lb ground pork
- ¼ cup diced fresh pear
- 1 tbsp minced sage leaves
- 1 garlic clove, minced
- 2 tbsp chopped chives
- Salt and pepper to taste

**Directions:**
1. Preheat the air fryer to 375°F. Combine the pork, pear, sage, chives, garlic, salt, and pepper in a bowl and mix gently but thoroughly with your hands, then make 8 patties about ½ inch thick. Lay the patties in the frying basket in a single layer and Air Fry for 15-20 minutes, flipping once halfway through. Remove and drain on paper towels, then serve. Serve and enjoy!

## Fajita Flank Steak Rolls

Servings:4
Cooking Time: 12 Minutes

**Ingredients:**
- 1 pound flank steak
- 4 slices pepper jack cheese
- 1 medium green bell pepper, seeded and chopped
- ½ medium red bell pepper, seeded and chopped
- ¼ cup finely chopped yellow onion
- 1 teaspoon salt
- ½ teaspoon ground black pepper
- Cooking spray

**Directions:**
1. Preheat the air fryer to 400°F.
2. Carefully butterfly steak, leaving the two halves connected. Place slices of cheese on top of steak. Scatter bell peppers and onion over cheese in an even layer.
3. Place steak so that the grain runs horizontally. Tightly roll up steak and secure it with eight evenly spaced toothpicks or eight sections of butcher's twine.
4. Slice steak into four even rolls. Spritz with cooking spray, then sprinkle with salt and black pepper. Place in the air fryer basket and cook 12 minutes until steak is brown on the edges and internal temperature reaches at least 160°F for well-done. Serve.

## Rosemary Lamb Chops

Servings: 4
Cooking Time: 6 Minutes
**Ingredients:**
- 8 lamb chops
- 1 tablespoon extra-virgin olive oil
- 1 teaspoon dried rosemary, crushed
- 2 cloves garlic, minced
- 1 teaspoon sea salt
- ¼ teaspoon black pepper

**Directions:**
1. In a large bowl, mix together the lamb chops, olive oil, rosemary, garlic, salt, and pepper. Let sit at room temperature for 10 minutes.
2. Meanwhile, preheat the air fryer to 380°F.
3. Cook the lamb chops for 3 minutes, flip them over, and cook for another 3 minutes.

## Lemon-butter Veal Cutlets

Servings: 2
Cooking Time: 4 Minutes
**Ingredients:**
- 3 strips Butter
- 3 Thinly pounded 2-ounce veal leg cutlets (less than ¼ inch thick)
- ¼ teaspoon Lemon-pepper seasoning

**Directions:**
1. Preheat the air fryer to 400°F.
2. Run a vegetable peeler lengthwise along a hard, cold stick of butter, making 2, 3, or 4 long strips as the recipe requires for the number of cutlets you're making.

3. Lay the veal cutlets on a clean, dry cutting board or work surface. Sprinkle about ⅛ teaspoon lemon-pepper seasoning over each. Set a strip of butter on top of each cutlet.

4. When the machine is at temperature, set the topped cutlets in the basket so that they don't overlap or even touch. Air-fry undisturbed for 4 minutes without turning.

5. Use a nonstick-safe spatula to transfer the cutlets to a serving plate or plates, taking care to keep as much of the butter on top as possible. Remove the basket from the drawer or from over the baking tray. Carefully pour the browned butter over the cutlets.

# Kielbasa Chunks With Pineapple & Peppers

Servings: 2
Cooking Time: 10 Minutes
**Ingredients:**
- ¾ pound kielbasa sausage
- 1 cup bell pepper chunks (any color)
- 1 8-ounce can pineapple chunks in juice, drained
- 1 tablespoon barbeque seasoning
- 1 tablespoon soy sauce
- cooking spray

**Directions:**
1. Cut sausage into ½-inch slices.
2. In a medium bowl, toss all ingredients together.
3. Spray air fryer basket with nonstick cooking spray.
4. Pour sausage mixture into the basket.
5. Cook at 390°F for approximately 5 minutes. Shake basket and cook an additional 5 minutes.

# Air-fried Roast Beef With Rosemary Roasted Potatoes

Servings: 8
Cooking Time: 60 Minutes
**Ingredients:**
- 1 top sirloin roast
- salt and freshly ground black pepper
- 1 teaspoon dried thyme
- 2 pounds red potatoes, halved or quartered
- 2 teaspoons olive oil
- 1 teaspoon very finely chopped fresh rosemary, plus more for garnish

**Directions:**
1. Start by making sure your roast will fit into the air fryer basket without touching the top element. Trim it if you have to in order to get it to fit nicely in your air fryer.
2. Preheat the air fryer to 360°F.
3. Season the beef all over with salt, pepper and thyme. Transfer the seasoned roast to the air fryer basket.
4. Air-fry at 360°F for 20 minutes. Turn the roast over and continue to air-fry at 360°F for another 20 minutes.

5. Toss the potatoes with the olive oil, salt, pepper and fresh rosemary. Turn the roast over again in the air fryer basket and toss the potatoes in around the sides of the roast. Air-fry the roast and potatoes at 360°F for another 20 minutes. Check the internal temperature of the roast with an instant-read thermometer, and continue to roast until the beef is 5° lower than your desired degree of doneness. Let the roast rest for 5 to 10 minutes before slicing and serving. While the roast is resting, continue to air-fry the potatoes if desired for extra browning and crispiness.

6. Slice the roast and serve with the potatoes, adding a little more fresh rosemary if desired.

# Corn Dogs

Servings:4
Cooking Time: 8 Minutes
**Ingredients:**
- 1½ cups shredded mozzarella cheese
- 1 ounce cream cheese
- ½ cup blanched finely ground almond flour
- 4 beef hot dogs

**Directions:**
1. Place mozzarella, cream cheese, and flour in a large microwave-safe bowl. Microwave on high 45 seconds, then stir with a fork until a soft ball of dough forms.
2. Press dough out into a 12" × 6" rectangle, then use a knife to separate into four smaller rectangles.
3. Wrap each hot dog in one rectangle of dough and place into ungreased air fryer basket. Adjust the temperature to 400°F and set the timer for 8 minutes, turning corn dogs halfway through cooking. Corn dogs will be golden brown when done. Serve warm.

# Egg Stuffed Pork Meatballs

Servings: 2
Cooking Time: 40 Minutes
**Ingredients:**
- 3 soft boiled eggs, peeled
- 8 oz ground pork
- 2 tsp dried tarragon
- ½ tsp hot paprika
- 2 tsp garlic powder
- Salt and pepper to taste

**Directions:**
1. Preheat air fryer to 350°F. Combine the pork, tarragon, hot paprika, garlic powder, salt, and pepper in a bowl and stir until all spices are evenly spread throughout the meat. Divide the meat mixture into three equal portions in the mixing bowl, and shape each into balls.
2. Flatten one of the meatballs on top to make a wide, flat meat circle. Place an egg in the middle. Use your hands to mold the mixture up and around to enclose the egg. Repeat with the remaining eggs. Place the stuffed balls in the air fryer. Air Fry for 18-20 minutes, shaking the basket once until the meat is crispy and golden brown. Serve.

# Lamb Burgers

Servings: 2
Cooking Time: 16 Minutes
**Ingredients:**
- 8 oz lamb, minced
- ½ teaspoon salt
- ½ teaspoon ground black pepper
- ½ teaspoon dried cilantro
- 1 tablespoon water
- Cooking spray

**Directions:**
1. In the mixing bowl mix up minced lamb, salt, ground black pepper, dried cilantro, and water.
2. Stir the meat mixture carefully with the help of the spoon and make 2 burgers.
3. Preheat the air fryer to 375°F.
4. Spray the air fryer basket with cooking spray and put the burgers inside.
5. Cook them for 8 minutes from each side.

# Garlic And Oregano Lamb Chops

Servings: 4
Cooking Time: 17 Minutes
**Ingredients:**
- 1½ tablespoons Olive oil
- 1 tablespoon Minced garlic
- 1 teaspoon Dried oregano
- 1 teaspoon Finely minced orange zest
- ¾ teaspoon Fennel seeds
- ¾ teaspoon Table salt
- ¾ teaspoon Ground black pepper
- 6 4-ounce, 1-inch-thick lamb loin chops

**Directions:**
1. Mix the olive oil, garlic, oregano, orange zest, fennel seeds, salt, and pepper in a large bowl. Add the chops and toss well to coat. Set aside as the air fryer heats, tossing one more time.
2. Preheat the air fryer to 400°F.
3. Set the chops bone side down in the basket with as much air space between them as possible. Air-fry undisturbed for 14 minutes for medium-rare, or until an instant-read meat thermometer inserted into the thickest part of a chop registers 132°F. Or air-fry undisturbed for 17 minutes for well done, or until an instant-read meat thermometer registers 145°F.
4. Use kitchen tongs to transfer the chops to a wire rack. Cool for 5 minutes before serving.

# Crispy Five-spice Pork Belly

Servings: 6
Cooking Time: 60-75 Minutes
**Ingredients:**
- 1½ pounds Pork belly with skin

- 3 tablespoons Shaoxing (Chinese cooking rice wine), dry sherry, or white grape juice
- 1½ teaspoons Granulated white sugar
- ¾ teaspoon Five-spice powder
- 1¼ cups Coarse sea salt or kosher salt

**Directions:**
1. Preheat the air fryer to 350°F .
2. Set the pork belly skin side up on a cutting board. Use a meat fork to make dozens and dozens of tiny holes all across the surface of the skin. You can hardly make too many holes. These will allow the skin to bubble up and keep it from becoming hard as it roasts.
3. Turn the pork belly over so that one of its longer sides faces you. Make four evenly spaced vertical slits in the meat. The slits should go about halfway into the meat toward the fat.
4. Mix the Shaoxing or its substitute, sugar, and five-spice powder in a small bowl until the sugar dissolves. Massage this mixture across the meat and into the cuts.
5. Turn the pork belly over again. Blot dry any moisture on the skin. Make a double-thickness aluminum foil tray by setting two 10-inch-long pieces of foil on top of another. Set the pork belly skin side up in the center of this tray. Fold the sides of the tray up toward the pork, crimping the foil as you work to make a high-sided case all around the pork belly. Seal the foil to the meat on all sides so that only the skin is exposed.
6. Pour the salt onto the skin and pat it down and in place to create a crust. Pick up the foil tray with the pork in it and set it in the basket.
7. Air-fry undisturbed for 35 minutes for a small batch, 45 minutes for a medium batch, or 50 minutes for a large batch.
8. Remove the foil tray with the pork belly still in it. Warning: The foil tray is full of scalding-hot fat. Discard the fat in the tray, as well as the tray itself. Transfer the pork belly to a cutting board.
9. Raise the air fryer temperature to 375°F. Brush the salt crust off the pork, removing any visible salt from the sides of the meat, too.
10. When the machine is at temperature, return the pork belly skin side up to the basket. Air-fry undisturbed for 25 minutes, or until crisp and very well browned. If the machine is at 390°F, you may be able to shave 5 minutes off the cooking time so that the skin doesn't blacken.
11. Use a nonstick-safe spatula, and perhaps a silicone baking mitt, to transfer the pork belly to a wire rack. Cool for 10 minutes before serving.

# London Broil

Servings:4
Cooking Time: 12 Minutes
**Ingredients:**
- 1 pound top round steak
- 1 tablespoon Worcestershire sauce
- ¼ cup soy sauce
- 2 cloves garlic, peeled and finely minced
- ½ teaspoon ground black pepper
- ½ teaspoon salt
- 2 tablespoons salted butter, melted

**Directions:**
1. Place steak in a large sealable bowl or bag. Pour in Worcestershire sauce and soy sauce, then add garlic, pepper, and salt. Toss to coat. Seal and place into refrigerator to let marinate 2 hours.
2. Remove steak from marinade and pat dry. Drizzle top side with butter, then place into ungreased air fryer basket. Adjust the temperature to 375°F and set the timer for 12 minutes, turning steak halfway through cooking. Steak will be done when browned at the edges and it has an internal temperature of 150°F for medium or 180°F for well-done.
3. Let steak rest on a large plate 10 minutes before slicing into thin pieces. Serve warm.

# Marinated Rib Eye

Servings:4
Cooking Time: 10 Minutes
**Ingredients:**
- 1 pound rib eye steak
- ¼ cup soy sauce
- 1 tablespoon Worcestershire sauce
- 1 tablespoon granular brown erythritol
- 2 tablespoons olive oil
- ½ teaspoon salt
- ¼ teaspoon ground black pepper

**Directions:**
1. Place rib eye in a large sealable bowl or bag and pour in soy sauce, Worcestershire sauce, erythritol, and olive oil. Seal and let marinate 30 minutes in the refrigerator.
2. Remove rib eye from marinade, pat dry, and sprinkle on all sides with salt and pepper. Place rib eye into ungreased air fryer basket. Adjust the temperature to 400°F and set the timer for 10 minutes. Steak will be done when browned at the edges and has an internal temperature of 150°F for medium or 180°F for well-done. Serve warm.

# Crispy Lamb Shoulder Chops

Servings: 3
Cooking Time: 28 Minutes
**Ingredients:**
- ¾ cup All-purpose flour or gluten-free all-purpose flour
- 2 teaspoons Mild paprika
- 2 teaspoons Table salt
- 1½ teaspoons Garlic powder
- 1½ teaspoons Dried sage leaves
- 3 6-ounce bone-in lamb shoulder chops, any excess fat trimmed
- Olive oil spray

**Directions:**
1. Whisk the flour, paprika, salt, garlic powder, and sage in a large bowl until the mixture is of a uniform color. Add the chops and toss well to coat. Transfer them to a cutting board.
2. Preheat the air fryer to 375°F .
3. When the machine is at temperature, again dredge the chops one by one in the flour mixture. Lightly coat both sides of each chop with olive oil spray before putting it in the basket. Continue on with the remaining chop(s), leaving air space between them in the basket.
4. Air-fry, turning once, for 25 minutes, or until the chops are well browned and tender when pierced with the point of a paring knife. If the machine is at 360°F, you may need to add up to 3 minutes to the cooking time.
5. Use kitchen tongs to transfer the chops to a wire rack. Cool for 5 minutes before serving.

# Baby Back Ribs

Servings: 4
Cooking Time: 36 Minutes
**Ingredients:**
- 2¼ pounds Pork baby back rib rack(s)
- 1 tablespoon Dried barbecue seasoning blend or rub (gluten-free, if a concern)
- 1 cup Water
- 3 tablespoons Purchased smooth barbecue sauce (gluten-free, if a concern)

**Directions:**
1. Preheat the air fryer to 350°F.
2. Cut the racks into 4- to 5-bone sections, about two sections for the small batch, three for the medium, and four for the large. Sprinkle both sides of these sections with the seasoning blend.
3. Pour the water into the bottom of the air-fryer drawer or into a tray placed under the rack. Set the rib sections in the basket so that they're not touching. Air-fry for 30 minutes, turning once.
4. If using a tray with water, check it a couple of times to make sure it still has water in it or hasn't overflowed from the rendered fat.
5. Brush half the barbecue sauce on the exposed side of the ribs. Air-fry undisturbed for 3 minutes. Turn the racks over, brush with the remaining sauce, and air-fry undisturbed for 3 minutes more, or until sizzling and brown.
6. Use kitchen tongs to transfer the racks to a cutting board. Let stand for 5 minutes, then slice between the bones to serve.

# Wasabi-coated Pork Loin Chops

Servings: 3
Cooking Time: 14 Minutes
**Ingredients:**
- 1½ cups Wasabi peas
- ¼ cup Plain panko bread crumbs
- 1 Large egg white(s)
- 2 tablespoons Water
- 3 5- to 6-ounce boneless center-cut pork loin chops (about ½ inch thick)

**Directions:**
1. Preheat the air fryer to 375°F.
2. Put the wasabi peas in a food processor. Cover and process until finely ground, about like panko bread crumbs. Add the bread crumbs and pulse a few times to blend.
3. Set up and fill two shallow soup plates or small pie plates on your counter: one for the egg white(s), whisked with the water until uniform; and one for the wasabi pea mixture.
4. Dip a pork chop in the egg white mixture, coating the chop on both sides as well as around the edge. Allow any excess egg white mixture to slip back into the rest, then set the chop in the wasabi pea mixture. Press gently and turn it several times to coat evenly on both sides and around the edge. Set aside, then dip and coat the remaining chop(s).
5. Set the chops in the basket with as much air space between them as possible. Air-fry, turning once at the 6-minute mark, for 12 minutes, or until the chops are crisp and browned and an instant-read meat thermometer inserted into the center of a chop registers 145°F. If the machine is at 360°F, you may need to add 2 minutes to the cooking time.
6. Use kitchen tongs to transfer the chops to a wire rack. Cool for a couple of minutes before serving.

# Pork Meatballs

Servings:18
Cooking Time: 12 Minutes
**Ingredients:**
- 1 pound ground pork
- 1 large egg, whisked
- ½ teaspoon garlic powder
- ½ teaspoon salt
- ½ teaspoon ground ginger
- ¼ teaspoon crushed red pepper flakes
- 1 medium scallion, trimmed and sliced

**Directions:**
1. Combine all ingredients in a large bowl. Spoon out 2 tablespoons mixture and roll into a ball. Repeat to form eighteen meatballs total.
2. Place meatballs into ungreased air fryer basket. Adjust the temperature to 400°F and set the timer for 12 minutes, shaking the basket three times throughout cooking. Meatballs will be browned and have an internal temperature of at least 145°F when done. Serve warm.

# Flatiron Steak Grill On Parsley Salad

Servings:4
Cooking Time: 45 Minutes
**Ingredients:**
- ½ cup parmesan cheese, grated
- 1 ½ pounds flatiron steak
- 1 tablespoon fresh lemon juice
- 2 cups parsley leaves
- 3 tablespoons olive oil
- Salt and pepper to taste

**Directions:**
1. Preheat the air fryer to 390°F.
2. Place the grill pan accessory in the air fryer.
3. Mix together the steak, oil, salt and pepper.
4. Grill for 15 minutes per batch and make sure to flip the meat halfway through the cooking time.
5. Meanwhile, prepare the salad by combining in a bowl the parsley leaves, parmesan cheese and lemon juice. Season with salt and pepper.

# Crunchy Veal Cutlets

Servings: 2
Cooking Time: 5 Minutes
**Ingredients:**
- ½ cup All-purpose flour or tapioca flour
- 1 Large egg(s), well beaten
- ¾ cup Seasoned Italian-style dried bread crumbs (gluten-free, if a concern)
- 2 tablespoons Yellow cornmeal
- 4 Thinly pounded 2-ounce veal leg cutlets (less than ¼ inch thick)
- Olive oil spray

**Directions:**
1. Preheat the air fryer to 400°F.
2. Set up and fill three shallow soup plates or small pie plates on your counter: one for the flour; one for the egg(s); and one for the bread crumbs, whisked with the cornmeal until well combined.
3. Dredge a veal cutlet in the flour, coating it on both sides. Gently shake off any excess flour, then gently dip it in the beaten egg(s), coating both sides. Let the excess egg slip back into the rest. Dip the cutlet in the bread-crumb mixture, turning it several times and pressing gently to make an even coating on both sides. Coat it on both sides with olive oil spray, then set it aside and continue dredging and coating more cutlets.
4. When the machine is at temperature, set the cutlets in the basket so that they don't touch each other. Air-fry undisturbed for 5 minutes, or until crisp and brown. (If only some of the veal cutlets will fit in one layer for any selected batch—the sizes of air fryer baskets vary dramatically—work in batches as necessary.)

5. Use kitchen tongs to transfer the cutlets to a wire rack. Cool for only 1 to 2 minutes before serving.

# Fried Spam

Servings: 2
Cooking Time: 12 Minutes
**Ingredients:**
- ½ cup All-purpose flour or gluten-free all-purpose flour
- 1 Large egg(s)
- 1 tablespoon Wasabi paste
- 1⅓ cups Plain panko bread crumbs (gluten-free, if a concern)
- 4 ½-inch-thick Spam slices
- Vegetable oil spray

**Directions:**
1. Preheat the air fryer to 400°F.
2. Set up and fill three shallow soup plates or small pie plates on your counter: one for the flour; one for the egg(s), whisked with the wasabi paste until uniform; and one for the bread crumbs.
3. Dip a slice of Spam in the flour, coating both sides. Slip it into the egg mixture and turn to coat on both sides, even along the edges. Let any excess egg mixture slip back into the rest, then set the slice in the bread crumbs. Turn it several times, pressing gently to make an even coating on both sides. Generously coat both sides of the slice with vegetable oil spray. Set aside so you can dip, coat, and spray the remaining slice(s).
4. Set the slices in the basket in a single layer so that they don't touch. Air-fry undisturbed for 12 minutes, or until very brown and quite crunchy.
5. Use kitchen tongs to transfer the slices to a wire rack. Cool for a minute or two before serving.

# Meatloaf

Servings:4
Cooking Time: 40 Minutes
**Ingredients:**
- 1 pound 80/20 lean ground beef
- 1 large egg
- 3 tablespoons Italian bread crumbs
- 1 teaspoon salt
- 2 tablespoons ketchup
- 2 tablespoons brown sugar

**Directions:**
1. Preheat the air fryer to 350°F.
2. In a large bowl, combine beef, egg, bread crumbs, and salt.
3. In a small bowl, mix ketchup and brown sugar.
4. Form meat mixture into a 6" × 3" loaf and brush with ketchup mixture.
5. Place in the air fryer basket and cook 40 minutes until internal temperature reaches at least 160°F. Serve warm.

# Beef Al Carbon (street Taco Meat)

Servings: 6
Cooking Time: 8 Minutes
**Ingredients:**
- 1½ pounds sirloin steak, cut into ½-inch cubes
- ¾ cup lime juice
- ½ cup extra-virgin olive oil
- 1 teaspoon ground cumin
- 2 teaspoons garlic powder
- 1 teaspoon salt

**Directions:**
1. In a large bowl, toss together the steak, lime juice, olive oil, cumin, garlic powder, and salt. Allow the meat to marinate for 30 minutes. Drain off all the marinade and pat the meat dry with paper towels.
2. Preheat the air fryer to 400°F.
3. Place the meat in the air fryer basket and spray with cooking spray. Cook the meat for 5 minutes, toss the meat, and continue cooking another 3 minutes, until slightly crispy.

# Roast Beef

Servings:6
Cooking Time: 60 Minutes
**Ingredients:**
- 1 top round beef roast
- 1 teaspoon salt
- ½ teaspoon ground black pepper
- 1 teaspoon dried rosemary
- ½ teaspoon garlic powder
- 1 tablespoon coconut oil, melted

**Directions:**
1. Sprinkle all sides of roast with salt, pepper, rosemary, and garlic powder. Drizzle with coconut oil. Place roast into ungreased air fryer basket, fatty side down. Adjust the temperature to 375°F and set the timer for 60 minutes, turning the roast halfway through cooking. Roast will be done when no pink remains and internal temperature is at least 180°F. Serve warm.

# Barbecue Country-style Pork Ribs

Servings: 3
Cooking Time: 30 Minutes
**Ingredients:**
- 3 8-ounce boneless country-style pork ribs
- 1½ teaspoons Mild smoked paprika
- 1½ teaspoons Light brown sugar
- ¾ teaspoon Onion powder
- ¾ teaspoon Ground black pepper
- ¼ teaspoon Table salt
- Vegetable oil spray

**Directions:**
1. Preheat the air fryer to 350°F . Set the ribs in a bowl on the counter as the machine heats.

2. Mix the smoked paprika, brown sugar, onion powder, pepper, and salt in a small bowl until well combined. Rub this mixture over all the surfaces of the country-style ribs. Generously coat the country-style ribs with vegetable oil spray.

3. Set the ribs in the basket with as much air space between them as possible. Air-fry undisturbed for 30 minutes, or until browned and sizzling and an instant-read meat thermometer inserted into one rib registers at least 145°F.

4. Use kitchen tongs to transfer the country-style ribs to a wire rack. Cool for 5 minutes before serving.

## Chicken-fried Steak

Servings: 2
Cooking Time: 12 Minutes
**Ingredients:**
- 1½ cups All-purpose flour
- 2 Large egg(s)
- 2 tablespoons Regular or low-fat sour cream
- 2 tablespoons Worcestershire sauce
- 2 ¼-pound thin beef cube steak(s)
- Vegetable oil spray

**Directions:**
1. Preheat the air fryer to 400°F.
2. Set up and fill two shallow soup plates or small pie plates on your counter: one for the flour; and one for the egg(s), whisked with the sour cream and Worcestershire sauce until uniform.
3. Dredge a piece of beef in the flour, coating it well on both sides and even along the edge. Shake off any excess; then dip the meat in the egg mixture, coating both sides while retaining the flour on the meat. Let any excess egg mixture slip back into the rest. Dredge the meat in the flour once again, coating all surfaces well. Gently shake off the excess coating and set the steak aside if you're coating another steak or two. Once done, coat the steak(s) on both sides with the vegetable oil spray.
4. Set the steak(s) in the basket. If there's more than one steak, make sure they do not overlap or even touch, although the smallest gap between them is enough to get them crunchy. Air-fry undisturbed for 6 minutes.
5. Use kitchen tongs to pick up one of the steaks. Coat it again on both sides with vegetable oil spray. Turn it upside down and set it back in the basket with that same regard for the space between them in larger batches. Repeat with any other steaks. Continue air-frying undisturbed for 6 minutes, or until golden brown and crunchy.
6. Use kitchen tongs to transfer the steak(s) to a wire rack. Cool for 5 minutes before serving.

## Easy Garlic Butter Steak

Servings: 2
Cooking Time: 6 Minutes
**Ingredients:**

- 2 steaks
- 2 tsp garlic butter
- 1/4 tsp Italian seasoning
- Pepper
- Salt

**Directions:**
1. Season steaks with Italian seasoning, pepper, and salt.
2. Rub steaks with garlic butter and place into the air fryer basket and cook at 350°F for 6 minutes.
3. Serve and enjoy.

## Spinach And Mushroom Steak Rolls

Servings:4
Cooking Time: 19 Minutes
**Ingredients:**
- ½ medium yellow onion, peeled and chopped
- ½ cup chopped baby bella mushrooms
- 1 cup chopped fresh spinach
- 1 pound flank steak
- 8 slices provolone cheese
- 1 teaspoon salt
- ½ teaspoon ground black pepper
- Cooking spray

**Directions:**
1. In a medium skillet over medium heat, sauté onion 2 minutes until fragrant and beginning to soften. Add mushrooms and spinach and continue cooking 5 more minutes until spinach is wilted and mushrooms are soft.
2. Preheat the air fryer to 400°F.
3. Carefully butterfly steak, leaving the two halves connected. Place slices of cheese on top of steak, then top with cooked vegetables.
4. Place steak so that the grain runs horizontally. Tightly roll up steak and secure it closed with eight evenly placed toothpicks or eight sections of butcher's twine.
5. Slice steak into four rolls. Spritz with cooking spray, then sprinkle with salt and pepper. Place in the air fryer basket and cook 12 minutes until steak is brown on the edges and internal temperature reaches at least 160°F for well-done. Serve.

## Cheddar Bacon Ranch Pinwheels

Servings:5
Cooking Time: 12 Minutes Per Batch
**Ingredients:**
- 4 ounces full-fat cream cheese, softened
- 1 tablespoon dry ranch seasoning
- ½ cup shredded Cheddar cheese
- 1 sheet frozen puff pastry dough, thawed
- 6 slices bacon, cooked and crumbled

**Directions:**
1. Preheat the air fryer to 320°F. Cut parchment paper to fit the air fryer basket.

2. In a medium bowl, mix cream cheese, ranch seasoning, and Cheddar. Unfold puff pastry and gently spread cheese mixture over pastry.

3. Sprinkle crumbled bacon on top. Starting from a long side, roll dough into a log, pressing in the edges to seal.

4. Cut log into ten pieces, then place on parchment in the air fryer basket, working in batches as necessary.

5. Cook 12 minutes, turning each piece after 7 minutes. Let cool 5 minutes before serving.

# Orange And Brown Sugar–glazed Ham

Servings:8
Cooking Time: 15 Minutes
**Ingredients:**
- ½ cup brown sugar
- ¼ cup orange juice
- 2 tablespoons yellow mustard
- 1 fully cooked boneless ham
- 1 teaspoon salt
- ½ teaspoon ground black pepper

**Directions:**
1. Preheat the air fryer to 375°F.
2. In a medium bowl, whisk together brown sugar, orange juice, and mustard until combined. Brush over ham until well coated. Sprinkle with salt and pepper.
3. Place in the air fryer basket and cook 15 minutes until heated through and edges are caramelized. Serve warm.

# Calzones

Servings:4
Cooking Time: 15 Minutes
**Ingredients:**
- 1 tube refrigerated pizza dough
- 28 slices pepperoni
- ½ cup full-fat ricotta cheese
- 1 cup shredded mozzarella cheese
- 1 large egg, whisked

**Directions:**
1. Preheat the air fryer to 350°F. Cut parchment paper to fit the air fryer basket.
2. Place dough on a work surface and unroll. Cut into four sections.
3. For each calzone, place 7 slices pepperoni on the bottom half of a dough section. Top pepperoni with 2 tablespoons ricotta and ¼ cup mozzarella.
4. Fold top half of dough over to cover the fillings and press the edges together. Gently roll the edges closed or press them with a fork to seal.
5. Brush calzones with egg. Place on parchment in the air fryer basket and cook 15 minutes, turning after about 10 minutes, until firm and golden brown. Serve warm.

# Peppered Steak Bites

Servings: 4
Cooking Time: 14 Minutes
**Ingredients:**
- 1 pound sirloin steak, cut into 1-inch cubes
- ½ teaspoon coarse sea salt
- 1 teaspoon coarse black pepper
- 2 teaspoons Worcestershire sauce
- ½ teaspoon garlic powder
- ¼ teaspoon red pepper flakes
- ¼ cup chopped parsley

**Directions:**
1. Preheat the air fryer to 390°F.
2. In a large bowl, place the steak cubes and toss with the salt, pepper, Worcestershire sauce, garlic powder, and red pepper flakes.
3. Pour the steak into the air fryer basket and cook for 10 to 14 minutes, depending on how well done you prefer your bites. Starting at the 8-minute mark, toss the steak bites every 2 minutes to check for doneness.
4. When the steak is cooked, remove it from the basket to a serving bowl and top with the chopped parsley. Allow the steak to rest for 5 minutes before serving.

# Herbed Beef Roast

Servings:5
Cooking Time:45 Minutes
**Ingredients:**
- 2 pounds beef roast
- 1 tablespoon olive oil
- 1 teaspoon dried rosemary, crushed
- 1 teaspoon dried thyme, crushed
- Salt, to taste

**Directions:**
1. Preheat the Air fryer to 360°F and grease an Air fryer basket.
2. Rub the roast generously with herb mixture and coat with olive oil.
3. Arrange the roast in the Air fryer basket and cook for about 45 minutes.
4. Dish out the roast and cover with foil for about 10 minutes.
5. Cut into desired size slices and serve.

# Steak Fingers

Servings: 4
Cooking Time: 8 Minutes
**Ingredients:**
- 4 small beef cube steaks
- salt and pepper
- ½ cup flour
- oil for misting or cooking spray

**Directions:**
1. Cut cube steaks into 1-inch-wide strips.

2. Sprinkle lightly with salt and pepper to taste.

3. Roll in flour to coat all sides.

4. Spray air fryer basket with cooking spray or oil.

5. Place steak strips in air fryer basket in single layer, very close together but not touching. Spray top of steak strips with oil or cooking spray.

6. Cook at 390°F for 4minutes, turn strips over, and spray with oil or cooking spray.

7. Cook 4 more minutes and test with fork for doneness. Steak fingers should be crispy outside with no red juices inside. If needed, cook an additional 4 minutes or until well done.

8. Repeat steps 5 through 7 to cook remaining strips.

## Marinated Steak Kebabs

Servings:4

Cooking Time: 5 Minutes

**Ingredients:**

- 1 pound strip steak, fat trimmed, cut into 1" cubes
- ½ cup soy sauce
- ¼ cup olive oil
- 1 tablespoon granular brown erythritol
- ½ teaspoon salt
- ¼ teaspoon ground black pepper
- 1 medium green bell pepper, seeded and chopped into 1" cubes

**Directions:**

1. Place steak into a large sealable bowl or bag and pour in soy sauce and olive oil. Add erythritol, then stir to coat steak. Marinate at room temperature 30 minutes.

2. Remove streak from marinade and sprinkle with salt and black pepper.

3. Place meat and vegetables onto 6" skewer sticks, alternating between steak and bell pepper.

4. Place kebabs into ungreased air fryer basket. Adjust the temperature to 400°F and set the timer for 5 minutes. Steak will be done when crispy at the edges and peppers are tender. Serve warm.

## Sweet And Spicy Pork Ribs

Servings:4

Cooking Time: 20 Minutes Per Batch

**Ingredients:**

- 1 rack pork spareribs, white membrane removed
- ¼ cup brown sugar
- 2 teaspoons salt
- 2 teaspoons ground black pepper
- 1 tablespoon chili powder
- 1 teaspoon garlic powder
- ½ teaspoon cayenne pepper

**Directions:**

1. Preheat the air fryer to 400°F.

2. Place ribs on a work surface and cut the rack into two pieces to fit in the air fryer basket.

3. In a medium bowl, whisk together brown sugar, salt, black pepper, chili powder, garlic powder, and cayenne to make a dry rub.

4. Massage dry rub onto both sides of ribs until well coated. Place a portion of ribs in the air fryer basket, working in batches as necessary.

5. Cook 20 minutes until internal temperature reaches at least 190°F and no pink remains. Let rest 5 minutes before cutting and serving.

## Pork Belly Marinated In Onion-coconut Cream

Servings:3

Cooking Time: 25 Minutes

**Ingredients:**

- ½ pork belly, sliced to thin strips
- 1 onion, diced
- 1 tablespoon butter
- 4 tablespoons coconut cream
- Salt and pepper to taste

**Directions:**

1. Place all ingredients in a mixing bowl and allow to marinate in the fridge for 2 hours.

2. Preheat the air fryer for 5 minutes.

3. Place the pork strips in the air fryer and bake for 25 minutes at 350°F.

## Honey Mesquite Pork Chops

Servings: 2

Cooking Time: 10 Minutes

**Ingredients:**

- 2 tablespoons mesquite seasoning
- ¼ cup honey
- 1 tablespoon olive oil
- 1 tablespoon water
- freshly ground black pepper
- 2 bone-in center cut pork chops

**Directions:**

1. Whisk the mesquite seasoning, honey, olive oil, water and freshly ground black pepper together in a shallow glass dish. Pierce the chops all over and on both sides with a fork or meat tenderizer. Add the pork chops to the marinade and massage the marinade into the chops. Cover and marinate for 30 minutes.

2. Preheat the air fryer to 330°F.

3. Transfer the pork chops to the air fryer basket and pour half of the marinade over the chops, reserving the remaining marinade. Air-fry the pork chops for 6 minutes. Flip the pork chops over and pour the remaining marinade on top. Air-fry for an additional 3 minutes at 330°F. Then, increase the air fryer temperature to 400°F and air-fry the pork chops for an additional minute.

4. Transfer the pork chops to a serving plate, and let them rest for 5 minutes before serving. If you'd like a sauce for

these chops, pour the cooked marinade from the bottom of the air fryer over the top.

## Italian Meatballs

Servings: 8
Cooking Time: 12 Minutes
**Ingredients:**
- ¾ pound Lean ground beef
- 6 ounces Bulk mild or hot Italian sausage meat
- ½ cup Seasoned Italian-style dried bread crumbs
- 1 Large egg
- 3 tablespoons Whole or low-fat milk
- Olive oil spray

**Directions:**
1. Preheat the air fryer to 375°F .
2. Mix the ground beef, Italian sausage meat, bread crumbs, egg, and milk in a bowl until well combined. Using clean hands, form this mixture into large meatballs, using a ¼ cup for each. Set the meatballs on a large cutting board and coat them on all sides with olive oil spray. Be gentle when you turn them. They're fragile.
3. When the machine is at temperature, set them in the basket with as much space between them as possible. The important thing is that they should not touch, even if there's only a fraction of an inch between them. Air-fry undisturbed for 12 minutes, or until an instant-read meat thermometer inserted into the center of a meatball registers 165°F.
4. Use kitchen tongs to gently pick up the meatballs one by one and transfer them to a cutting board or a serving platter. Cool for a few minutes before serving.

## Mexican-style Shredded Beef

Servings:6
Cooking Time: 35 Minutes
**Ingredients:**
- 1 beef chuck roast, cut into 2" cubes
- 1 teaspoon salt
- ½ teaspoon ground black pepper
- ½ cup no-sugar-added chipotle sauce

**Directions:**
1. In a large bowl, sprinkle beef cubes with salt and pepper and toss to coat. Place beef into ungreased air fryer basket. Adjust the temperature to 400°F and set the timer for 30 minutes, shaking the basket halfway through cooking. Beef will be done when internal temperature is at least 160°F.
2. Place cooked beef into a large bowl and shred with two forks. Pour in chipotle sauce and toss to coat.
3. Return beef to air fryer basket for an additional 5 minutes at 400°F to crisp with sauce. Serve warm.

## Pepperoni Pockets

Servings: 4
Cooking Time: 8 Minutes
**Ingredients:**
- 4 bread slices, 1-inch thick
- olive oil for misting
- 24 slices pepperoni
- 1 ounce roasted red peppers, drained and patted dry
- 1 ounce Pepper Jack cheese cut into 4 slices
- pizza sauce (optional)

**Directions:**
1. Spray both sides of bread slices with olive oil.
2. Stand slices upright and cut a deep slit in the top to create a pocket—almost to the bottom crust but not all the way through.
3. Stuff each bread pocket with 6 slices of pepperoni, a large strip of roasted red pepper, and a slice of cheese.
4. Place bread pockets in air fryer basket, standing up. Cook at 360°F for 8 minutes, until filling is heated through and bread is lightly browned. Serve while hot as is or with pizza sauce for dipping.

## Mustard Herb Pork Tenderloin

Servings:6
Cooking Time: 20 Minutes
**Ingredients:**
- ¼ cup mayonnaise
- 2 tablespoons Dijon mustard
- ½ teaspoon dried thyme
- ¼ teaspoon dried rosemary
- 1 pork tenderloin
- ½ teaspoon salt
- ¼ teaspoon ground black pepper

**Directions:**
1. In a small bowl, mix mayonnaise, mustard, thyme, and rosemary. Brush tenderloin with mixture on all sides, then sprinkle with salt and pepper on all sides.
2. Place tenderloin into ungreased air fryer basket. Adjust the temperature to 400°F and set the timer for 20 minutes, turning tenderloin halfway through cooking. Tenderloin will be golden and have an internal temperature of at least 145°F when done. Serve warm.

## Cheeseburgers

Servings:4
Cooking Time: 10 Hours
**Ingredients:**
- 1 pound 70/30 ground beef
- ½ teaspoon salt
- ¼ teaspoon ground black pepper
- 4 slices American cheese
- 4 hamburger buns

**Directions:**
1. Preheat the air fryer to 360°F.
2. Separate beef into four equal portions and form into patties.
3. Sprinkle both sides of patties with salt and pepper. Place in the air fryer basket and cook 10 minutes, turning halfway

through cooking time, until internal temperature reaches at least 160°F.

4. For each burger, place a slice of cheese on a patty and place on a hamburger bun. Serve warm.

# Caramelized Pork

Servings:6
Cooking Time:17 Minutes
**Ingredients:**
- 2 pounds pork shoulder, cut into 1½-inch thick slices
- 1/3 cup soy sauce
- 2 tablespoons sugar
- 1 tablespoon honey

**Directions:**
1. Preheat the Air fryer to 335°F and grease an Air fryer basket.
2. Mix all the ingredients in a large bowl and coat chops well.
3. Cover and refrigerate for about 8 hours.
4. Arrange the chops in the Air fryer basket and cook for about 10 minutes, flipping once in between.
5. Set the Air fryer to 390°F and cook for 7 more minutes.
6. Dish out in a platter and serve hot.

# Lamb Chops

Servings: 2
Cooking Time: 20 Minutes
**Ingredients:**
- 2 teaspoons oil
- ½ teaspoon ground rosemary
- ½ teaspoon lemon juice
- 1 pound lamb chops, approximately 1-inch thick
- salt and pepper
- cooking spray

**Directions:**
1. Mix the oil, rosemary, and lemon juice together and rub into all sides of the lamb chops. Season to taste with salt and pepper.
2. For best flavor, cover lamb chops and allow them to rest in the fridge for 20 minutes.
3. Spray air fryer basket with nonstick spray and place lamb chops in it.
4. Cook at 360°F for approximately 20minutes. This will cook chops to medium. The meat will be juicy but have no remaining pink. Cook for a minute or two longer for well done chops. For rare chops, stop cooking after about 12minutes and check for doneness.

# Rib Eye Steak Seasoned With Italian Herb

Servings:4
Cooking Time: 45 Minutes
**Ingredients:**
- 1 packet Italian herb mix
- 1 tablespoon olive oil
- 2 pounds bone-in rib eye steak
- Salt and pepper to taste

**Directions:**
1. Preheat the air fryer to 390°F.
2. Place the grill pan accessory in the air fryer.
3. Season the steak with salt, pepper, Italian herb mix, and olive oil. Cover top with foil.
4. Grill for 45 minutes and flip the steak halfway through the cooking time.

# City "chicken"

Servings: 3
Cooking Time: 10 Minutes
**Ingredients:**
- 1 pound Pork tenderloin, cut into 2-inch cubes
- ½ cup All-purpose flour or tapioca flour
- 1 Large egg(s)
- 1 teaspoon Dried poultry seasoning blend
- 1¼ cups Plain panko bread crumbs (gluten-free, if a concern)
- Vegetable oil spray

**Directions:**
1. Preheat the air fryer to 350°F .
2. Thread 3 or 4 pieces of pork on a 4-inch bamboo skewer. You'll need 2 or 3 skewers for a small batch, 3 or 4 for a medium, and up to 6 for a large batch.
3. Set up and fill three shallow soup plates or small pie plates on your counter: one for the flour; one for the egg(s), beaten with the poultry seasoning until foamy; and one for the bread crumbs.
4. Dip and roll one skewer into the flour, coating all sides of the meat. Gently shake off any excess flour, then dip and roll the skewer in the egg mixture. Let any excess egg mixture slip back into the rest, then set the skewer in the bread crumbs and roll it around, pressing gently, until the exterior surfaces of the meat are evenly coated. Generously coat the meat on the skewer with vegetable oil spray. Set aside and continue dredging, dipping, coating, and spraying the remaining skewers.
5. Set the skewers in the basket in one layer and air-fry undisturbed for 10 minutes, or until brown and crunchy.
6. Use kitchen tongs to transfer the skewers to a wire rack. Cool for a minute or two before serving.

# Garlic Fillets

Servings: 4
Cooking Time: 15 Minutes
**Ingredients:**
- 1-pound beef filet mignon
- 1 teaspoon minced garlic
- 1 tablespoon peanut oil
- ½ teaspoon salt
- 1 teaspoon dried oregano

**Directions:**

1. Chop the beef into the medium size pieces and sprinkle with salt and dried oregano. Then add minced garlic and peanut oil and mix up the meat well. Place the bowl with meat in the fridge for 10 minutes to marinate. Meanwhile, preheat the air fryer to 400°F. Put the marinated beef pieces in the air fryer and cook them for 10 minutes Then flip the beef on another side and cook for 5 minutes more.

## Parmesan-crusted Pork Chops

Servings:4
Cooking Time: 12 Minutes
**Ingredients:**
- 1 large egg
- ½ cup grated Parmesan cheese
- 4 boneless pork chops
- ½ teaspoon salt
- ¼ teaspoon ground black pepper

**Directions:**
1. Whisk egg in a medium bowl and place Parmesan in a separate medium bowl.
2. Sprinkle pork chops on both sides with salt and pepper. Dip each pork chop into egg, then press both sides into Parmesan.
3. Place pork chops into ungreased air fryer basket. Adjust the temperature to 400°F and set the timer for 12 minutes, turning chops halfway through cooking. Pork chops will be golden and have an internal temperature of at least 145°F when done. Serve warm.

## Steak Bites And Spicy Dipping Sauce

Servings:4
Cooking Time: 8 Minutes
**Ingredients:**
- 2 pounds sirloin steak, cut into 2" cubes
- 2 teaspoons salt
- 1 teaspoon ground black pepper
- 1 teaspoon garlic powder
- ½ cup mayonnaise
- 2 tablespoons sriracha

**Directions:**
1. Preheat the air fryer to 400°F.
2. Sprinkle steak with salt, pepper, and garlic powder.
3. Place steak in the air fryer basket and cook 8 minutes, shaking the basket twice during cooking, until internal temperature reaches at least 160°F.
4. In a small bowl, combine mayonnaise and sriracha. Serve with steak bites for dipping.

## Pork Tenderloin With Bacon And Veggies

Servings:3
Cooking Time:28 Minutes
**Ingredients:**
- 3 potatoes

- ¾ pound frozen green beans
- 6 bacon slices
- 3 pork tenderloins
- 2 tablespoons olive oil

**Directions:**
1. Preheat the Air fryer to 390°F and grease an Air fryer basket.
2. Wrap 4-6 green beans with one bacon slice and coat the pork tenderloins with olive oil.
3. Pierce the potatoes with a fork and arrange in the Air fryer basket.
4. Cook for about 15 minutes and add the pork tenderloins.
5. Cook for about 6 minutes and dish out in a bowl.
6. Arrange the bean rolls into the Air fryer basket and top with the pork tenderloins.
7. Cook for about 7 minutes and dish out in a platter.
8. Cut each tenderloin into desired size slices to serve alongside the potatoes and green beans rolls.

## Cheese-stuffed Steak Burgers

Servings:4
Cooking Time: 10 Minutes
**Ingredients:**
- 1 pound 80/20 ground sirloin
- 4 ounces mild Cheddar cheese, cubed
- ½ teaspoon salt
- ¼ teaspoon ground black pepper

**Directions:**
1. Form ground sirloin into four equal balls, then separate each ball in half and flatten into two thin patties, for eight total patties. Place 1 ounce Cheddar into center of one patty, then top with a second patty and press edges to seal burger closed. Repeat with remaining patties and Cheddar to create four burgers.
2. Sprinkle salt and pepper over both sides of burgers and carefully place burgers into ungreased air fryer basket. Adjust the temperature to 350°F and set the timer for 10 minutes. Burgers will be done when browned on the edges and top. Serve warm.

## Pesto-rubbed Veal Chops

Servings: 2
Cooking Time: 12-15 Minutes
**Ingredients:**
- ¼ cup Purchased pesto
- 2 10-ounce bone-in veal loin or rib chop(s)
- ½ teaspoon Ground black pepper

**Directions:**
1. Preheat the air fryer to 400°F.
2. Rub the pesto onto both sides of the veal chop(s). Sprinkle one side of the chop(s) with the ground black pepper. Set aside at room temperature as the machine comes up to temperature.
3. Set the chop(s) in the basket. If you're cooking more than one chop, leave as much air space between them as

possible. Air-fry undisturbed for 12 minutes for medium-rare, or until an instant-read meat thermometer inserted into the center of a chop registers 135°F. Or air-fry undisturbed for 15 minutes for medium-well, or until an instant-read meat thermometer registers 145°F.

4. Use kitchen tongs to transfer the chops to a cutting board or a wire rack. Cool for 5 minutes before serving.

## Greek Pork Chops

Servings: 4
Cooking Time: 30 Minutes
**Ingredients:**
- 3 tbsp grated Halloumi cheese
- 4 pork chops
- 1 tsp Greek seasoning
- Salt and pepper to taste
- ¼ cup all-purpose flour
- 2 tbsp bread crumbs
- Cooking spray

**Directions:**
1. Preheat air fryer to 380°F. Season the pork chops with Greek seasoning, salt and pepper. In a shallow bowl, add flour. In another shallow bowl, combine the crumbs and Halloumi. Dip the chops in the flour, then in the bread crumbs. Place them in the fryer and spray with cooking oil. Bake for 12-14 minutes, flipping once. Serve warm.

## Mustard And Rosemary Pork Tenderloin With Fried Apples

Servings: 2
Cooking Time: 26 Minutes
**Ingredients:**
- 1 pork tenderloin
- 2 tablespoons coarse brown mustard
- salt and freshly ground black pepper
- 1½ teaspoons finely chopped fresh rosemary, plus sprigs for garnish
- 2 apples, cored and cut into 8 wedges
- 1 tablespoon butter, melted
- 1 teaspoon brown sugar

**Directions:**
1. Preheat the air fryer to 370°F.
2. Cut the pork tenderloin in half so that you have two pieces that fit into the air fryer basket. Brush the mustard onto both halves of the pork tenderloin and then season with salt, pepper and the fresh rosemary. Place the pork tenderloin halves into the air fryer basket and air-fry for 10 minutes. Turn the pork over and air-fry for an additional 8 minutes or until the internal temperature of the pork registers 155°F on an instant read thermometer. If your pork tenderloin is especially thick, you may need to add a minute or two, but it's better to check the pork and add time, than to overcook it.

3. Let the pork rest for 5 minutes. In the meantime, toss the apple wedges with the butter and brown sugar and air-fry at 400°F for 8 minutes, shaking the basket once or twice during the cooking process so the apples cook and brown evenly.
4. Slice the pork on the bias. Serve with the fried apples scattered over the top and a few sprigs of rosemary as garnish.

## Spinach And Provolone Steak Rolls

Servings:8
Cooking Time: 12 Minutes
**Ingredients:**
- 1 flank steak, butterflied
- 8 deli slices provolone cheese
- 1 cup fresh spinach leaves
- ½ teaspoon salt
- ¼ teaspoon ground black pepper

**Directions:**
1. Place steak on a large plate. Place provolone slices to cover steak, leaving 1" at the edges. Lay spinach leaves over cheese. Gently roll steak and tie with kitchen twine or secure with toothpicks. Carefully slice into eight pieces. Sprinkle each with salt and pepper.
2. Place rolls into ungreased air fryer basket, cut side up. Adjust the temperature to 400°F and set the timer for 12 minutes. Steak rolls will be browned and cheese will be melted when done and have an internal temperature of at least 150°F for medium steak and 180°F for well-done steak. Serve warm.

## Steakhouse Filets Mignons

Servings: 3
Cooking Time: 12-15 Minutes
**Ingredients:**
- ¾ ounce Dried porcini mushrooms
- ¼ teaspoon Granulated white sugar
- ¼ teaspoon Ground white pepper
- ¼ teaspoon Table salt
- 6 ¼-pound filets mignons or beef tenderloin steaks
- 6 Thin-cut bacon strips (gluten-free, if a concern)

**Directions:**
1. Preheat the air fryer to 400°F.
2. Grind the dried mushrooms in a clean spice grinder until powdery. Add the sugar, white pepper, and salt. Grind to blend.
3. Rub this mushroom mixture into both cut sides of each filet. Wrap the circumference of each filet with a strip of bacon.
4. Set the filets mignons in the basket on their sides with the bacon seam side down. Do not let the filets touch; keep at least ¼ inch open between them. Air-fry undisturbed for 12 minutes for rare, or until an instant-read meat thermometer inserted into the center of a filet registers 125°F; 13 minutes for medium-rare, or until an instant-read meat thermometer inserted into the center of a filet registers

132°F; or 15 minutes for medium, or until an instant-read meat thermometer inserted into the center of a filet registers 145°F.

5. Use kitchen tongs to transfer the filets to a wire rack, setting them cut side down. Cool for 5 minutes before serving.

## Pork Spare Ribs

Servings:4
Cooking Time: 30 Minutes
**Ingredients:**
- 1 rack pork spare ribs
- 1 teaspoon ground cumin
- 2 teaspoons salt
- 1 teaspoon ground black pepper
- 1 teaspoon garlic powder

- ½ teaspoon dry ground mustard
- ½ cup low-carb barbecue sauce

**Directions:**
1. Place ribs on ungreased aluminum foil sheet. Carefully use a knife to remove membrane and sprinkle meat evenly on both sides with cumin, salt, pepper, garlic powder, and ground mustard.
2. Cut rack into portions that will fit in your air fryer, and wrap each portion in one layer of aluminum foil, working in batches if needed.
3. Place ribs into ungreased air fryer basket. Adjust the temperature to 400°F and set the timer for 25 minutes.
4. When the timer beeps, carefully remove ribs from foil and brush with barbecue sauce. Return to air fryer and cook at 400°F for an additional 5 minutes to brown. Ribs will be done when no pink remains and internal temperature is at least 180°F. Serve warm.

# Chapter 6. Fish And Seafood Recipes

## Ahi Tuna Steaks

Servings:2
Cooking Time: 14 Minutes
**Ingredients:**
- 2 ahi tuna steaks
- 2 tablespoons olive oil
- 3 tablespoons everything bagel seasoning

**Directions:**
1. Preheat the air fryer to 400°F.
2. Drizzle both sides of steaks with oil. Place seasoning on a medium plate and press each side of tuna steaks into seasoning to form a thick layer.
3. Place steaks in the air fryer basket and cook 14 minutes, turning halfway through cooking time, until internal temperature reaches at least 145°F for well-done. Serve warm.

## Horseradish-crusted Salmon Fillets

Servings:3
Cooking Time: 8 Minutes
**Ingredients:**
- ½ cup Fresh bread crumbs
- 4 tablespoons (¼ cup/½ stick) Butter, melted and cooled
- ¼ cup Jarred prepared white horseradish
- Vegetable oil spray
- 4 6-ounce skin-on salmon fillets

**Directions:**
1. Preheat the air fryer to 400°F.

2. Mix the bread crumbs, butter, and horseradish in a bowl until well combined.
3. Take the basket out of the machine. Generously spray the skin side of each fillet. Pick them up one by one with a nonstick-safe spatula and set them in the basket skin side down with as much air space between them as possible. Divide the bread-crumb mixture between the fillets, coating the top of each fillet with an even layer. Generously coat the bread-crumb mixture with vegetable oil spray.
4. Return the basket to the machine and air-fry undisturbed for 8 minutes, or until the topping has lightly browned and the fish is firm but not hard.
5. Use a nonstick-safe spatula to transfer the salmon fillets to serving plates. Cool for 5 minutes before serving. Because of the butter in the topping, it will stay very hot for quite a while. Take care, especially if you're serving these fillets to children.

## Super Crunchy Flounder Fillets

Servings:2
Cooking Time: 6 Minutes
**Ingredients:**
- ½ cup All-purpose flour or tapioca flour
- 1 Large egg white(s)
- 1 tablespoon Water
- ¾ teaspoon Table salt
- 1 cup Plain panko bread crumbs (gluten-free, if a concern)
- 2 4-ounce skinless flounder fillet(s)

- Vegetable oil spray

**Directions:**

1. Preheat the air fryer to 400°F.

2. Set up and fill three shallow soup plates or small pie plates on your counter: one for the flour; one for the egg white(s), beaten with the water and salt until foamy; and one for the bread crumbs.

3. Dip one fillet in the flour, turning it to coat both sides. Gently shake off any excess flour, then dip the fillet in the egg white mixture, turning it to coat. Let any excess egg white mixture slip back into the rest, then set the fish in the bread crumbs. Turn it several times, gently pressing it into the crumbs to create an even crust. Generously coat both sides of the fillet with vegetable oil spray. If necessary, set it aside and continue coating the remaining fillet(s) in the same way.

4. Set the fillet(s) in the basket. If working with more than one fillet, they should not touch, although they may be quite close together, depending on the basket's size. Air-fry undisturbed for 6 minutes, or until lightly browned and crunchy.

5. Use a nonstick-safe spatula to transfer the fillet(s) to a wire rack. Cool for only a minute or two before serving.

## Herbed Haddock

Servings:2
Cooking Time:8 Minutes
**Ingredients:**

- 2 haddock fillets
- 2 tablespoons pine nuts
- 3 tablespoons fresh basil, chopped
- 1 tablespoon Parmesan cheese, grated
- ½ cup extra-virgin olive oil
- Salt and black pepper, to taste

**Directions:**

1. Preheat the Air fryer to 355°F and grease an Air fryer basket.

2. Coat the haddock fillets evenly with olive oil and season with salt and black pepper.

3. Place the haddock fillets in the Air fryer basket and cook for about 8 minutes.

4. Dish out the haddock fillets in serving plates.

5. Meanwhile, put remaining ingredients in a food processor and pulse until smooth.

6. Top this cheese sauce over the haddock fillets and serve hot.

## French Clams

Servings: 5
Cooking Time: 3 Minutes
**Ingredients:**

- 2-pounds clams, raw, shells removed
- 1 tablespoon Herbs de Provence
- 1 tablespoon sesame oil
- 1 garlic clove, diced

**Directions:**

1. Put the clams in the bowl and sprinkle with Herbs de Provence, sesame oil, and diced garlic. Shake the seafood well. Preheat the air fryer to 390°F. Put the clams in the air fryer and cook them for 3 minutes. When the clams are cooked, shake them well and transfer in the serving plates.

## Fish Taco Bowl

Servings:4
Cooking Time: 12 Minutes
**Ingredients:**

- 2 cups finely shredded cabbage
- ½ cup mayonnaise
- Juice of 1 medium lime, divided
- 4 boneless, skinless tilapia fillets
- 2 teaspoons chili powder
- 1 teaspoon salt
- ½ teaspoon ground black pepper

**Directions:**

1. In a large bowl, mix cabbage, mayonnaise, and half of lime juice to make a slaw. Cover and refrigerate while the fish cooks.

2. Preheat the air fryer to 400°F.

3. Sprinkle tilapia with chili powder, salt, and pepper. Spritz each side with cooking spray.

4. Place fillets in the air fryer basket and cook 12 minutes, turning halfway through cooking time, until fish is opaque, flakes easily, and reaches an internal temperature of 145°F.

5. Allow fish to cool 5 minutes before chopping into bite-sized pieces. To serve, place ½ cup slaw into each bowl and top with one-fourth of fish. Squeeze remaining lime juice over fish. Serve warm.

## Chili Blackened Shrimp

Servings: 4
Cooking Time: 15 Minutes
**Ingredients:**

- 1 lb peeled shrimp, deveined
- 1 tsp paprika
- ½ tsp dried dill
- ½ tsp red chili flakes
- ½ lemon, juiced
- Salt and pepper to taste

**Directions:**

1. Preheat air fryer to 400°F. In a resealable bag, add shrimp, paprika, dill, red chili flakes, lemon juice, salt and pepper. Seal and shake well. Place the shrimp in the greased frying basket and Air Fry for 7-8 minutes, shaking the basket once until blackened. Let cool slightly and serve.

# Catfish Nuggets

Servings: 4
Cooking Time: 7 Minutes Per Batch
**Ingredients:**
- 2 medium catfish fillets, cut in chunks
- salt and pepper
- 2 eggs
- 2 tablespoons skim milk
- ½ cup cornstarch
- 1 cup panko breadcrumbs, crushed
- oil for misting or cooking spray

**Directions:**
1. Season catfish chunks with salt and pepper to your liking.
2. Beat together eggs and milk in a small bowl.
3. Place cornstarch in a second small bowl.
4. Place breadcrumbs in a third small bowl.
5. Dip catfish chunks in cornstarch, dip in egg wash, shake off excess, then roll in breadcrumbs.
6. Spray all sides of catfish chunks with oil or cooking spray.
7. Place chunks in air fryer basket in a single layer, leaving space between for air circulation.
8. Cook at 390°F for 4minutes, turn, and cook an additional 3 minutes, until fish flakes easily and outside is crispy brown.
9. Repeat steps 7 and 8 to cook remaining catfish nuggets.

# Bacon-wrapped Cajun Scallops

Servings:4
Cooking Time: 13 Minutes
**Ingredients:**
- 8 slices bacon
- 8 sea scallops, rinsed and patted dry
- 1 teaspoon Cajun seasoning
- 4 tablespoons salted butter, melted

**Directions:**
1. Preheat the air fryer to 375°F.
2. Place bacon in the air fryer basket and cook 3 minutes. Remove bacon and wrap each scallop in one slice bacon before securing with a toothpick.
3. Sprinkle Cajun seasoning evenly over scallops. Spritz scallops lightly with cooking spray and place in the air fryer basket in a single layer. Cook 10 minutes, turning halfway through cooking time, until scallops are opaque and firm and internal temperature reaches at least 130°F. Drizzle with butter. Serve warm.

# Shrimp Al Pesto

Servings: 4
Cooking Time: 10 Minutes
**Ingredients:**
- 1 lb peeled shrimp, deveined
- ¼ cup pesto sauce
- 1 lime, sliced
- 2 cups cooked farro

**Directions:**
1. Preheat air fryer to 360°F. Coat the shrimp with the pesto sauce in a bowl. Put the shrimp in a single layer in the frying basket. Put the lime slices over the shrimp and Roast for 5 minutes. Remove lime and discard. Serve the shrimp over a bed of farro pilaf. Enjoy!

# Crab Cakes

Servings:4
Cooking Time: 12 Minutes
**Ingredients:**
- 2 cans lump crabmeat, drained
- ½ cup plain bread crumbs
- ½ cup mayonnaise
- 1 ½ teaspoons Old Bay Seasoning
- Zest and juice of ½ medium lemon
- ½ teaspoon salt
- ½ teaspoon ground black pepper
- Cooking spray

**Directions:**
1. Preheat the air fryer to 375°F.
2. In a large bowl, mix all ingredients.
3. Scoop ¼ cup mixture and form into a 4" patty. Repeat to make eight crab cakes. Spritz cakes with cooking spray.
4. Place in the air fryer basket and cook 12 minutes, turning halfway through cooking time, until edges are brown and center is firm. Serve warm.

# Crispy Sweet-and-sour Cod Fillets

Servings:3
Cooking Time: 12 Minutes
**Ingredients:**
- 1½ cups Plain panko bread crumbs (gluten-free, if a concern)
- 2 tablespoons Regular or low-fat mayonnaise (not fat-free; gluten-free, if a concern)
- ¼ cup Sweet pickle relish
- 3 4- to 5-ounce skinless cod fillets

**Directions:**
1. Preheat the air fryer to 400°F.
2. Pour the bread crumbs into a shallow soup plate or a small pie plate. Mix the mayonnaise and relish in a small bowl until well combined. Smear this mixture all over the cod fillets. Set them in the crumbs and turn until evenly coated on all sides, even on the ends.
3. Set the coated cod fillets in the basket with as much air space between them as possible. They should not touch. Air-fry undisturbed for 12 minutes, or until browned and crisp.
4. Use a nonstick-safe spatula to transfer the cod pieces to a wire rack. Cool for only a minute or two before serving hot.

# Almond Topped Trout

Servings: 4
Cooking Time: 20 Minutes
**Ingredients:**
- 4 trout fillets
- 2 tbsp olive oil
- Salt and pepper to taste
- 2 garlic cloves, sliced
- 1 lemon, sliced
- 1 tbsp flaked almonds

**Directions:**
1. Preheat air fryer to 380°F. Lightly brush each fillet with olive oil on both sides and season with salt and pepper. Put the fillets in a single layer in the frying basket. Put the sliced garlic over the tops of the trout fillets, then top with lemon slices and cook for 12-15 minutes. Serve topped with flaked almonds and enjoy!

# Swordfish With Capers And Tomatoes

Servings: 2
Cooking Time: 10 Minutes
**Ingredients:**
- 2 1-inch thick swordfish steaks
- A pinch of salt and black pepper
- 30 ounces tomatoes, chopped
- 2 tablespoons capers, drained
- 1 tablespoon red vinegar
- 2 tablespoons oregano, chopped

**Directions:**
1. In a pan that fits the air fryer, combine all the ingredients, toss, put the pan in the fryer and cook at 390°F for 10 minutes, flipping the fish halfway. Divide the mix between plates and serve.

# Tuna-stuffed Tomatoes

Servings:2
Cooking Time: 5 Minutes
**Ingredients:**
- 2 medium beefsteak tomatoes, tops removed, seeded, membranes removed
- 2 pouches tuna packed in water, drained
- 1 medium stalk celery, trimmed and chopped
- 2 tablespoons mayonnaise
- ¼ teaspoon salt
- ¼ teaspoon ground black pepper
- 2 teaspoons coconut oil
- ¼ cup shredded mild Cheddar cheese

**Directions:**
1. Scoop pulp out of each tomato, leaving ½" shell.
2. In a medium bowl, mix tuna, celery, mayonnaise, salt, and pepper. Drizzle with coconut oil. Spoon ½ mixture into each tomato and top each with 2 tablespoons Cheddar.

3. Place tomatoes into ungreased air fryer basket. Adjust the temperature to 320°F and set the timer for 5 minutes. Cheese will be melted when done. Serve warm.

# Perfect Soft-shelled Crabs

Servings:2
Cooking Time: 12 Minutes
**Ingredients:**
- ½ cup All-purpose flour
- 1 tablespoon Old Bay seasoning
- 1 Large egg(s), well beaten
- 1 cup Ground oyster crackers
- 2 2½-ounce cleaned soft-shelled crab(s), about 4 inches across
- Vegetable oil spray

**Directions:**
1. Preheat the air fryer to 375°F.
2. Set up and fill three shallow soup plates or small pie plates on your counter: one for the flour, whisked with the Old Bay until well combined; one for the beaten egg(s); and one for the cracker crumbs.
3. Set a soft-shelled crab in the flour mixture and turn to coat evenly and well on all sides, even inside the legs. Dip the crab into the egg(s) and coat well, turning at least once, again getting some of the egg between the legs. Let any excess egg slip back into the rest, then set the crab in the cracker crumbs. Turn several times, pressing very gently to get the crab evenly coated with crumbs, even between the legs. Generously coat the crab on all sides with vegetable oil spray. Set it aside if you're making more than one and coat these in the same way.
4. Set the crab(s) in the basket with as much air space between them as possible. They may overlap slightly, particularly at the ends of their legs, depending on the basket's size. Air-fry undisturbed for 12 minutes, or until very crisp and golden brown. If the machine is at 390°F, the crabs may be done in only 10 minutes.
5. Use kitchen tongs to gently transfer the crab(s) to a wire rack. Cool for a couple of minutes before serving.

# Easy Lobster Tail With Salted Butetr

Servings:4
Cooking Time: 6 Minutes
**Ingredients:**
- 2 tablespoons melted butter
- 4 lobster tails
- Salt and pepper to taste

**Directions:**
1. Preheat the air fryer to 390°F.
2. Place the grill pan accessory.
3. Cut the lobster through the tail section using a pair of kitchen scissors.
4. Brush the lobster tails with melted butter and season with salt and pepper to taste.
5. Place on the grill pan and cook for 6 minutes.

# Miso-rubbed Salmon Fillets

Servings:3
Cooking Time: 5 Minutes
**Ingredients:**
- ¼ cup White (shiro) miso paste (usually made from rice and soy beans)
- 1½ tablespoons Mirin or a substitute
- 2½ teaspoons Unseasoned rice vinegar
- Vegetable oil spray
- 3 6-ounce skin-on salmon fillets

**Directions:**
1. Preheat the air fryer to 400°F.
2. Mix the miso, mirin, and vinegar in a small bowl until uniform.
3. Remove the basket from the machine. Generously spray the skin side of each fillet. Pick them up one by one with a nonstick-safe spatula and set them in the basket skin side down with as much air space between them as possible. Coat the top of each fillet with the miso mixture, dividing it evenly between them.
4. Return the basket to the machine. Air-fry undisturbed for 5 minutes, or until lightly browned and firm.
5. Use a nonstick-safe spatula to transfer the fillets to serving plates. Cool for only a minute or so before serving.

# Snow Crab Legs

Servings:6
Cooking Time: 15 Minutes Per Batch
**Ingredients:**
- 8 pounds fresh shell-on snow crab legs
- 2 tablespoons olive oil
- 2 teaspoons Old Bay Seasoning
- 4 tablespoons salted butter, melted
- 2 teaspoons lemon juice

**Directions:**
1. Preheat the air fryer to 400°F.
2. Drizzle crab legs with oil and sprinkle with Old Bay. Place in the air fryer basket, working in batches as necessary. Cook 15 minutes, turning halfway through cooking time, until crab turns a bright red-orange.
3. In a small bowl, whisk together butter and lemon juice. Serve as a dipping sauce with warm crab legs.

# Shrimp "scampi"

Servings:4
Cooking Time: 5 Minutes
**Ingredients:**
- 1½ pounds Large shrimp, peeled and deveined
- ¼ cup Olive oil
- 2 tablespoons Minced garlic
- 1 teaspoon Dried oregano
- Up to 1 teaspoon Red pepper flakes
- ½ teaspoon Table salt
- 2 tablespoons White balsamic vinegar

**Directions:**
1. Preheat the air fryer to 400°F.
2. Stir the shrimp, olive oil, garlic, oregano, red pepper flakes, and salt in a large bowl until the shrimp are well coated.
3. When the machine is at temperature, transfer the shrimp to the basket. They will overlap and even sit on top of each other. Air-fry for 5 minutes, tossing and rearranging the shrimp twice to make sure the covered surfaces are exposed, until pink and firm.
4. Pour the contents of the basket into a serving bowl. Pour the vinegar over the shrimp while hot and toss to coat.

# Chili Lime Shrimp

Servings:4
Cooking Time: 5 Minutes
**Ingredients:**
- 1 pound medium shrimp, peeled and deveined
- 1 tablespoon salted butter, melted
- 2 teaspoons chili powder
- ¼ teaspoon garlic powder
- ¼ teaspoon salt
- ¼ teaspoon ground black pepper
- ½ small lime, zested and juiced, divided

**Directions:**
1. In a medium bowl, toss shrimp with butter, then sprinkle with chili powder, garlic powder, salt, pepper, and lime zest.
2. Place shrimp into ungreased air fryer basket. Adjust the temperature to 400°F and set the timer for 5 minutes. Shrimp will be firm and form a "C" shape when done.
3. Transfer shrimp to a large serving dish and drizzle with lime juice. Serve warm.

# Chili-lime Shrimp

Servings:4
Cooking Time: 10 Minutes
**Ingredients:**
- 1 pound medium shrimp, peeled and deveined
- ½ cup lime juice
- 2 tablespoons olive oil
- 2 tablespoons sriracha
- 1 teaspoon salt
- ¼ teaspoon ground black pepper

**Directions:**
1. Preheat the air fryer to 375°F.
2. In an 6" round cake pan, combine all ingredients.
3. Place pan in the air fryer and cook 10 minutes, stirring halfway through cooking time, until the inside of shrimp are pearly white and opaque and internal temperature reaches at least 145°F. Serve warm.

# Garlic And Dill Salmon

Servings: 2
Cooking Time: 8 Minutes
**Ingredients:**
- 12 ounces salmon filets with skin
- 2 tablespoons melted butter
- 1 tablespoon extra-virgin olive oil
- 2 garlic cloves, minced
- 1 tablespoon fresh dill
- ½ teaspoon sea salt
- ½ lemon

**Directions:**
1. Pat the salmon dry with paper towels.
2. In a small bowl, mix together the melted butter, olive oil, garlic, and dill.
3. Sprinkle the top of the salmon with sea salt. Brush all sides of the salmon with the garlic and dill butter.
4. Preheat the air fryer to 350°F.
5. Place the salmon, skin side down, in the air fryer basket. Cook for 6 to 8 minutes, or until the fish flakes in the center.
6. Remove the salmon and plate on a serving platter. Squeeze fresh lemon over the top of the salmon. Serve immediately.

# Fish Sticks For Kids

Servings: 8
Cooking Time: 6 Minutes
**Ingredients:**
- 8 ounces fish fillets (pollock or cod)
- salt (optional)
- ½ cup plain breadcrumbs
- oil for misting or cooking spray

**Directions:**
1. Cut fish fillets into "fingers" about ½ x 3 inches. Sprinkle with salt to taste, if desired.
2. Roll fish in breadcrumbs. Spray all sides with oil or cooking spray.
3. Place in air fryer basket in single layer and cook at 390°F for 6 minutes, until golden brown and crispy.

# Lemon And Thyme Sea Bass

Servings: 3
Cooking Time: 15 Minutes
**Ingredients:**
- 8 oz sea bass, trimmed, peeled
- 4 lemon slices
- 1 tablespoon thyme
- 2 teaspoons sesame oil
- 1 teaspoon salt

**Directions:**
1. Fill the sea bass with lemon slices and rub with thyme, salt, and sesame oil. Then preheat the air fryer to 385°F and put the fish in the air fryer basket. Cook it for 12 minutes.

Then flip the fish on another side and cook it for 3 minutes more.

# Lemon-basil On Cod Filet

Servings:4
Cooking Time: 15 Minutes
**Ingredients:**
- ¼ cup olive oil
- 4 cod fillets
- A bunch of basil, torn
- Juice from 1 lemon, freshly squeezed
- Salt and pepper to taste

**Directions:**
1. Preheat the air fryer for 5 minutes.
2. Season the cod fillets with salt and pepper to taste. Place on lightly greased air fryer baking pan.
3. Mix the rest of the ingredients in a bowl and toss to combine. Pour over fish.
4. Cook for 15 minutes at 330°F.
5. Serve and enjoy.

# Miso Fish

Servings: 2
Cooking Time: 10 Minutes
**Ingredients:**
- 2 cod fish fillets
- 1 tbsp garlic, chopped
- 2 tsp swerve
- 2 tbsp miso

**Directions:**
1. Add all ingredients to the zip-lock bag. Shake well place in the refrigerator for overnight.
2. Place marinated fish fillets into the air fryer basket and cook at 350°F for 10 minutes.
3. Serve and enjoy.

# Butternut Squash–wrapped Halibut Fillets

Servings:3
Cooking Time: 11 Minutes
**Ingredients:**
- 15 Long spiralized peeled and seeded butternut squash strands
- 3 5- to 6-ounce skinless halibut fillets
- 3 tablespoons Butter, melted
- ¾ teaspoon Mild paprika
- ¾ teaspoon Table salt
- ¾ teaspoon Ground black pepper

**Directions:**
1. Preheat the air fryer to 375°F .
2. Hold 5 long butternut squash strands together and wrap them around a fillet. Set it aside and wrap any remaining fillet(s).

3. Mix the melted butter, paprika, salt, and pepper in a small bowl. Brush this mixture over the squash-wrapped fillets on all sides.

4. When the machine is at temperature, set the fillets in the basket with as much air space between them as possible. Air-fry undisturbed for 10 minutes, or until the squash strands have browned but not burned. If the machine is at 360°F, you may need to add 1 minute to the cooking time. In any event, watch the fish carefully after the 8-minute mark.

5. Use a nonstick-safe spatula to gently transfer the fillets to a serving platter or plates. Cool for only a minute or so before serving.

## Fish-in-chips

Servings:4
Cooking Time: 11 Minutes
**Ingredients:**
- 1 cup All-purpose flour or potato starch
- 2 Large egg(s), well beaten
- 1½ cups Crushed plain potato chips, preferably thick-cut or ruffled (gluten-free, if a concern)
- 4 4-ounce skinless cod fillets

**Directions:**
1. Preheat the air fryer to 400°F.
2. Set up and fill three shallow soup plates or small pie plates on your counter: one for the flour, one for the beaten egg(s), and one for the crushed potato chips.
3. Dip a piece of cod in the flour, turning it to coat on all sides, even the ends and sides. Gently shake off any excess flour, then dip it in the beaten egg(s). Gently turn to coat it on all sides, then let any excess egg slip back into the rest. Set the fillet in the crushed potato chips and turn several times and onto all sides, pressing gently to coat the fish. Dip it back in the egg(s), coating all sides but taking care that the coating doesn't slip off; then dip it back in the potato chips for a thick, even coating. Set it aside and coat more fillets in the same way.
4. When the machine is at temperature, set the fillets in the basket with as much air space between them as possible. Air-fry undisturbed for 11 minutes, until golden brown and firm but not hard.
5. Use kitchen tongs to transfer the fillets to a wire rack. Cool for just a minute or two before serving.

## Sesame Tuna Steak

Servings: 2
Cooking Time: 12 Minutes
**Ingredients:**
- 1 tbsp. coconut oil, melted
- 2 x 6-oz. tuna steaks
- ½ tsp. garlic powder
- 2 tsp. black sesame seeds
- 2 tsp. white sesame seeds

**Directions:**

1. Apply the coconut oil to the tuna steaks with a brunch, then season with garlic powder.
2. Combine the black and white sesame seeds. Embed them in the tuna steaks, covering the fish all over. Place the tuna into your air fryer.
3. Cook for eight minutes at 400°F, turning the fish halfway through.
4. The tuna steaks are ready when they have reached a temperature of 145°F. Serve straightaway.

## Kid´s Flounder Fingers

Servings: 4
Cooking Time: 45 Minutes
**Ingredients:**
- 1 lb catfish flounder fillets, cut into 1-inch chunks
- ½ cup seasoned fish fry breading mix

**Directions:**
1. Preheat air fryer to 400°F. In a resealable bag, add flounder and breading mix. Seal bag and shake until the fish is coated. Place the nuggets in the greased frying basket and Air Fry for 18-20 minutes, shaking the basket once until crisp. Serve warm and enjoy!

## Flounder Fillets

Servings: 4
Cooking Time: 8 Minutes
**Ingredients:**
- 1 egg white
- 1 tablespoon water
- 1 cup panko breadcrumbs
- 2 tablespoons extra-light virgin olive oil
- 4 4-ounce flounder fillets
- salt and pepper
- oil for misting or cooking spray

**Directions:**
1. Preheat air fryer to 390°F.
2. Beat together egg white and water in shallow dish.
3. In another shallow dish, mix panko crumbs and oil until well combined and crumbly.
4. Season flounder fillets with salt and pepper to taste. Dip each fillet into egg mixture and then roll in panko crumbs, pressing in crumbs so that fish is nicely coated.
5. Spray air fryer basket with nonstick cooking spray and add fillets. Cook at 390°F for 3minutes.
6. Spray fish fillets but do not turn. Cook 5 minutes longer or until golden brown and crispy. Using a spatula, carefully remove fish from basket and serve.

## Bacon-wrapped Scallops

Servings: 4
Cooking Time: 8 Minutes
**Ingredients:**
- 16 large scallops
- 8 bacon strips
- ½ teaspoon black pepper
- ¼ teaspoon smoked paprika

**Directions:**
1. Pat the scallops dry with a paper towel. Slice each of the bacon strips in half. Wrap 1 bacon strip around 1 scallop and secure with a toothpick. Repeat with the remaining scallops. Season the scallops with pepper and paprika.
2. Preheat the air fryer to 350°F.
3. Place the bacon-wrapped scallops in the air fryer basket and cook for 4 minutes, shake the basket, cook another 3 minutes, shake the basket, and cook another 1 to 3 to minutes. When the bacon is crispy, the scallops should be cooked through and slightly firm, but not rubbery. Serve immediately.

## Snapper Fillets With Thai Sauce

Servings: 2
Cooking Time: 30 Minutes + Marinating Time
**Ingredients:**
- 1/2 cup full-fat coconut milk
- 2 tablespoons lemon juice
- 1 teaspoon fresh ginger, grated
- 2 snapper fillets
- 1 tablespoon olive oil
- Salt and white pepper, to taste

**Directions:**
1. Place the milk, lemon juice, and ginger in a glass bowl; add fish and let it marinate for 1 hour.
2. Removed the fish from the milk mixture and place in the Air Fryer basket. Drizzle olive oil all over the fish fillets.
3. Cook in the preheated Air Fryer at 390°F for 15 minutes.
4. Meanwhile, heat the milk mixture over medium-high heat; bring to a rapid boil, stirring continuously. Reduce to simmer and add the salt, and pepper; continue to cook 12 minutes more.
5. Spoon the sauce over the warm snapper fillets and serve immediately. Bon appétit!

## Fried Catfish Fillets

Servings:2
Cooking Time: 40 Minutes
**Ingredients:**
- 3 tbsp breadcrumbs
- 1 tsp cayenne pepper
- 1 tsp dry fish seasoning, of choice
- 2 sprigs parsley, chopped
- Salt to taste, optional
- Cooking spray

**Directions:**
1. Preheat air fryer to 400°F. Pour all the dry ingredients, except the parsley, in a zipper bag. Pat dry and add the fish pieces. Close the bag and shake to coat the fish well. Do this with one fish piece at a time.
2. Lightly spray the fish with olive oil. Arrange them in the fryer basket, one at a time depending on the size of the fish. Close the air fryer and cook for 10 minutes. Flip the fish and cook further for 10 minutes. For extra crispiness, cook for 3 more minutes. Garnish with parsley and serve.

## Thyme Scallops

Servings: 1
Cooking Time: 12 Minutes
**Ingredients:**
- 1 lb. scallops
- Salt and pepper
- ½ tbsp. butter
- ½ cup thyme, chopped

**Directions:**
1. Wash the scallops and dry them completely. Season with pepper and salt, then set aside while you prepare the pan.
2. Grease a foil pan in several spots with the butter and cover the bottom with the thyme. Place the scallops on top.
3. Pre-heat the fryer at 400°F and set the rack inside.
4. Place the foil pan on the rack and allow to cook for seven minutes.
5. Take care when removing the pan from the fryer and transfer the scallops to a serving dish. Spoon any remaining butter in the pan over the fish and enjoy.

## Italian Tuna Roast

Servings: 8
Cooking Time: 21 Minutes
**Ingredients:**
- cooking spray
- 1 tablespoon Italian seasoning
- ⅛ teaspoon ground black pepper
- 1 tablespoon extra-light olive oil
- 1 teaspoon lemon juice
- 1 tuna loin

**Directions:**
1. Spray baking dish with cooking spray and place in air fryer basket. Preheat air fryer to 390°F.
2. Mix together the Italian seasoning, pepper, oil, and lemon juice.
3. Using a dull table knife or butter knife, pierce top of tuna about every half inch: Insert knife into top of tuna roast and pierce almost all the way to the bottom.
4. Spoon oil mixture into each of the holes and use the knife to push seasonings into the tuna as deeply as possible.
5. Spread any remaining oil mixture on all outer surfaces of tuna.

6. Place tuna roast in baking dish and cook at 390°F for 20 minutes. Check temperature with a meat thermometer. Cook for an additional 1 minutes or until temperature reaches 145°F.

7. Remove basket from fryer and let tuna sit in basket for 10minutes.

# Teriyaki Salmon

Servings:4
Cooking Time: 27 Minutes
**Ingredients:**
- ½ cup teriyaki sauce
- ¼ teaspoon salt
- 1 teaspoon ground ginger
- ½ teaspoon garlic powder
- 4 boneless, skinless salmon fillets
- 2 tablespoons toasted sesame seeds

**Directions:**
1. In a large bowl, whisk teriyaki sauce, salt, ginger, and garlic powder. Add salmon to the bowl, being sure to coat each side with marinade. Cover and let marinate in refrigerator 15 minutes.
2. Preheat the air fryer to 375°F.
3. Spritz fillets with cooking spray and place in the air fryer basket. Cook 12 minutes, turning halfway through cooking time, until glaze has caramelized to a dark brown color, salmon flakes easily, and internal temperature reaches at least 145°F. Sprinkle sesame seeds on salmon and serve warm.

# Mediterranean-style Cod

Servings:4
Cooking Time: 12 Minutes
**Ingredients:**
- 4 cod fillets
- 3 tablespoons fresh lemon juice
- 1 tablespoon olive oil
- ¼ teaspoon salt
- 6 cherry tomatoes, halved
- ¼ cup pitted and sliced kalamata olives

**Directions:**
1. Place cod into an ungreased 6" round nonstick baking dish. Pour lemon juice into dish and drizzle cod with olive oil. Sprinkle with salt. Place tomatoes and olives around baking dish in between fillets.
2. Place dish into air fryer basket. Adjust the temperature to 350°F and set the timer for 12 minutes, carefully turning cod halfway through cooking. Fillets will be lightly browned, easily flake, and have an internal temperature of at least 145°F when done. Serve warm.

# Sweet Potato–wrapped Shrimp

Servings:3
Cooking Time: 6 Minutes
**Ingredients:**

- 24 Long spiralized sweet potato strands
- Olive oil spray
- ¼ teaspoon Garlic powder
- ¼ teaspoon Table salt
- Up to a ⅛ teaspoon Cayenne
- 12 Large shrimp, peeled and deveined

**Directions:**
1. Preheat the air fryer to 400°F.
2. Lay the spiralized sweet potato strands on a large swath of paper towels and straighten out the strands to long ropes. Coat them with olive oil spray, then sprinkle them with the garlic powder, salt, and cayenne.
3. Pick up 2 strands and wrap them around the center of a shrimp, with the ends tucked under what now becomes the bottom side of the shrimp. Continue wrapping the remainder of the shrimp.
4. Set the shrimp bottom side down in the basket with as much air space between them as possible. Air-fry undisturbed for 6 minutes, or until the sweet potato strands are crisp and the shrimp are pink and firm.
5. Use kitchen tongs to transfer the shrimp to a wire rack. Cool for only a minute or two before serving.

# Air Fried Cod With Basil Vinaigrette

Servings:4
Cooking Time: 15 Minutes
**Ingredients:**
- ¼ cup olive oil
- 4 cod fillets
- A bunch of basil, torn
- Juice from 1 lemon, freshly squeezed
- Salt and pepper to taste

**Directions:**
1. Preheat the air fryer for 5 minutes.
2. Season the cod fillets with salt and pepper to taste.
3. Place in the air fryer and cook for 15 minutes at 350°F.
4. Meanwhile, mix the rest of the ingredients in a bowl and toss to combine.
5. Serve the air fried cod with the basil vinaigrette.

# Coconut Shrimp

Servings:4
Cooking Time: 10 Minutes
**Ingredients:**
- 1 cup all-purpose flour
- 1 teaspoon salt
- 2 large eggs
- ½ cup panko bread crumbs
- 1 cup shredded unsweetened coconut flakes
- 1 pound large shrimp, peeled and deveined
- Cooking spray

**Directions:**
1. Preheat the air fryer to 375°F.

2. In a medium bowl, mix flour and salt. In a separate medium bowl, whisk eggs. In a third medium bowl, mix bread crumbs and coconut flakes.

3. Dredge shrimp first in flour mixture, shaking off excess, then in eggs, letting any additional egg drip off, and finally in bread crumb mixture. Spritz with cooking spray.

4. Place shrimp in the air fryer basket. Cook 10 minutes, turning and spritzing opposite side with cooking spray halfway through cooking, until insides are pearly white and opaque and internal temperature reaches at least 145°F. Serve warm.

## Quick And Easy Shrimp

Servings:2
Cooking Time:5 Minutes
**Ingredients:**
- ½ pound tiger shrimp
- 1 tablespoon olive oil
- ½ teaspoon old bay seasoning
- ¼ teaspoon smoked paprika
- ¼ teaspoon cayenne pepper
- Salt, to taste

**Directions:**
1. Preheat the Air fryer to 390°F and grease an Air fryer basket.
2. Mix all the ingredients in a large bowl until well combined.
3. Place the shrimps in the Air fryer basket and cook for about 5 minutes.
4. Dish out and serve warm.

## Simple Salmon Fillets

Servings: 2
Cooking Time: 7 Minutes
**Ingredients:**
- 2 salmon fillets
- 2 tsp olive oil
- 2 tsp paprika
- Pepper
- Salt

**Directions:**
1. Rub salmon fillet with oil, paprika, pepper, and salt.
2. Place salmon fillets in the air fryer basket and cook at 390°F for 7 minutes.
3. Serve and enjoy.

## Garlic-lemon Steamer Clams

Servings:2
Cooking Time: 30 Minutes
**Ingredients:**
- 25 Manila clams, scrubbed
- 2 tbsp butter, melted
- 1 garlic clove, minced
- 2 lemon wedges

**Directions:**
1. Add the clams to a large bowl filled with water and let sit for 10 minutes. Drain. Pour more water and let sit for 10 more minutes. Drain. Preheat air fryer to 350°F. Place clams in the basket and Air Fry for 7 minutes. Discard any clams that don't open. Remove clams from shells and place them into a large serving dish. Drizzle with melted butter and garlic and squeeze lemon on top. Serve.

## Cajun Flounder Fillets

Servings:2
Cooking Time: 5 Minutes
**Ingredients:**
- 2 4-ounce skinless flounder fillet(s)
- 2 teaspoons Peanut oil
- 1 teaspoon Purchased or homemade Cajun dried seasoning blend

**Directions:**
1. Preheat the air fryer to 400°F.
2. Oil the fillet(s) by drizzling on the peanut oil, then gently rubbing in the oil with your clean, dry fingers. Sprinkle the seasoning blend evenly over both sides of the fillet(s).
3. When the machine is at temperature, set the fillet(s) in the basket. If working with more than one fillet, they should not touch, although they may be quite close together, depending on the basket's size. Air-fry undisturbed for 5 minutes, or until lightly browned and cooked through.
4. Use a nonstick-safe spatula to transfer the fillets to a serving platter or plate(s). Serve at once.

## Spicy Mackerel

Servings: 2
Cooking Time: 20 Minutes
**Ingredients:**
- 2 mackerel fillets
- 2 tbsp. red chili flakes
- 2 tsp. garlic, minced
- 1 tsp. lemon juice

**Directions:**
1. Season the mackerel fillets with the red pepper flakes, minced garlic, and a drizzle of lemon juice. Allow to sit for five minutes.
2. Preheat your fryer at 350°F.
3. Cook the mackerel for five minutes, before opening the drawer, flipping the fillets, and allowing to cook on the other side for another five minutes.
4. Plate the fillets, making sure to spoon any remaining juice over them before serving.

# Simple Sesame Squid On The Grill

Servings:3
Cooking Time: 10 Minutes
**Ingredients:**
- 1 ½ pounds squid, cleaned
- 2 tablespoon toasted sesame oil
- Salt and pepper to taste

**Directions:**
1. Preheat the air fryer at 390°F.
2. Place the grill pan accessory in the air fryer.
3. Season the squid with sesame oil, salt and pepper.
4. Grill the squid for 10 minutes.

# Lime Flaming Halibut

Servings:2
Cooking Time: 20 Minutes
**Ingredients:**
- 2 tbsp butter, melted
- ½ tsp chili powder
- ½ cup bread crumbs
- 2 halibut fillets

**Directions:**
1. Preheat air fryer to 350ºF. In a bowl, mix the butter, chili powder and bread crumbs. Press mixture onto tops of halibut fillets. Place halibut in the greased frying basket and Air Fry for 10 minutes or until the fish is opaque and flake easily with a fork. Serve right away.

# Coconut Jerk Shrimp

Servings:3
Cooking Time: 8 Minutes
**Ingredients:**
- 1 Large egg white(s)
- 1 teaspoon Purchased or homemade jerk dried seasoning blend
- ¾ cup Plain panko bread crumbs (gluten-free, if a concern)
- ¾ cup Unsweetened shredded coconut
- 12 Large shrimp, peeled and deveined
- Coconut oil spray

**Directions:**
1. Preheat the air fryer to 375°F .
2. Whisk the egg white(s) and seasoning blend in a bowl until foamy. Add the shrimp and toss well to coat evenly.
3. Mix the bread crumbs and coconut on a dinner plate until well combined. Use kitchen tongs to pick up a shrimp, letting the excess egg white mixture slip back into the rest. Set the shrimp in the bread-crumb mixture. Turn several times to coat evenly and thoroughly. Set on a cutting board and continue coating the remainder of the shrimp.
4. Lightly coat all the shrimp on both sides with the coconut oil spray. Set them in the basket in one layer with as much space between them as possible. Air-fry undisturbed for 6 minutes, or until the coating is lightly browned. If the air fryer is at 360°F, you may need to add 2 minutes to the cooking time.
5. Use clean kitchen tongs to transfer the shrimp to a wire rack. Cool for only a minute or two before serving.

# Great Cat Fish

Servings:4
Cooking Time: 25 Minutes
**Ingredients:**
- ¼ cup seasoned fish fry
- 1 tbsp olive oil
- 1 tbsp parsley, chopped

**Directions:**
1. Preheat your air fryer to 400°F, and add seasoned fish fry, and fillets in a large Ziploc bag; massage well to coat. Place the fillets in your air fryer's cooking basket and cook for 10 minutes. Flip the fish and cook for 2-3 more minutes. Top with parsley and serve.

# Restaurant-style Flounder Cutlets

Servings: 2
Cooking Time: 15 Minutes
**Ingredients:**
- 1 egg
- 1 cup Pecorino Romano cheese, grated
- Sea salt and white pepper, to taste
- 1/2 teaspoon cayenne pepper
- 1 teaspoon dried parsley flakes
- 2 flounder fillets

**Directions:**
1. To make a breading station, whisk the egg until frothy.
2. In another bowl, mix Pecorino Romano cheese, and spices.
3. Dip the fish in the egg mixture and turn to coat evenly; then, dredge in the cracker crumb mixture, turning a couple of times to coat evenly.
4. Cook in the preheated Air Fryer at 390°F for 5 minutes; turn them over and cook another 5 minutes. Enjoy!

# Air Fried Calamari

Servings:3
Cooking Time: 30 Minutes
**Ingredients:**
- ½ cup cornmeal or cornstarch
- 2 large eggs, beaten
- 2 mashed garlic cloves
- 1 cup breadcrumbs
- lemon juice

**Directions:**
1. Coat calamari with the cornmeal. The first mixture is prepared by mixing the eggs and garlic. Dip the calamari in the eggs' mixture. Then dip them in the breadcrumbs. Put the rings in the fridge for 2 hours.
2. Then, line them in the air fryer and add oil generously. Fry for 10 to 13 minutes at 390°F, shaking once halfway

through. Serve with garlic mayonnaise and top with lemon juice.

## Lemon Butter Scallops

Servings: 1
Cooking Time: 30 Minutes
**Ingredients:**
- 1 lemon
- 1 lb. scallops
- ½ cup butter
- ¼ cup parsley, chopped

**Directions:**
1. Juice the lemon into a Ziploc bag.
2. Wash your scallops, dry them, and season to taste. Put them in the bag with the lemon juice. Refrigerate for an hour.
3. Remove the bag from the refrigerator and leave for about twenty minutes until it returns to room temperature. Transfer the scallops into a foil pan that is small enough to be placed inside the fryer.
4. Pre-heat the fryer at 400°F and put the rack inside.
5. Place the foil pan on the rack and cook for five minutes.
6. In the meantime, melt the butter in a saucepan over a medium heat. Zest the lemon over the saucepan, then add in the chopped parsley. Mix well.
7. Take care when removing the pan from the fryer. Transfer the contents to a plate and drizzle with the lemon-butter mixture. Serve hot.

## Zesty Mahi Mahi

Servings:3
Cooking Time:8 Minutes
**Ingredients:**
- 1½ pounds Mahi Mahi fillets
- 1 lemon, cut into slices
- 1 tablespoon fresh dill, chopped
- ½ teaspoon red chili powder
- Salt and ground black pepper, as required

**Directions:**
1. Preheat the Air fryer to 375°F and grease an Air fryer basket.
2. Season the Mahi Mahi fillets evenly with chili powder, salt, and black pepper.
3. Arrange the Mahi Mahi fillets into the Air fryer basket and top with the lemon slices.
4. Cook for about 8 minutes and dish out
5. Place the lemon slices over the salmon the salmon fillets in the serving plates.
6. Garnish with fresh dill and serve warm.

## Seared Scallops In Beurre Blanc

Servings: 4
Cooking Time: 15 Minutes
**Ingredients:**
- 1 lb sea scallops
- Salt and pepper to taste

- 2 tbsp butter, melted
- 1 lemon, zested and juiced
- 2 tbsp dry white wine

**Directions:**
1. Preheat the air fryer to 400°F. Sprinkle the scallops with salt and pepper, then set in a bowl. Combine the butter, lemon zest, lemon juice, and white wine in another bowl; mix well. Put the scallops in a baking pan and drizzle over them the mixture. Air Fry for 8-11 minutes, flipping over at about 5 minutes until opaque. Serve and enjoy!

## Nacho Chips Crusted Prawns

Servings:2
Cooking Time: 8 Minutes
**Ingredients:**
- ¾ pound prawns, peeled and deveined
- 1 large egg
- 5 ounces Nacho flavored chips, finely crushed

**Directions:**
1. In a shallow bowl, beat the egg.
2. In another bowl, place the nacho chips
3. Dip each prawn into the beaten egg and then, coat with the crushed nacho chips.
4. Set the temperature of air fryer to 350°F. Grease an air fryer basket.
5. Arrange prawns into the prepared air fryer basket.
6. Air fry for about 8 minutes.
7. Remove from air fryer and transfer the prawns onto serving plates.
8. Serve hot.

## Garlic Lemon Scallops

Servings:4
Cooking Time: 10 Minutes
**Ingredients:**
- 4 tablespoons salted butter, melted
- 4 teaspoons peeled and finely minced garlic
- ½ small lemon, zested and juiced
- 8 sea scallops, cleaned and patted dry
- ¼ teaspoon salt
- ¼ teaspoon ground black pepper

**Directions:**
1. In a small bowl, mix butter, garlic, lemon zest, and lemon juice. Place scallops in an ungreased 6" round nonstick baking dish. Pour butter mixture over scallops, then sprinkle with salt and pepper.
2. Place dish into air fryer basket. Adjust the temperature to 360°F and set the timer for 10 minutes. Scallops will be opaque and firm, and have an internal temperature of 130°F when done. Serve warm.

# Lime Bay Scallops

Servings:4
Cooking Time: 10 Minutes
**Ingredients:**
- 2 tbsp butter, melted
- 1 lime, juiced
- ¼ tsp salt
- 1 lb bay scallops
- 2 tbsp chopped cilantro

**Directions:**
1. Preheat air fryer to 350ºF. Combine all ingredients in a bowl, except for the cilantro. Place scallops in the frying basket and Air Fry for 5 minutes, tossing once. Serve immediately topped with cilantro.

# Italian Shrimp

Servings: 4
Cooking Time: 12 Minutes
**Ingredients:**
- 1 pound shrimp, peeled and deveined
- A pinch of salt and black pepper
- 1 tablespoon sesame seeds, toasted
- ½ teaspoon Italian seasoning
- 1 tablespoon olive oil

**Directions:**
1. In a bowl, mix the shrimp with the rest of the ingredients and toss well. Put the shrimp in the air fryer's basket, cook at 370°F for 12 minutes, divide into bowls and serve,

# Mahi-mahi "burrito" Fillets

Servings:3
Cooking Time: 10 Minutes
**Ingredients:**
- 1 Large egg white
- 1½ cups Crushed corn tortilla chips (gluten-free, if a concern)
- 1 tablespoon Chile powder
- 3 5-ounce skinless mahi-mahi fillets
- 6 tablespoons Canned refried beans
- Vegetable oil spray

**Directions:**
1. Preheat the air fryer to 400°F.
2. Set up and fill two shallow soup plates or small pie plates on your counter: one with the egg white, beaten until foamy; and one with the crushed tortilla chips.
3. Gently rub ½ teaspoon chile powder on each side of each fillet.

4. Spread 1 tablespoon refried beans over both sides and the edges of a fillet. Dip the fillet in the egg white, turning to coat it on both sides. Let any excess egg white slip back into the rest, then set the fillet in the crushed tortilla chips. Turn several times, pressing gently to coat it evenly. Coat the fillet on all sides with the vegetable oil spray, then set it aside. Prepare the remaining fillet(s) in the same way.
5. When the machine is at temperature, set the fillets in the basket with as much air space between them as possible. Air-fry undisturbed for 10 minutes, or until crisp and browned.
6. Use a nonstick-safe spatula to transfer the fillets to a serving platter or plates. Cool for only a minute or so, then serve hot.

# Buttery Lobster Tails

Servings:4
Cooking Time: 6 Minutes
**Ingredients:**
- 4 6- to 8-ounce shell-on raw lobster tails
- 2 tablespoons Butter, melted and cooled
- 1 teaspoon Lemon juice
- ½ teaspoon Finely grated lemon zest
- ½ teaspoon Garlic powder
- ½ teaspoon Table salt
- ½ teaspoon Ground black pepper

**Directions:**
1. Preheat the air fryer to 375°F .
2. To give the tails that restaurant look, you need to butterfly the meat. To do so, place a tail on a cutting board so that the shell is convex. Use kitchen shears to cut a line down the middle of the shell from the larger end to the smaller, cutting only the shell and not the meat below, and stopping before the back fins. Pry open the shell, leaving it intact. Use your clean fingers to separate the meat from the shell's sides and bottom, keeping it attached to the shell at the back near the fins. Pull the meat up and out of the shell through the cut line, laying the meat on top of the shell and closing the shell under the meat. Make two equidistant cuts down the meat from the larger end to near the smaller end, each about ¼ inch deep, for the classic restaurant look on the plate. Repeat this procedure with the remaining tail(s).
3. Stir the butter, lemon juice, zest, garlic powder, salt, and pepper in a small bowl until well combined. Brush this mixture over the lobster meat set atop the shells.
4. When the machine is at temperature, place the tails shell side down in the basket with as much air space between them as possible. Air-fry undisturbed for 6 minutes, or until the lobster meat has pink streaks over it and is firm.
5. Use kitchen tongs to transfer the tails to a wire rack. Cool for only a minute or two before serving.

# Chapter 7. Vegetarians Recipes

## Pepper-pineapple With Butter-sugar Glaze

Servings:2
Cooking Time: 10 Minutes
**Ingredients:**
- 1 medium-sized pineapple, peeled and sliced
- 1 red bell pepper, seeded and julienned
- 1 teaspoon brown sugar
- 2 teaspoons melted butter
- Salt to taste

**Directions:**
1. Preheat the air fryer to 390°F.
2. Place the grill pan accessory in the air fryer.
3. Mix all ingredients in a Ziploc bag and give a good shake.
4. Dump onto the grill pan and cook for 10 minutes making sure that you flip the pineapples every 5 minutes.

## Brussels Sprouts With Balsamic Oil

Servings:4
Cooking Time: 15 Minutes
**Ingredients:**
- ¼ teaspoon salt
- 1 tablespoon balsamic vinegar
- 2 cups Brussels sprouts, halved
- 2 tablespoons olive oil

**Directions:**
1. Preheat the air fryer for 5 minutes.
2. Mix all ingredients in a bowl until the zucchini fries are well coated.
3. Place in the air fryer basket.
4. Close and cook for 15 minutes for 350°F.

## Colorful Vegetable Medley

Servings: 4
Cooking Time: 20 Minutes
**Ingredients:**
- 1 lb green beans, chopped
- 2 carrots, cubed
- Salt and pepper to taste
- 1 zucchini, cut into chunks
- 1 red bell pepper, sliced
- Cooking spray

**Directions:**
1. Preheat air fryer to 390°F. Combine green beans, carrots, salt and pepper in a large bowl. Spray with cooking oil and transfer to the frying basket. Roast for 6 minutes.
2. Combine zucchini and red pepper in a bowl. Season to taste and spray with cooking oil; set aside. When the cooking time is up, add the zucchini and red pepper to the basket. Cook for another 6 minutes. Serve and enjoy.

## Pesto Vegetable Skewers

Servings:8
Cooking Time: 8 Minutes
**Ingredients:**
- 1 medium zucchini, trimmed and cut into ½" slices
- ½ medium yellow onion, peeled and cut into 1" squares
- 1 medium red bell pepper, seeded and cut into 1" squares
- 16 whole cremini mushrooms
- ⅓ cup basil pesto
- ½ teaspoon salt
- ¼ teaspoon ground black pepper

**Directions:**
1. Divide zucchini slices, onion, and bell pepper into eight even portions. Place on 6" skewers for a total of eight kebabs. Add 2 mushrooms to each skewer and brush kebabs generously with pesto.
2. Sprinkle each kebab with salt and black pepper on all sides, then place into ungreased air fryer basket. Adjust the temperature to 375°F and set the timer for 8 minutes, turning kebabs halfway through cooking. Vegetables will be browned at the edges and tender-crisp when done. Serve warm.

## Italian Seasoned Easy Pasta Chips

Servings:2
Cooking Time:10 Minutes
**Ingredients:**
- ½ teaspoon salt
- 1 ½ teaspoon Italian seasoning blend
- 1 tablespoon nutritional yeast
- 1 tablespoon olive oil
- 2 cups whole wheat bowtie pasta

**Directions:**
1. Place the baking dish accessory in the air fryer.
2. Give a good stir.
3. Close the air fryer and cook for 10 minutes at 390°F.

## Sweet And Spicy Barbecue Tofu

Servings:4
Cooking Time: 1 Hour 15 Minutes
**Ingredients:**
- 1 package extra-firm tofu, drained
- ½ cup barbecue sauce
- ½ cup brown sugar
- 1 teaspoon liquid smoke
- 1 teaspoon crushed red pepper flakes
- ½ teaspoon salt

- Cooking spray

**Directions:**

1. Press tofu block to remove excess moisture. If you don't have a tofu press, line a baking sheet with paper towels and set tofu on top. Set a second baking sheet on top of tofu and weight it with a heavy item such as a skillet. Let tofu sit at least 30 minutes, changing paper towels if necessary.
2. Cut pressed tofu into twenty-four equal pieces. Set aside.
3. In a large bowl, combine barbecue sauce, brown sugar, liquid smoke, red pepper flakes, and salt. Mix well and add tofu, coating completely. Cover and let marinate at least 30 minutes on the counter.
4. Preheat the air fryer to 400°F.
5. Spray the air fryer basket with cooking spray and add marinated tofu. Cook 15 minutes, shaking the basket twice during cooking.
6. Let cool 10 minutes before serving warm.

## Zucchini Gratin

Servings: 2
Cooking Time: 15 Minutes
**Ingredients:**

- 5 oz. parmesan cheese, shredded
- 1 tbsp. coconut flour
- 1 tbsp. dried parsley
- 2 zucchinis
- 1 tsp. butter, melted

**Directions:**

1. Mix the parmesan and coconut flour together in a bowl, seasoning with parsley to taste.
2. Cut the zucchini in half lengthwise and chop the halves into four slices.
3. Pre-heat the fryer at 400°F.
4. Pour the melted butter over the zucchini and then dip the zucchini into the parmesan-flour mixture, coating it all over. Cook the zucchini in the fryer for thirteen minutes.

## Eggplant Parmesan

Servings:4
Cooking Time: 17 Minutes
**Ingredients:**

- 1 medium eggplant, ends trimmed, sliced into ½" rounds
- ¼ teaspoon salt
- 2 tablespoons coconut oil
- ½ cup grated Parmesan cheese
- 1 ounce 100% cheese crisps, finely crushed
- ½ cup low-carb marinara sauce
- ½ cup shredded mozzarella cheese

**Directions:**

1. Sprinkle eggplant rounds with salt on both sides and wrap in a kitchen towel for 30 minutes. Press to remove excess water, then drizzle rounds with coconut oil on both sides.
2. In a medium bowl, mix Parmesan and cheese crisps. Press each eggplant slice into mixture to coat both sides.

3. Place rounds into ungreased air fryer basket. Adjust the temperature to 350°F and set the timer for 15 minutes, turning rounds halfway through cooking. They will be crispy around the edges when done.
4. When timer beeps, spoon marinara over rounds and sprinkle with mozzarella. Continue cooking an additional 2 minutes at 350°F until cheese is melted. Serve warm.

## Garlic Okra Chips

Servings: 4
Cooking Time: 20 Minutes
**Ingredients:**

- 2 cups okra, cut into rounds
- 1 ½ tbsp. melted butter
- 1 garlic clove, minced
- 1 tsp powdered paprika
- Salt and pepper to taste

**Directions:**

1. Preheat air fryer to 350°F. Toss okra, melted butter, paprika, garlic, salt and pepper in a medium bowl until okra is coated. Place okra in the frying basket and Air Fry for 5 minutes. Shake the basket and Air Fry for another 5 minutes. Shake one more time and Air Fry for 2 minutes until crispy. Serve warm and enjoy.

## Grilled 'n Glazed Strawberries

Servings:2
Cooking Time: 20 Minutes
**Ingredients:**

- 1 tbsp honey
- 1 tsp lemon zest
- 1-lb large strawberries
- 3 tbsp melted butter
- Lemon wedges
- Pinch kosher salt

**Directions:**

1. Thread strawberries in 4 skewers.
2. In a small bowl, mix well remaining ingredients except for lemon wedges. Brush all over strawberries.
3. Place skewer on air fryer skewer rack.
4. For 10 minutes, cook on 360°F. Halfway through cooking time, brush with honey mixture and turnover skewer.
5. Serve and enjoy with a squeeze of lemon.

## Vegetable Nuggets

Servings:6
Cooking Time: 10 Minutes Per Batch
**Ingredients:**

- 1 cup shredded carrots
- 2 cups broccoli florets
- 2 large eggs
- 1 cup shredded Cheddar cheese
- 1 cup Italian bread crumbs

- 1 teaspoon salt
- ½ teaspoon ground black pepper

**Directions:**
1. Preheat the air fryer to 400°F.
2. In a food processor, combine carrots and broccoli and pulse five times. Add eggs, Cheddar, bread crumbs, salt, and pepper, and pulse ten times.
3. Carefully scoop twenty-four balls, about 1 heaping tablespoon each, out of the mixture. Spritz balls with cooking spray.
4. Place balls in the air fryer basket, working in batches as necessary, and cook 10 minutes, shaking the basket twice during cooking to ensure even browning. Serve warm.

## Cauliflower Rice–stuffed Peppers

Servings:4
Cooking Time: 15 Minutes
**Ingredients:**
- 2 cups uncooked cauliflower rice
- ¾ cup drained canned petite diced tomatoes
- 2 tablespoons olive oil
- 1 cup shredded mozzarella cheese
- ¼ teaspoon salt
- ¼ teaspoon ground black pepper
- 4 medium green bell peppers, tops removed, seeded

**Directions:**
1. In a large bowl, mix all ingredients except bell peppers. Scoop mixture evenly into peppers.
2. Place peppers into ungreased air fryer basket. Adjust the temperature to 350°F and set the timer for 15 minutes. Peppers will be tender and cheese will be melted when done. Serve warm.

## Crispy Eggplant Rounds

Servings:4
Cooking Time: 10 Minutes
**Ingredients:**
- 1 large eggplant, ends trimmed, cut into ½" slices
- ½ teaspoon salt
- 2 ounces Parmesan 100% cheese crisps, finely ground
- ½ teaspoon paprika
- ¼ teaspoon garlic powder
- 1 large egg

**Directions:**
1. Sprinkle eggplant rounds with salt. Place rounds on a kitchen towel for 30 minutes to draw out excess water. Pat rounds dry.
2. In a medium bowl, mix cheese crisps, paprika, and garlic powder. In a separate medium bowl, whisk egg. Dip each eggplant round in egg, then gently press into cheese crisps to coat both sides.
3. Place eggplant rounds into ungreased air fryer basket. Adjust the temperature to 400°F and set the timer for 10

minutes, turning rounds halfway through cooking. Eggplant will be golden and crispy when done. Serve warm.

## Wine Infused Mushrooms

Servings:6
Cooking Time: 32 Minutes
**Ingredients:**
- 1 tablespoon butter
- 2 teaspoons Herbs de Provence
- ½ teaspoon garlic powder
- 2 pounds fresh mushrooms, quartered
- 2 tablespoons white vermouth

**Directions:**
1. Set the temperature of air fryer to 320°F.
2. In an air fryer pan, mix together the butter, Herbs de Provence, and garlic powder and air fry for about 2 minutes.
3. Stir in the mushrooms and air fry for about 25 minutes.
4. Stir in the vermouth and air fry for 5 more minutes.
5. Remove from air fryer and transfer the mushrooms onto serving plates.
6. Serve hot.

## Spaghetti Squash

Servings:4
Cooking Time: 45 Minutes
**Ingredients:**
- 1 large spaghetti squash, halved lengthwise and seeded
- 1 teaspoon salt
- ½ teaspoon ground black pepper
- 1 teaspoon garlic powder
- 1 teaspoon dried parsley
- 2 tablespoons salted butter, melted

**Directions:**
1. Preheat the air fryer to 350°F.
2. Sprinkle squash with salt, pepper, garlic powder, and parsley. Spritz with cooking spray.
3. Place skin side down in the air fryer basket and cook 30 minutes.
4. Turn squash skin side up and cook an additional 15 minutes until fork-tender. You should be able to easily use a fork to scrape across the surface to separate the strands.
5. Place strands in a medium bowl, top with butter, and toss. Serve warm.

## Crispy Cabbage Steaks

Servings:4
Cooking Time: 10 Minutes
**Ingredients:**
- 1 small head green cabbage, cored and cut into ½"-thick slices
- ¼ teaspoon salt
- ¼ teaspoon ground black pepper
- 2 tablespoons olive oil
- 1 clove garlic, peeled and finely minced

- ½ teaspoon dried thyme
- ½ teaspoon dried parsley

**Directions:**

1. Sprinkle each side of cabbage with salt and pepper, then place into ungreased air fryer basket, working in batches if needed.

2. Drizzle each side of cabbage with olive oil, then sprinkle with remaining ingredients on both sides. Adjust the temperature to 350°F and set the timer for 10 minutes, turning "steaks" halfway through cooking. Cabbage will be browned at the edges and tender when done. Serve warm.

# Broccoli & Parmesan Dish

Servings:4
Cooking Time: 25 Minutes
**Ingredients:**

- 1 tbsp olive oil
- 1 lemon, Juiced
- Salt and pepper to taste
- 1-ounce Parmesan cheese, grated

**Directions:**

1. In a bowl, mix all ingredients. Add the mixture to your air fryer and cook for 20 minutes at 360°F. Serve.

# Broccoli Salad

Servings: 2
Cooking Time: 15 Minutes
**Ingredients:**

- 3 cups fresh broccoli florets
- 2 tbsp. coconut oil, melted
- ¼ cup sliced s
- ½ medium lemon, juiced

**Directions:**

1. Take a six-inch baking dish and fill with the broccoli florets. Pour the melted coconut oil over the broccoli and add in the sliced s. Toss together. Put the dish in the air fryer.

2. Cook at 380°F for seven minutes, stirring at the halfway point.

3. Place the broccoli in a bowl and drizzle the lemon juice over it.

# Easy Baked Root Veggies

Servings:4
Cooking Time: 45 Minutes
**Ingredients:**

- ¼ cup olive oil
- 1 head broccoli, cut into florets
- 1 tablespoon dry onion powder
- 2 sweet potatoes, peeled and cubed
- 4 carrots, cut into chunks
- 4 zucchinis, sliced thickly
- salt and pepper to taste

**Directions:**

1. Preheat the air fryer to 400°F.

2. In a baking dish that can fit inside the air fryer, mix all the ingredients and bake for 45 minutes or until the vegetables are tender and the sides have browned.

# Roasted Cauliflower

Servings: 2
Cooking Time: 20 Minutes
**Ingredients:**

- medium head cauliflower
- 2 tbsp. salted butter, melted
- 1 medium lemon
- 1 tsp. dried parsley
- ½ tsp. garlic powder

**Directions:**

1. Having removed the leaves from the cauliflower head, brush it with the melted butter. Grate the rind of the lemon over it and then drizzle some juice. Finally add the parsley and garlic powder on top.

2. Transfer the cauliflower to the basket of the fryer.

3. Cook for fifteen minutes at 350°F, checking regularly to ensure it doesn't overcook. The cauliflower is ready when it is hot and fork tender.

4. Take care when removing it from the fryer, cut up and serve.

# Chewy Glazed Parsnips

Servings:6
Cooking Time:44 Minutes
**Ingredients:**

- 2 pounds parsnips, peeled and cut into 1-inch chunks
- 1 tablespoon butter, melted
- 2 tablespoons maple syrup
- 1 tablespoon dried parsley flakes, crushed
- ¼ teaspoon red pepper flakes, crushed

**Directions:**

1. Preheat the Air fryer to 355°F and grease an Air fryer basket.

2. Mix parsnips and butter in a bowl and toss to coat well.

3. Arrange the parsnips in the Air fryer basket and cook for about 40 minutes.

4. Meanwhile, mix remaining ingredients in a large bowl.

5. Transfer this mixture into the Air fryer basket and cook for about 4 more minutes.

6. Dish out and serve warm.

# Cheese & Bean Burgers

Servings: 2
Cooking Time: 35 Minutes
**Ingredients:**

- 1 cup cooked black beans
- ½ cup shredded cheddar
- 1 egg, beaten
- Salt and pepper to taste
- 1 cup bread crumbs

- ½ cup grated carrots

**Directions:**

1. Preheat air fryer to 350°F. Mash the beans with a fork in a bowl. Mix in the cheese, salt, and pepper until evenly combined. Stir in half of the bread crumbs and egg. Shape the mixture into 2 patties. Coat each patty with the remaining bread crumbs and spray with cooking oil. Air Fry for 14-16 minutes, turning once. When ready, remove to a plate. Top with grated carrots and serve.

# Curried Eggplant

Servings:2

Cooking Time:10 Minutes

**Ingredients:**

- 1 large eggplant, cut into ½-inch thick slices
- 1 garlic clove, minced
- ½ fresh red chili, chopped
- 1 tablespoon vegetable oil
- ¼ teaspoon curry powder
- Salt, to taste

**Directions:**

1. Preheat the Air fryer to 300°F and grease an Air fryer basket.
2. Mix all the ingredients in a bowl and toss to coat well.
3. Arrange the eggplant slices in the Air fryer basket and cook for about 10 minutes, tossing once in between.
4. Dish out onto serving plates and serve hot.

# Cauliflower Steak With Thick Sauce

Servings:2

Cooking Time: 15 Minutes

**Ingredients:**

- ¼ cup almond milk
- ¼ teaspoon vegetable stock powder
- 1 cauliflower, sliced into two
- 1 tablespoon olive oil
- 2 tablespoons onion, chopped
- salt and pepper to taste

**Directions:**

1. Soak the cauliflower in salted water or brine for at least 2 hours.
2. Preheat the air fryer to 400°F.
3. Rinse the cauliflower and place inside the air fryer and cook for 15 minutes.
4. Meanwhile, heat oil in a skillet over medium flame. Sauté the onions and stir until translucent. Add the vegetable stock powder and milk.
5. Bring to boil and adjust the heat to low.
6. Allow the sauce to reduce and season with salt and pepper.
7. Place cauliflower steak on a plate and pour over sauce.

# Sesame Seeds Bok Choy

Servings:4

Cooking Time: 6 Minutes

**Ingredients:**

- 4 bunches baby bok choy, bottoms removed and leaves separated
- Olive oil cooking spray
- 1 teaspoon garlic powder
- 1 teaspoon sesame seeds

**Directions:**

1. Set the temperature of air fryer to 325°F.
2. Arrange bok choy leaves into the air fryer basket in a single layer.
3. Spray with the cooking spray and sprinkle with garlic powder.
4. Air fry for about 5-6 minutes, shaking after every 2 minutes.
5. Remove from air fryer and transfer the bok choy onto serving plates.
6. Garnish with sesame seeds and serve hot.

# Toasted Ravioli

Servings:4

Cooking Time: 8 Minutes

**Ingredients:**

- 1 cup Italian bread crumbs
- 2 tablespoons grated vegetarian Parmesan cheese
- 1 large egg
- ¼ cup whole milk
- 1 package fresh cheese ravioli
- Cooking spray

**Directions:**

1. Preheat the air fryer to 400°F.
2. In a large bowl, whisk together bread crumbs and Parmesan.
3. In a medium bowl, whisk together egg and milk.
4. Dip each ravioli into egg mixture, shaking off the excess, then press into bread crumb mixture until well coated. Spritz each side with cooking spray.
5. Place in the air fryer basket and cook 8 minutes, turning halfway through cooking time, until ravioli is brown at the edges and crispy. Serve warm.

# Lemony Green Beans

Servings:3

Cooking Time:12 Minutes

**Ingredients:**

- 1 pound green beans, trimmed and halved
- 1 teaspoon butter, melted
- 1 tablespoon fresh lemon juice
- ¼ teaspoon garlic powder

**Directions:**

1. Preheat the Air fryer to 400°F and grease an Air fryer basket.
2. Mix all the ingredients in a bowl and toss to coat well.
3. Arrange the green beans into the Air fryer basket and cook for about 12 minutes.
4. Dish out in a serving plate and serve hot.

# Effortless Mac `n´ Cheese

Servings: 4
Cooking Time: 15 Minutes
**Ingredients:**
* 1 cup heavy cream
* 1 cup milk
* ½ cup mozzarella cheese
* 2 tsp grated Parmesan cheese
* 16 oz cooked elbow macaroni

**Directions:**
1. Preheat air fryer to 400°F. Whisk the heavy cream, milk, mozzarella cheese, and Parmesan cheese until smooth in a bowl. Stir in the macaroni and pour into a baking dish. Cover with foil and Bake in the air fryer for 6 minutes. Remove foil and Bake until cooked through and bubbly, 3-5 minutes. Serve warm.

# Layered Ravioli Bake

Servings:4
Cooking Time: 20 Minutes
**Ingredients:**
* 2 cups marinara sauce, divided
* 2 packages fresh cheese ravioli
* 12 slices provolone cheese
* ½ cup Italian bread crumbs
* ½ cup grated vegetarian Parmesan cheese

**Directions:**
1. Preheat the air fryer to 350°F.
2. In the bottom of a 3-quart baking pan, spread ⅓ cup marinara. Place 6 ravioli on top of the sauce, then add 3 slices provolone on top, then another layer of ⅓ cup marinara. Repeat these layers three times to use up remaining ravioli, provolone, and sauce.
3. In a small bowl, mix bread crumbs and Parmesan. Sprinkle over the top of dish.
4. Cover pan with foil, being sure to tuck foil under the bottom of the pan to ensure the air fryer fan does not blow it off. Place pan in the air fryer basket and cook 15 minutes.
5. Remove foil and cook an additional 5 minutes until the top is brown and bubbling. Serve warm.

# Sweet And Sour Brussel Sprouts

Servings:2
Cooking Time:10 Minutes
**Ingredients:**
* 2 cups Brussels sprouts, trimmed and halved lengthwise
* 1 tablespoon balsamic vinegar
* 1 tablespoon maple syrup
* Salt, as required

**Directions:**
1. Preheat the Air fryer to 400°F and grease an Air fryer basket.
2. Mix all the ingredients in a bowl and toss to coat well.
3. Arrange the Brussel sprouts in the Air fryer basket and cook for about 10 minutes, shaking once halfway through.
4. Dish out in a bowl and serve hot.

# Healthy Apple-licious Chips

Servings:1
Cooking Time: 6 Minutes
**Ingredients:**
* ½ teaspoon ground cumin
* 1 apple, cored and sliced thinly
* 1 tablespoon sugar
* A pinch of salt

**Directions:**
1. Place all ingredients in a bowl and toss to coat everything.
2. Put the grill pan accessory in the air fryer and place the sliced apples on the grill pan.
3. Close the air fryer and cook for 6 minutes at 390°F.

# Spinach Pesto Flatbread

Servings:4
Cooking Time: 8 Minutes Per Batch
**Ingredients:**
* 1 cup basil pesto
* 4 round flatbreads
* ½ cup chopped frozen spinach, thawed and drained
* 8 ounces fresh mozzarella cheese, sliced
* 1 teaspoon crushed red pepper flakes

**Directions:**
1. Preheat the air fryer to 350°F.
2. For each flatbread, spread ¼ cup pesto across flatbread, then scatter 2 tablespoons spinach over pesto. Top with 2 ounces mozzarella slices and ¼ teaspoon red pepper flakes. Repeat with remaining flatbread and toppings.
3. Place in the air fryer basket, working in batches as necessary, and cook 8 minutes until cheese is brown and bubbling. Serve warm.

# Baked Polenta With Chili-cheese

Servings:3
Cooking Time: 10 Minutes
**Ingredients:**
* 1 commercial polenta roll, sliced
* 1 cup cheddar cheese sauce
* 1 tablespoon chili powder

**Directions:**
1. Place the baking dish accessory in the air fryer.
2. Arrange the polenta slices in the baking dish.
3. Add the chili powder and cheddar cheese sauce.
4. Close the air fryer and cook for 10 minutes at 390°F.

# Thyme Lentil Patties

Servings: 2
Cooking Time: 35 Minutes
**Ingredients:**
- ½ cup grated American cheese
- 1 cup cooked lentils
- ¼ tsp dried thyme
- 2 eggs, beaten
- Salt and pepper to taste
- 1 cup bread crumbs

**Directions:**
1. Preheat air fryer to 350°F. Put the eggs, lentils, and cheese in a bowl and mix to combine. Stir in half the bread crumbs, thyme, salt, and pepper. Form the mixture into 2 patties and coat them in the remaining bread crumbs. Transfer to the greased frying basket. Air Fry for 14-16 minutes until brown, flipping once. Serve.

# Spicy Roasted Cashew Nuts

Servings: 4
Cooking Time: 20 Minutes
**Ingredients:**
- 1 cup whole cashews
- 1 teaspoon olive oil
- Salt and ground black pepper, to taste
- 1/2 teaspoon smoked paprika
- 1/2 teaspoon ancho chili powder

**Directions:**
1. Toss all ingredients in the mixing bowl.
2. Line the Air Fryer basket with baking parchment. Spread out the spiced cashews in a single layer in the basket.
3. Roast at 350°F for 6 to 8 minutes, shaking the basket once or twice. Work in batches. Enjoy!

# Caramelized Carrots

Servings:3
Cooking Time:15 Minutes
**Ingredients:**
- 1 small bag baby carrots
- ½ cup butter, melted
- ½ cup brown sugar

**Directions:**
1. Preheat the Air fryer to 400°F and grease an Air fryer basket.
2. Mix the butter and brown sugar in a bowl.
3. Add the carrots and toss to coat well.
4. Arrange the carrots in the Air fryer basket and cook for about 15 minutes.
5. Dish out and serve warm.

# Broccoli With Olives

Servings:4
Cooking Time:19 Minutes
**Ingredients:**
- 2 pounds broccoli, stemmed and cut into 1-inch florets
- 1/3 cup Kalamata olives, halved and pitted
- ¼ cup Parmesan cheese, grated
- 2 tablespoons olive oil
- Salt and ground black pepper, as required
- 2 teaspoons fresh lemon zest, grated

**Directions:**
1. Preheat the Air fryer to 400°F and grease an Air fryer basket.
2. Boil the broccoli for about 4 minutes and drain well.
3. Mix broccoli, oil, salt, and black pepper in a bowl and toss to coat well.
4. Arrange broccoli into the Air fryer basket and cook for about 15 minutes.
5. Stir in the olives, lemon zest and cheese and dish out to serve.

# Roasted Vegetable Grilled Cheese

Servings:4
Cooking Time: 6 Minutes
**Ingredients:**
- 8 slices sourdough bread
- 4 slices provolone cheese
- ½ cup chopped roasted red peppers
- ¼ cup chopped yellow onion
- 4 slices white American cheese

**Directions:**
1. Preheat the air fryer to 300°F.
2. Place a slice of bread on a work surface. Top with a slice of provolone, then with 2 tablespoons roasted red peppers and 1 tablespoon onion. Repeat with three more bread slices and remaining provolone and vegetables.
3. Place loaded bread slices in the air fryer basket and cook 1 minute until cheese is melted and onion is softened.
4. Remove the air fryer basket and carefully place 1 slice of American cheese on top of each slice of bread, finishing each with a second slice of bread to complete each sandwich.
5. Spritz the top with cooking spray. Increase the air fryer temperature to 400°F and cook 5 minutes, turning carefully after 3 minutes, until bread is golden and cheese is melted. Serve warm.

# Basil Tomatoes

Servings:2
Cooking Time:10 Minutes
**Ingredients:**
- 2 tomatoes, halved
- 1 tablespoon fresh basil, chopped
- Olive oil cooking spray
- Salt and black pepper, as required

**Directions:**
1. Preheat the Air fryer to 320°F and grease an Air fryer basket.

2. Spray the tomato halves evenly with olive oil cooking spray and season with salt, black pepper and basil.
3. Arrange the tomato halves into the Air fryer basket, cut sides up.
4. Cook for about 10 minutes and dish out onto serving plates.

# Gorgeous Jalapeño Poppers

Servings: 6
Cooking Time: 25 Minutes
**Ingredients:**
- 6 center-cut bacon slices, halved
- 6 jalapeños, halved lengthwise
- 4 oz cream cheese
- ¼ cup grated Gruyere cheese
- 2 tbsp chives, chopped

**Directions:**
1. Scoop out seeds and membranes of the jalapeño halves, discard. Combine cream cheese, Gruyere cheese, and chives in a bowl. Fill the jalapeño halves with the cream cheese filling using a small spoon. Wrap each pepper with a slice of bacon and secure with a toothpick.
2. Preheat air fryer to 325°F. Put the stuffed peppers in a single layer on the greased frying basket and Bake until the peppers are tender, cheese is melted, and the bacon is brown, 11-13 minutes. Serve warm and enjoy!

# Twice-baked Broccoli-cheddar Potatoes

Servings:4
Cooking Time: 35 Minutes
**Ingredients:**
- 4 large russet potatoes
- 2 tablespoons plus 2 teaspoons ranch dressing
- 1 teaspoon salt
- ½ teaspoon ground black pepper
- ¼ cup chopped cooked broccoli florets
- 1 cup shredded sharp Cheddar cheese

**Directions:**
1. Preheat the air fryer to 400°F.
2. Using a fork, poke several holes in potatoes. Place in the air fryer basket and cook 30 minutes until fork-tender.
3. Once potatoes are cool enough to handle, slice lengthwise and scoop out the cooked potato into a large bowl, being careful to maintain the structural integrity of potato skins. Add ranch dressing, salt, pepper, broccoli, and Cheddar to potato flesh and stir until well combined.
4. Scoop potato mixture back into potato skins and return to the air fryer basket. Cook an additional 5 minutes until cheese is melted. Serve warm.

# Cheesy Brussel Sprouts

Servings:3
Cooking Time:10 Minutes

**Ingredients:**
- 1 pound Brussels sprouts, trimmed and halved
- ¼ cup whole wheat breadcrumbs
- ¼ cup Parmesan cheese, shredded
- 1 tablespoon balsamic vinegar
- 1 tablespoon extra-virgin olive oil
- Salt and black pepper, to taste

**Directions:**
1. Preheat the Air fryer to 400°F and grease an Air fryer basket.
2. Mix Brussel sprouts, vinegar, oil, salt, and black pepper in a bowl and toss to coat well.
3. Arrange the Brussel sprouts in the Air fryer basket and cook for about 5 minutes.
4. Sprinkle with breadcrumbs and cheese and cook for about 5 more minutes.
5. Dish out and serve hot.

# Falafels

Servings: 12
Cooking Time: 10 Minutes
**Ingredients:**
- 1 pouch falafel mix
- 2–3 tablespoons plain breadcrumbs
- oil for misting or cooking spray

**Directions:**
1. Prepare falafel mix according to package directions.
2. Preheat air fryer to 390°F.
3. Place breadcrumbs in shallow dish or on wax paper.
4. Shape falafel mixture into 12 balls and flatten slightly. Roll in breadcrumbs to coat all sides and mist with oil or cooking spray.
5. Place falafels in air fryer basket in single layer and cook for 5 minutes. Shake basket, and continue cooking for 5 minutes, until they brown and are crispy.

# Cheesy Cauliflower Crust Pizza

Servings:2
Cooking Time: 12 Minutes Per Batch
**Ingredients:**
- 2 steamer bags cauliflower florets
- 1 large egg
- 1 cup grated vegetarian Parmesan cheese
- 3 cups shredded mozzarella cheese, divided
- 1 cup pizza sauce

**Directions:**
1. Preheat the air fryer to 375°F. Cut two pieces of parchment paper to fit the air fryer basket, one for each crust.
2. Cook cauliflower in the microwave according to package instructions, then drain in a colander. Run under cold water until cool to the touch. Use a cheesecloth to squeeze the excess water from cauliflower, removing as much as possible.

3. In a food processor, combine cauliflower, egg, Parmesan, and 1 cup mozzarella. Process on low about 15 seconds until a sticky ball forms.

4. Separate dough into two pieces. Working with damp hands to prevent dough from sticking, press each dough ball into a 6" round.

5. Place crust on parchment in the air fryer basket, working in batches as necessary. Cook 6 minutes, then flip over with a spatula and top the crust with ½ cup pizza sauce and 1 cup mozzarella. Cook an additional 6 minutes until edges are dark brown and cheese is brown and bubbling. Let cool at least 5 minutes before serving. The crust firms up as it cools.

## Roasted Spaghetti Squash

Servings:6
Cooking Time: 45 Minutes
**Ingredients:**
- 1 spaghetti squash, halved and seeded
- 2 tablespoons coconut oil
- 4 tablespoons salted butter, melted
- 1 teaspoon garlic powder
- 2 teaspoons dried parsley

**Directions:**
1. Brush shell of spaghetti squash with coconut oil. Brush inside with butter. Sprinkle inside with garlic powder and parsley.

2. Place squash skin side down into ungreased air fryer basket, working in batches if needed. Adjust the temperature to 350°F and set the timer for 30 minutes. When the timer beeps, flip squash and cook an additional 15 minutes until fork-tender.

3. Use a fork to remove spaghetti strands from shell and serve warm.

## Cheesy Broccoli Sticks

Servings:2
Cooking Time: 16 Minutes
**Ingredients:**
- 1 steamer bag broccoli florets, cooked according to package instructions
- 1 large egg
- 1 ounce Parmesan 100% cheese crisps, finely ground
- ½ cup shredded sharp Cheddar cheese
- ½ teaspoon salt
- ½ cup ranch dressing

**Directions:**
1. Let cooked broccoli cool 5 minutes, then place into a food processor with egg, cheese crisps, Cheddar, and salt. Process on low for 30 seconds until all ingredients are combined and begin to stick together.

2. Cut a sheet of parchment paper to fit air fryer basket. Take one scoop of mixture, about 3 tablespoons, and roll into a 4" stick shape, pressing down gently to flatten the top.

Place stick on ungreased parchment into air fryer basket. Repeat with remaining mixture to form eight sticks.

3. Adjust the temperature to 350°F and set the timer for 16 minutes, turning sticks halfway through cooking. Sticks will be golden brown when done.

4. Serve warm with ranch dressing on the side for dipping.

## Home-style Cinnamon Rolls

Servings: 4
Cooking Time: 40 Minutes
**Ingredients:**
- ½ pizza dough
- 1/3 cup dark brown sugar
- ¼ cup butter, softened
- ½ tsp ground cinnamon

**Directions:**
1. Preheat air fryer to 360°F. Roll out the dough into a rectangle. Using a knife, spread the brown sugar and butter, covering all the edges, and sprinkle with cinnamon. Fold the long side of the dough into a log, then cut it into 8 equal pieces, avoiding compression. Place the rolls, spiral-side up, onto a parchment-lined sheet. Let rise for 20 minutes. Grease the rolls with cooking spray and Bake for 8 minutes until golden brown. Serve right away.

## Broccoli With Cauliflower

Servings:4
Cooking Time:20 Minutes
**Ingredients:**
- 1½ cups broccoli, cut into 1-inch pieces
- 1½ cups cauliflower, cut into 1-inch pieces
- 1 tablespoon olive oil
- Salt, as required

**Directions:**
1. Preheat the Air fryer to 375°F and grease an Air fryer basket.

2. Mix the vegetables, olive oil, and salt in a bowl and toss to coat well.

3. Arrange the veggie mixture in the Air fryer basket and cook for about 20 minutes, tossing once in between.

4. Dish out in a bowl and serve hot.

## Sweet Roasted Carrots

Servings: 4
Cooking Time: 25 Minutes
**Ingredients:**
- 6 carrots, cut into ½-inch pieces
- 2 tbsp butter, melted
- 2 tbsp parsley, chopped
- 1 tsp honey

**Directions:**
1. Preheat air fryer to 390°F. Add carrots to a baking pan and pour over butter, honey, and 2-3 tbsp of water. Mix well. Transfer the carrots to the greased frying basket and Roast

for 12 minutes, shaking the basket once. Sprinkle with parsley and serve warm.

# Breadcrumbs Stuffed Mushrooms

Servings:4
Cooking Time:10 Minutes
**Ingredients:**
- 1½ spelt bread slices
- 1 tablespoon flat-leaf parsley, finely chopped
- 16 small button mushrooms, stemmed and gills removed
- 1½ tablespoons olive oil
- 1 garlic clove, crushed
- Salt and black pepper, to taste

**Directions:**
1. Preheat the Air fryer to 390°F and grease an Air fryer basket.
2. Put the bread slices in a food processor and pulse until fine crumbs form.
3. Transfer the crumbs into a bowl and stir in the olive oil, garlic, parsley, salt, and black pepper.
4. Stuff the breadcrumbs mixture in each mushroom cap and arrange the mushrooms in the Air fryer basket.
5. Cook for about 10 minutes and dish out in a bowl to serve warm.

# Turmeric Crispy Chickpeas

Servings:4
Cooking Time: 22 Minutes
**Ingredients:**
- 1 tbsp butter, melted
- ½ tsp dried rosemary
- ¼ tsp turmeric
- Salt to taste

**Directions:**
1. Preheat the Air fryer to 380°F.
2. In a bowl, combine together chickpeas, butter, rosemary, turmeric, and salt; toss to coat. Place the prepared chickpeas in your Air Fryer's cooking basket and cook for 6 minutes. Slide out the basket and shake; cook for another 6 minutes until crispy.

# Stuffed Portobellos

Servings:4
Cooking Time: 8 Minutes
**Ingredients:**
- 3 ounces cream cheese, softened
- ½ medium zucchini, trimmed and chopped
- ¼ cup seeded and chopped red bell pepper
- 1½ cups chopped fresh spinach leaves
- 4 large portobello mushrooms, stems removed
- 2 tablespoons coconut oil, melted
- ½ teaspoon salt

**Directions:**

1. In a medium bowl, mix cream cheese, zucchini, pepper, and spinach.
2. Drizzle mushrooms with coconut oil and sprinkle with salt. Scoop ¼ zucchini mixture into each mushroom.
3. Place mushrooms into ungreased air fryer basket. Adjust the temperature to 400°F and set the timer for 8 minutes. Portobellos will be tender and tops will be browned when done. Serve warm.

# Sweet Pepper Nachos

Servings:2
Cooking Time: 5 Minutes
**Ingredients:**
- 6 mini sweet peppers, seeded and sliced in half
- ¾ cup shredded Colby jack cheese
- ¼ cup sliced pickled jalapeños
- ½ medium avocado, peeled, pitted, and diced
- 2 tablespoons sour cream

**Directions:**
1. Place peppers into an ungreased 6" round nonstick baking dish. Sprinkle with Colby and top with jalapeños.
2. Place dish into air fryer basket. Adjust the temperature to 350°F and set the timer for 5 minutes. Cheese will be melted and bubbly when done.
3. Remove dish from air fryer and top with avocado. Drizzle with sour cream. Serve warm.

# Roasted Vegetable Pita Pizza

Servings: 4
Cooking Time: 20 Minutes
**Ingredients:**
- 1 medium red bell pepper, seeded and cut into quarters
- 1 teaspoon extra-virgin olive oil
- ⅛ teaspoon black pepper
- ⅛ teaspoon salt
- Two 6-inch whole-grain pita breads
- 6 tablespoons pesto sauce
- ¼ small red onion, thinly sliced
- ½ cup shredded part-skim mozzarella cheese

**Directions:**
1. Preheat the air fryer to 400°F.
2. In a small bowl, toss the bell peppers with the olive oil, pepper, and salt.
3. Place the bell peppers in the air fryer and cook for 15 minutes, shaking every 5 minutes to prevent burning.
4. Remove the peppers and set aside. Turn the air fryer temperature down to 350°F.
5. Lay the pita bread on a flat surface. Cover each with half the pesto sauce; then top with even portions of the red bell peppers and onions. Sprinkle cheese over the top. Spray the air fryer basket with olive oil mist.
6. Carefully lift the pita bread into the air fryer basket with a spatula.
7. Cook for 5 to 8 minutes, or until the outer edges begin to brown and the cheese is melted.

8. Serve warm with desired sides.

## Garlicky Roasted Mushrooms

Servings: 4
Cooking Time: 30 Minutes
**Ingredients:**
- 16 garlic cloves, peeled
- 2 tsp olive oil
- 16 button mushrooms
- 2 tbsp fresh chives, snipped
- Salt and pepper to taste
- 1 tbsp white wine

**Directions:**
1. Preheat air fryer to 350°F. Coat the garlic with some olive oil in a baking pan, then Roast in the air fryer for 12 minutes. When done, take the pan out and stir in the mushrooms, salt, and pepper. Then add the remaining olive oil and white wine. Put the pan back into the fryer and Bake for 10-15 minutes until the mushrooms and garlic soften. Sprinkle with chives and serve warm.

## Tortilla Pizza Margherita

Servings: 1
Cooking Time: 15 Minutes
**Ingredients:**
- 1 flour tortilla
- ¼ cup tomato sauce
- 1/3 cup grated mozzarella
- 3 basil leaves

**Directions:**
1. Preheat air fryer to 350°F. Put the tortilla in the greased basket and pour the sauce in the center. Spread across the whole tortilla. Sprinkle with cheese and Bake for 8-10 minutes or until crisp. Remove carefully and top with basil leaves. Serve hot.

## Easy Glazed Carrots

Servings:4
Cooking Time:12 Minutes
**Ingredients:**
- 3 cups carrots, peeled and cut into large chunks
- 1 tablespoon olive oil
- 1 tablespoon honey
- Salt and black pepper, to taste

**Directions:**
1. Preheat the Air fryer to 390°F and grease an Air fryer basket.
2. Mix all the ingredients in a bowl and toss to coat well.
3. Transfer into the Air fryer basket and cook for about 12 minutes.
4. Dish out and serve hot.

## Garden Fresh Green Beans

Servings:4
Cooking Time:12 Minutes

**Ingredients:**
- 1 pound green beans, washed and trimmed
- 1 teaspoon butter, melted
- 1 tablespoon fresh lemon juice
- ¼ teaspoon garlic powder
- Salt and freshly ground pepper, to taste

**Directions:**
1. Preheat the Air fryer to 400°F and grease an Air fryer basket.
2. Put all the ingredients in a large bowl and transfer into the Air fryer basket.
3. Cook for about 8 minutes and dish out in a bowl to serve warm.

## Green Bean Sautée

Servings: 4
Cooking Time: 25 Minutes
**Ingredients:**
- 1 ½ lb green beans, trimmed
- 1 tbsp olive oil
- ½ tsp garlic powder
- Salt and pepper to taste
- 4 garlic cloves, thinly sliced
- 1 tbsp fresh basil, chopped

**Directions:**
1. Preheat the air fryer to 375°F. Toss the beans with the olive oil, garlic powder, salt, and pepper in a bowl, then add to the frying basket. Air Fry for 6 minutes, shaking the basket halfway through the cooking time. Add garlic to the air fryer and cook for 3-6 minutes or until the green beans are tender and the garlic slices start to brown. Sprinkle with basil and serve warm.

## Pizza Dough

Servings:4
Cooking Time: 1 Hour 10 Minutes, Plus 10 Minutes For Additional Batches
**Ingredients:**
- 2 cups all-purpose flour
- 1 tablespoon granulated sugar
- 1 tablespoon quick-rise yeast
- 4 tablespoons olive oil, divided
- ¾ cup warm water

**Directions:**
1. In a large bowl, mix flour, sugar, and yeast until combined. Add 2 tablespoons oil and warm water and mix until dough becomes smooth.
2. On a lightly floured surface, knead dough 10 minutes, then form into a smooth ball. Drizzle with remaining 2 tablespoons oil, then cover with plastic. Let dough rise 1 hour until doubled in size.
3. Preheat the air fryer to 320°F.

4. Separate dough into four pieces and press each into a 6" pan or air fryer pizza tray that has been spritzed with cooking oil.

5. Add any desired toppings. Place in the air fryer basket, working in batches as necessary, and cook 10 minutes until crust is brown at the edges and toppings are heated through. Serve warm.

## Cool Mini Zucchini's

Servings:4
Cooking Time: 25 Minutes
**Ingredients:**
- 4 large eggs, beaten
- 1 medium zucchini, sliced
- 4 ounces feta cheese, drained and crumbled
- 2 tbsp fresh dill, chopped
- Cooking spray
- Salt and pepper as needed

**Directions:**
1. Preheat the air fryer to 360°F, and un a bowl, add the beaten eggs and season with salt and pepper.
2. Stir in zucchini, dill and feta cheese. Grease 8 muffin tins with cooking spray. Roll pastry and arrange them to cover the sides of the muffin tins. Divide the egg mixture evenly between the holes. Place the prepared tins in your air fryer and cook for 15 minutes. Serve and enjoy!

## Stuffed Mushrooms

Servings:4
Cooking Time: 10 Minutes
**Ingredients:**
- 12 baby bella mushrooms, stems removed
- 4 ounces full-fat cream cheese, softened
- ¼ cup grated vegetarian Parmesan cheese
- ¼ cup Italian bread crumbs
- 1 teaspoon crushed red pepper flakes

**Directions:**
1. Preheat the air fryer to 400°F.
2. Use a spoon to hollow out mushroom caps.
3. In a medium bowl, combine cream cheese, Parmesan, bread crumbs, and red pepper flakes. Scoop approximately 1 tablespoon mixture into each mushroom cap.
4. Place stuffed mushrooms in the air fryer basket and cook 10 minutes until stuffing is brown. Let cool 5 minutes before serving.

# Chapter 8. Vegetable Side Dishes Recipes

## Grilled Cheese

Servings: 2
Cooking Time: 25 Minutes
**Ingredients:**
- 4 slices bread
- ½ cup sharp cheddar cheese
- ¼ cup butter, melted

**Directions:**
1. Pre-heat the Air Fryer at 360°F.
2. Put cheese and butter in separate bowls.
3. Apply the butter to each side of the bread slices with a brush.
4. Spread the cheese across two of the slices of bread and make two sandwiches. Transfer both to the fryer.
5. Cook for 5 – 7 minutes or until a golden brown color is achieved and the cheese is melted.

## Polenta

Servings: 4
Cooking Time: 15 Minutes
**Ingredients:**
- 1 pound polenta
- ¼ cup flour
- oil for misting or cooking spray

**Directions:**
1. Cut polenta into ½-inch slices.
2. Dip slices in flour to coat well. Spray both sides with oil or cooking spray.
3. Cook at 390°F for 5minutes. Turn polenta and spray both sides again with oil.
4. Cook 10 more minutes or until brown and crispy.

## Spiced Pumpkin Wedges

Servings: 4
Cooking Time: 35 Minutes
**Ingredients:**
- 2 ½ cups pumpkin, cubed
- 2 tbsp olive oil
- Salt and pepper to taste
- ¼ tsp pumpkin pie spice
- 1 tbsp thyme
- ¼ cup grated Parmesan

**Directions:**
1. Preheat air fryer to 360°F. Put the cubed pumpkin with olive oil, salt, pumpkin pie spice, black pepper, and thyme in

a bowl and stir until the pumpkin is well coated. Pour this mixture into the frying basket and Roast for 18-20 minutes, stirring once. Sprinkle the pumpkin with grated Parmesan. Serve and enjoy!

## Spicy Fried Green Beans

Servings: 2
Cooking Time: 8 Minutes
**Ingredients:**
- 12 ounces green beans, trimmed
- 2 small dried hot red chili peppers (like árbol)
- ¼ cup panko breadcrumbs
- 1 tablespoon olive oil
- ½ teaspoon salt
- ⅛ teaspoon crushed red pepper flakes
- 2 scallions, thinly sliced

**Directions:**
1. Preheat the air fryer to 400°F.
2. Toss the green beans, chili peppers and panko breadcrumbs with the olive oil, salt and crushed red pepper flakes.
3. Air-fry for 8 minutes, shaking the basket once during the cooking process. The crumbs will fall into the bottom drawer – don't worry.
4. Transfer the green beans to a serving dish, sprinkle the scallions and the toasted crumbs from the air fryer drawer on top and serve. The dried peppers are not to be eaten, but they do look nice with the green beans. You can leave them in, or take them out as you please.

## Asparagus Wrapped In Pancetta

Servings: 4
Cooking Time: 30 Minutes
**Ingredients:**
- 20 asparagus trimmed
- Salt and pepper pepper
- 4 pancetta slices
- 1 tbsp fresh sage, chopped

**Directions:**
1. Sprinkle the asparagus with fresh sage, salt and pepper. Toss to coat. Make 4 bundles of 5 spears by wrapping the center of the bunch with one slice of pancetta.
2. Preheat air fryer to 400°F. Put the bundles in the greased frying basket and Air Fry for 8-10 minutes or until the pancetta is brown and the asparagus are starting to char on the edges. Serve immediately.

## Perfect French Fries

Servings: 3
Cooking Time: 37 Minutes
**Ingredients:**
- 1 pound Large russet potato(es)
- Vegetable oil or olive oil spray
- ½ teaspoon Table salt

**Directions:**

1. Cut each potato lengthwise into ¼-inch-thick slices. Cut each of these lengthwise into ¼-inch-thick matchsticks.
2. Set the potato matchsticks in a big bowl of cool water and soak for 5 minutes. Drain in a colander set in the sink, then spread the matchsticks out on paper towels and dry them very well.
3. Preheat the air fryer to 225°F.
4. When the machine is at temperature, arrange the matchsticks in an even layer in the basket. Air-fry for 20 minutes, tossing and rearranging the fries twice.
5. Pour the contents of the basket into a big bowl. Increase the air fryer's temperature to 325°F.
6. Generously coat the fries with vegetable or olive oil spray. Toss well, then coat them again to make sure they're covered on all sides, tossing a couple of times to make sure.
7. When the machine is at temperature, pour the fries into the basket and air-fry for 12 minutes, tossing and rearranging the fries at least twice.
8. Increase the machine's temperature to 375°F. Air-fry for 5 minutes more, tossing and rearranging the fries at least twice to keep them from burning and to make sure they all get an even measure of the heat, until brown and crisp.
9. Pour the contents of the basket into a serving bowl. Toss the fries with the salt and serve hot.

## Wilted Brussels Sprout Slaw

Servings: 4
Cooking Time: 18 Minutes
**Ingredients:**
- 2 Thick-cut bacon strip(s), halved widthwise (gluten-free, if a concern)
- 4½ cups Bagged shredded Brussels sprouts
- ¼ teaspoon Table salt
- 2 tablespoons White balsamic vinegar
- 2 teaspoons Worcestershire sauce (gluten-free, if a concern)
- 1 teaspoon Dijon mustard (gluten-free, if a concern)
- ¼ teaspoon Ground black pepper

**Directions:**
1. Preheat the air fryer to 375°F .
2. When the machine is at temperature, lay the bacon strip halves in the basket in one layer and air-fry for 10 minutes, or until crisp.
3. Use kitchen tongs to transfer the bacon pieces to a wire rack. Put the shredded Brussels sprouts in a large bowl. Drain any fat from the basket or the tray under the basket onto the Brussels sprouts. Add the salt and toss well to coat.
4. Put the Brussels sprout shreds in the basket, spreading them out into as close to an even layer as you can. Air-fry for 8 minutes, tossing the basket's contents at least three times, until wilted and lightly browned.
5. Pour the contents of the basket into a serving bowl. Chop the bacon and add it to the Brussels sprouts. Add the vinegar, Worcestershire sauce, mustard, and pepper. Toss

well to blend the dressing and coat the Brussels sprout shreds. Serve warm.

## Caraway Seed Pretzel Sticks

Servings: 4
Cooking Time: 30 Minutes
**Ingredients:**
- ½ pizza dough
- 1 tsp baking soda
- 2 tbsp caraway seeds
- 1 cup of hot water
- Cooking spray

**Directions:**
1. Preheat air fryer to 400°F. Roll out the dough, on parchment paper, into a rectangle, then cut it into 8 strips. Whisk the baking soda and 1 cup of hot water until well dissolved in a bowl. Submerge each strip, shake off any excess, and stretch another 1 to 2 inches. Scatter with caraway seeds and let rise for 10 minutes in the frying basket. Grease with cooking spray and Air Fry for 8 minutes until golden brown, turning once. Serve.

## Chili-oiled Brussels Sprouts

Servings: 4
Cooking Time: 30 Minutes
**Ingredients:**
- 1 cup Brussels sprouts, quartered
- 1 tsp olive oil
- 1 tsp chili oil
- Salt and pepper to taste

**Directions:**
1. Preheat air fryer to 350°F. Coat the Brussels sprouts with olive oil, chili oil, salt, and black pepper in a bowl. Transfer to the frying basket. Bake for 20 minutes, shaking the basket several times throughout cooking until the sprouts are crispy, browned on the outside, and juicy inside. Serve and enjoy!

## Sweet Roasted Pumpkin Rounds

Servings: 4
Cooking Time: 35 Minutes
**Ingredients:**
- 1 pumpkin
- 1 tbsp honey
- 1 tbsp melted butter
- ¼ tsp cardamom
- ¼ tsp sea salt

**Directions:**
1. Preheat the air fryer to 370°F. Cut the pumpkin in half lengthwise and remove the seeds. Slice each half crosswise into 1-inch-wide half-circles, then cut each half-circle in half again to make quarter rounds. Combine the honey, butter, cardamom, and salt in a bowl and mix well. Toss the pumpkin in the mixture until coated, then put into the frying basket. Bake for 15-20 minutes, shaking once during

cooking until the edges start to brown and the squash is tender.

## Bacon-balsamic Brussels Sprouts

Servings:4
Cooking Time: 12 Minutes
**Ingredients:**
- 2 cups trimmed and halved fresh Brussels sprouts
- 2 tablespoons olive oil
- ¼ teaspoon salt
- ¼ teaspoon ground black pepper
- 2 tablespoons balsamic vinegar
- 2 slices cooked sugar-free bacon, crumbled

**Directions:**
1. In a large bowl, toss Brussels sprouts in olive oil, then sprinkle with salt and pepper. Place into ungreased air fryer basket. Adjust the temperature to 375°F and set the timer for 12 minutes, shaking the basket halfway through cooking. Brussels sprouts will be tender and browned when done.
2. Place sprouts in a large serving dish and drizzle with balsamic vinegar. Sprinkle bacon over top. Serve warm.

## Mini Spinach And Sweet Pepper Poppers

Servings:16
Cooking Time: 8 Minutes
**Ingredients:**
- 4 ounces cream cheese, softened
- 1 cup chopped fresh spinach leaves
- ½ teaspoon garlic powder
- 8 mini sweet bell peppers, tops removed, seeded, and halved lengthwise

**Directions:**
1. In a medium bowl, mix cream cheese, spinach, and garlic powder. Place 1 tablespoon mixture into each sweet pepper half and press down to smooth.
2. Place poppers into ungreased air fryer basket. Adjust the temperature to 400°F and set the timer for 8 minutes. Poppers will be done when cheese is browned on top and peppers are tender-crisp. Serve warm.

## Dinner Rolls

Servings:6
Cooking Time: 12 Minutes
**Ingredients:**
- 1 cup shredded mozzarella cheese
- 1 ounce cream cheese, broken into small pieces
- 1 cup blanched finely ground almond flour
- ¼ cup ground flaxseed
- ½ teaspoon baking powder
- 1 large egg, whisked

**Directions:**

1. Place mozzarella, cream cheese, and flour in a large microwave-safe bowl. Microwave on high 1 minute. Mix until smooth.
2. Add flaxseed, baking powder, and egg to mixture until fully combined and smooth. Microwave an additional 15 seconds if dough becomes too firm.
3. Separate dough into six equal pieces and roll each into a ball. Place rolls into ungreased air fryer basket. Adjust the temperature to 320°F and set the timer for 12 minutes, turning rolls halfway through cooking. Allow rolls to cool completely before serving, about 5 minutes.

## Asparagus

Servings: 4
Cooking Time: 9 Minutes
**Ingredients:**
- 1 bunch asparagus, washed and trimmed
- ⅛ teaspoon dried tarragon, crushed
- salt and pepper
- 1 to 2 teaspoons extra-light olive oil

**Directions:**
1. Spread asparagus spears on cookie sheet or cutting board.
2. Sprinkle with tarragon, salt, and pepper.
3. Drizzle with 1 teaspoon of oil and roll the spears or mix by hand. If needed, add up to 1 more teaspoon of oil and mix again until all spears are lightly coated.
4. Place spears in air fryer basket. If necessary, bend the longer spears to make them fit. It doesn't matter if they don't lie flat.
5. Cook at 390°F for 5minutes. Shake basket or stir spears with a spoon.
6. Cook for an additional 4 minutes or just until crisp-tender.

## Simple Zucchini Ribbons

Servings:4
Cooking Time: 15 Minutes
**Ingredients:**
- 2 zucchini
- 2 tsp butter, melted
- ¼ tsp garlic powder
- ¼ tsp chili flakes
- 8 cherry tomatoes, halved
- Salt and pepper to taste

**Directions:**
1. Preheat air fryer to 275ºF. Cut the zucchini into ribbons with a vegetable peeler. Mix them with butter, garlic, chili flakes, salt, and pepper in a bowl. Transfer to the frying basket and Air Fry for 2 minutes. Toss and add the cherry tomatoes. Cook for another 2 minutes. Serve.

## Spicy Kale

Servings: 4
Cooking Time: 10 Minutes

**Ingredients:**
- 1 pound kale, torn
- 1 tablespoon olive oil
- 1 teaspoon hot paprika
- A pinch of salt and black pepper
- 2 tablespoons oregano, chopped

**Directions:**
1. In a pan that fits the air fryer, combine all the ingredients and toss. Put the pan in the air fryer and cook at 380ºF for 10 minutes. Divide between plates and serve.

## Corn Muffins

Servings: 12
Cooking Time: 10 Minutes
**Ingredients:**
- ½ cup all-purpose flour
- ½ cup cornmeal
- ¼ cup granulated sugar
- ½ teaspoon baking powder
- ¼ cup salted butter, melted
- ½ cup buttermilk
- 1 large egg

**Directions:**
1. Preheat the air fryer to 350°F.
2. In a large bowl, whisk together flour, cornmeal, sugar, and baking powder.
3. Add butter, buttermilk, and egg to dry mixture. Stir until well combined.
4. Divide batter evenly among twelve silicone or aluminum muffin cups, filling cups about halfway. Working in batches as needed, place in the air fryer and cook 10 minutes until golden brown. Let cool 5 minutes before serving.

## Fried Corn On The Cob

Servings: 2
Cooking Time: 10 Minutes
**Ingredients:**
- 1½ tablespoons Regular or low-fat mayonnaise (not fat-free; gluten-free, if a concern)
- 1½ teaspoons Minced garlic
- ¼ teaspoon Table salt
- ¾ cup Plain panko bread crumbs (gluten-free, if a concern)
- 3 4-inch lengths husked and de-silked corn on the cob
- Vegetable oil spray

**Directions:**
1. Preheat the air fryer to 400°F.
2. Stir the mayonnaise, garlic, and salt in a small bowl until well combined. Spread the panko on a dinner plate.
3. Brush the mayonnaise mixture over the kernels of a piece of corn on the cob. Set the corn in the bread crumbs, then roll, pressing gently, to coat it. Lightly coat with

vegetable oil spray. Set it aside, then coat the remaining piece(s) of corn in the same way.

4.  Set the coated corn on the cob in the basket with as much air space between the pieces as possible. Air-fry undisturbed for 10 minutes, or until brown and crisp along the coating.

5.  Use kitchen tongs to gently transfer the pieces of corn to a wire rack. Cool for 5 minutes before serving.

## Roasted Rhubarb

Servings: 4

Cooking Time: 15 Minutes

**Ingredients:**

*   1 pound rhubarb, cut in chunks
*   2 teaspoons olive oil
*   2 tablespoons orange zest
*   ½ cup walnuts, chopped
*   ½ teaspoon sugar

**Directions:**

1.  In your air fryer, mix all the listed ingredients, and toss.
2.  Cook at 380ºF for 15 minutes.
3.  Divide the rhubarb between plates and serve as a side dish.

## Crispy Brussels Sprouts

Servings: 3

Cooking Time: 12 Minutes

**Ingredients:**

*   1¼ pounds Medium, 2-inch-in-length Brussels sprouts
*   1½ tablespoons Olive oil
*   ¾ teaspoon Table salt

**Directions:**

1.  Preheat the air fryer to 400°F.
2.  Halve each Brussels sprout through the stem end, pulling off and discarding any discolored outer leaves. Put the sprout halves in a large bowl, add the oil and salt, and stir well to coat evenly, until the Brussels sprouts are glistening.
3.  When the machine is at temperature, scrape the contents of the bowl into the basket, gently spreading the Brussels sprout halves into as close to one layer as possible. Air-fry for 12 minutes, gently tossing and rearranging the vegetables twice to get all covered or touching parts exposed to the air currents, until crisp and browned at the edges.
4.  Gently pour the contents of the basket onto a wire rack. Cool for a minute or two before serving.

## Flatbread Dippers

Servings:12

Cooking Time: 8 Minutes

**Ingredients:**

*   1 cup shredded mozzarella cheese
*   1 ounce cream cheese, broken into small pieces
*   ½ cup blanched finely ground almond flour

**Directions:**

1.  Place mozzarella into a large microwave-safe bowl. Add cream cheese pieces. Microwave on high 60 seconds, then stir to combine. Add flour and stir until a soft ball of dough forms.
2.  Cut dough ball into two equal pieces. Cut a piece of parchment to fit into air fryer basket. Press each dough piece into a 5" round on ungreased parchment.
3.  Place parchment with dough into air fryer basket. Adjust the temperature to 350°F and set the timer for 8 minutes. Carefully flip the flatbread over halfway through cooking. Flatbread will be golden brown when done.
4.  Let flatbread cool 5 minutes, then slice each round into six triangles. Serve warm.

## Yeast Rolls

Servings:16

Cooking Time: 1 Hour 10 Minutes

**Ingredients:**

*   4 tablespoons salted butter
*   ¼ cup granulated sugar
*   1 cup hot water
*   1 tablespoon quick-rise yeast
*   1 large egg
*   1 teaspoon salt
*   2 ½ cups all-purpose flour, divided
*   Cooking spray

**Directions:**

1.  In a microwave-safe bowl, microwave butter 30 seconds until melted. Pour 2 tablespoons of butter into a large bowl. Add sugar, hot water, and yeast. Mix until yeast is dissolved.
2.  Using a rubber spatula, mix in egg, salt, and 2 ¼ cups flour. Dough will be very sticky.
3.  Cover bowl with plastic wrap and let rise in a warm place 1 hour.
4.  Sprinkle remaining ¼ cup flour on dough and turn onto a lightly floured surface. Knead 2 minutes, then cut into sixteen even pieces.
5.  Preheat the air fryer to 350°F. Spray a 6" round cake pan with cooking spray.
6.  Sprinkle each roll with flour and arrange in pan. Brush with remaining melted butter. Place pan in the air fryer basket and cook 10 minutes until fluffy and golden on top. Serve warm.

## Yellow Squash And Zucchinis Dish

Servings: 4

Cooking Time:45 Minutes

**Ingredients:**

*   1 yellow squash; halved, deseeded and cut into chunks
*   6 tsp. olive oil
*   1 lb. zucchinis; sliced
*   1/2 lb. carrots; cubed
*   1 tbsp. tarragon; chopped
*   Salt and white pepper to the taste

**Directions:**

1. In your air fryer's basket; mix zucchinis with carrots, squash, salt, pepper and oil; toss well and cook at 400 °F, for 25 minutes. Divide them on plates and serve as a side dish with tarragon sprinkled on top.

## Mediterranean Zucchini Boats

Servings:4
Cooking Time: 10 Minutes
**Ingredients:**
- 1 large zucchini, ends removed, halved lengthwise
- 6 grape tomatoes, quartered
- ¼ teaspoon salt
- ¼ cup feta cheese
- 1 tablespoon balsamic vinegar
- 1 tablespoon olive oil

**Directions:**
1. Use a spoon to scoop out 2 tablespoons from center of each zucchini half, making just enough space to fill with tomatoes and feta.
2. Place tomatoes evenly in centers of zucchini halves and sprinkle with salt. Place into ungreased air fryer basket. Adjust the temperature to 350°F and set the timer for 10 minutes. When done, zucchini will be tender.
3. Transfer boats to a serving tray and sprinkle with feta, then drizzle with vinegar and olive oil. Serve warm.

## Spicy Roasted Potatoes

Servings: 2
Cooking Time: 15 Minutes
**Ingredients:**
- 4 potatoes, peeled and cut into wedges
- 2 tablespoons olive oil
- Sea salt and ground black pepper, to taste
- 1 teaspoon cayenne pepper
- 1/2 teaspoon ancho chili powder

**Directions:**
1. Toss all ingredients in a mixing bowl until the potatoes are well covered.
2. Transfer them to the Air Fryer basket and cook at 400ºF for 6 minutes; shake the basket and cook for a further 6 minutes.
3. Serve warm with your favorite sauce for dipping. Bon appétit!

## Crunchy Roasted Potatoes

Servings: 5
Cooking Time: 25 Minutes
**Ingredients:**
- 2 pounds Small red, white, or purple potatoes
- 2 tablespoons Olive oil
- 2 teaspoons Table salt
- ¾ teaspoon Garlic powder
- ½ teaspoon Ground black pepper

**Directions:**

1. Preheat the air fryer to 400°F.
2. Toss the potatoes, oil, salt, garlic powder, and pepper in a large bowl until the spuds are evenly and thoroughly coated.
3. When the machine is at temperature, pour the potatoes into the basket, spreading them into an even layer. Air-fry for 25 minutes, tossing twice, until the potatoes are tender but crunchy.
4. Pour the contents of the basket into a serving bowl. Cool for 5 minutes before serving.

## Chipotle Chickpea Tacos

Servings: 4
Cooking Time: 10 Minutes
**Ingredients:**
- 2 cans chickpeas, drained and rinsed
- ¼ cup adobo sauce
- ¾ teaspoon salt
- ¼ teaspoon ground black pepper
- 8 medium flour tortillas, warmed
- 1 ½ cups chopped avocado
- ½ cup chopped fresh cilantro

**Directions:**
1. Preheat the air fryer to 375°F.
2. In a large bowl, toss chickpeas, adobo, salt, and pepper to fully coat.
3. Using a slotted spoon, place chickpeas in the air fryer basket and cook 10 minutes, shaking the basket twice during cooking, until tender.
4. To assemble, scoop ¼ cup chickpeas into a tortilla, then top with avocado and cilantro. Repeat with remaining tortillas and filling. Serve warm.

## Roasted Garlic

Servings: 20
Cooking Time: 40 Minutes
**Ingredients:**
- 20 Peeled medium garlic cloves
- 2 tablespoons, plus more Olive oil

**Directions:**
1. Preheat the air fryer to 400°F.
2. Set a 10-inch sheet of aluminum foil on your work surface for a small batch, a 14-inch sheet for a medium batch, or a 16-inch sheet for a large batch. Put the garlic cloves in its center in one layer without bunching the cloves together. Drizzle the small batch with 1 tablespoon oil, the medium batch with 2 tablespoons, or the large one with 3 tablespoons. Fold up the sides and seal the foil into a packet.
3. When the machine is at temperature, put the packet in the basket. Air-fry for 40 minutes, or until very fragrant. The cloves inside should be golden and soft.
4. Transfer the packet to a cutting board. Cool for 5 minutes, then open and use the cloves hot. Or cool them to room temperature, set them in a small container or jar, pour

in enough olive oil to cover them, seal or cover the container, and refrigerate for up to 2 weeks.

## Green Beans And Potatoes Recipe

Servings: 5
Cooking Time:25 Minutes
**Ingredients:**
- 2 lbs. green beans
- 6 new potatoes; halved
- Salt and black pepper to the taste
- 6 bacon slices; cooked and chopped.
- A drizzle of olive oil

**Directions:**
1.  In a bowl; mix green beans with potatoes, salt, pepper and oil, toss, transfer to your air fryer and cook at 390 °F, for 15 minutes. Divide among plates and serve with bacon sprinkled on top.

## Zucchini Fries

Servings: 3
Cooking Time: 12 Minutes
**Ingredients:**
- 1 large Zucchini
- ½ cup All-purpose flour or tapioca flour
- 2 Large egg(s), well beaten
- 1 cup Seasoned Italian-style dried bread crumbs (gluten-free, if a concern)
- Olive oil spray

**Directions:**
1.  Preheat the air fryer to 400°F.
2.  Trim the zucchini into a long rectangular block, taking off the ends and four "sides" to make this shape. Cut the block lengthwise into ½-inch-thick slices. Lay these slices flat and cut in half widthwise. Slice each of these pieces into ½-inch-thick batons.
3.  Set up and fill three shallow soup plates or small pie plates on your counter: one for the flour, one for the beaten egg(s), and one for the bread crumbs.
4.  Set a zucchini baton in the flour and turn it several times to coat all sides. Gently shake off any excess flour, then dip it in the egg(s), turning it to coat. Let any excess egg slip back into the rest, then set the baton in the bread crumbs and turn it several times, pressing gently to coat all sides, even the ends. Set aside on a cutting board and continue coating the remainder of the batons in the same way.
5.  Lightly coat the batons on all sides with olive oil spray. Set them in two flat layers in the basket, the top layer at a 90-degree angle to the bottom one, with a little air space between the batons in each layer. In the end, the whole thing will look like a crosshatch pattern. Air-fry undisturbed for 6 minutes.
6.  Use kitchen tongs to gently rearrange the batons so that any covered parts are now uncovered. The batons no longer need to be in a crosshatch pattern. Continue air-frying undisturbed for 6 minutes, or until lightly browned and crisp.

7.  Gently pour the contents of the basket onto a wire rack. Spread the batons out and cool for only a minute or two before serving.

## Roasted Asparagus

Servings:4
Cooking Time: 12 Minutes
**Ingredients:**
- 1 tablespoon olive oil
- 1 pound asparagus spears, ends trimmed
- ¼ teaspoon salt
- ¼ teaspoon ground black pepper
- 1 tablespoon salted butter, melted

**Directions:**
1.  In a large bowl, drizzle olive oil over asparagus spears and sprinkle with salt and pepper.
2.  Place spears into ungreased air fryer basket. Adjust the temperature to 375°F and set the timer for 12 minutes, shaking the basket halfway through cooking. Asparagus will be lightly browned and tender when done.
3.  Transfer to a large dish and drizzle with butter. Serve warm.

## Tandoori Cauliflower

Servings: 4
Cooking Time: 10 Minutes
**Ingredients:**
- ½ cup Plain full-fat yogurt (not Greek yogurt)
- 1½ teaspoons Yellow curry powder, purchased or homemade
- 1½ teaspoons Lemon juice
- ¾ teaspoon Table salt (optional)
- 4½ cups 2-inch cauliflower florets

**Directions:**
1.  Preheat the air fryer to 400°F.
2.  Whisk the yogurt, curry powder, lemon juice, and salt (if using) in a large bowl until uniform. Add the florets and stir gently to coat the florets well and evenly. Even better, use your clean, dry hands to get the yogurt mixture down into all the nooks of the florets.
3.  When the machine is at temperature, transfer the florets to the basket, spreading them gently into as close to one layer as you can. Air-fry for 10 minutes, tossing and rearranging the florets twice so that any covered or touching parts are exposed to the air currents, until lightly browned and tender if still a bit crunchy.
4.  Pour the contents of the basket onto a wire rack. Cool for at least 5 minutes before serving, or serve at room temperature.

# Balsamic Green Beans With Bacon

Servings:4
Cooking Time: 15 Minutes
**Ingredients:**
- 2 cups green beans, trimmed
- 1 tbsp butter, melted
- Salt and pepper to taste
- 1 bacon slice, diced
- 1 clove garlic, minced
- 1 tbsp balsamic vinegar

**Directions:**
1. Preheat air fryer to 375ºF. Combine green beans, butter, salt, and pepper in a bowl. Put the bean mixture in the frying basket and Air Fry for 5 minutes. Stir in bacon and Air Fry for 4 more minutes. Mix in garlic and cook for 1 minute. Transfer it to a serving dish, drizzle with balsamic vinegar and combine. Serve right away.

# Roasted Peppers With Balsamic Vinegar And Basil

Servings: 6
Cooking Time: 12 Minutes
**Ingredients:**
- 4 Small or medium red or yellow bell peppers
- 3 tablespoons Olive oil
- 1 tablespoon Balsamic vinegar
- Up to 6 Fresh basil leaves, torn up

**Directions:**
1. Preheat the air fryer to 400°F.
2. When the machine is at temperature, put the peppers in the basket with at least ¼ inch between them. Air-fry undisturbed for 12 minutes, until blistered, even blackened in places.
3. Use kitchen tongs to transfer the peppers to a medium bowl. Cover the bowl with plastic wrap. Set aside at room temperature for 30 minutes.
4. Uncover the bowl and use kitchen tongs to transfer the peppers to a cutting board or work surface. Peel off the filmy exterior skin. If there are blackened bits under it, these can stay on the peppers. Cut off and remove the stem ends. Split open the peppers and discard any seeds and their spongy membranes. Slice the peppers into ½-inch- to 1-inch-wide strips.
5. Put these in a clean bowl and gently toss them with the oil, vinegar, and basil. Serve at once. Or cover and store at room temperature for up to 4 hours or in the refrigerator for up to 5 days.

# Parmesan Asparagus

Servings: 2
Cooking Time: 5 Minutes
**Ingredients:**
- 1 bunch asparagus, stems trimmed
- 1 teaspoon olive oil
- salt and freshly ground black pepper
- ¼ cup coarsely grated Parmesan cheese
- ½ lemon

**Directions:**
1. Preheat the air fryer to 400°F.
2. Toss the asparagus with the oil and season with salt and freshly ground black pepper.
3. Transfer the asparagus to the air fryer basket and air-fry at 400°F for 5 minutes, shaking the basket to turn the asparagus once or twice during the cooking process.
4. When the asparagus is cooked to your liking, sprinkle the asparagus generously with the Parmesan cheese and close the air fryer drawer again. Let the asparagus sit for 1 minute in the turned-off air fryer. Then, remove the asparagus, transfer it to a serving dish and finish with a grind of black pepper and a squeeze of lemon juice.

# Roasted Belgian Endive With Pistachios And Lemon

Servings: 2
Cooking Time: 7 Minutes
**Ingredients:**
- 2 Medium 3-ounce Belgian endive head(s)
- 2 tablespoons Olive oil
- ½ teaspoon Table salt
- ¼ cup Finely chopped unsalted shelled pistachios
- Up to 2 teaspoons Lemon juice

**Directions:**
1. Preheat the air fryer to 325°F.
2. Trim the Belgian endive head(s), removing the little bit of dried-out stem end but keeping the leaves intact. Quarter the head(s) through the stem. Brush the endive quarters with oil, getting it down between the leaves. Sprinkle the quarters with salt.
3. When the machine is at temperature, set the endive quarters cut sides up in the basket with as much air space between them as possible. They should not touch. Air-fry undisturbed for 7 minutes, or until lightly browned along the edges.
4. Use kitchen tongs to transfer the endive quarters to serving plates or a platter. Sprinkle with the pistachios and lemon juice. Serve warm or at room temperature.

# Acorn Squash Halves With Maple Butter Glaze

Servings: 2
Cooking Time: 33 Minutes
**Ingredients:**
- 1 medium Acorn squash
- Vegetable oil spray
- ¼ teaspoon Table salt
- 1½ tablespoons Butter, melted
- 1½ tablespoons Maple syrup

**Directions:**

1. Preheat the air fryer to 325°F.
2. Cut a squash in half through the stem end. Use a flatware spoon to scrape out and discard the seeds and membranes in each half. Use a paring knife to make a crisscross pattern of cuts about ½ inch apart and ¼ inch deep across the "meat" of the squash. If working with a second squash, repeat this step for that one.
3. Generously coat the cut side of the squash halves with vegetable oil spray. Sprinkle the halves with the salt. Set them in the basket cut side up with at least ¼ inch between them. Air-fry undisturbed for 30 minutes.
4. Increase the machine's temperature to 400°F. Mix the melted butter and syrup in a small bowl until uniform. Brush this mixture over the cut sides of the squash(es), letting it pool in the center. Air-fry undisturbed for 3 minutes, or until the glaze is bubbling.
5. Use a nonstick-safe spatula and kitchen tongs to transfer the squash halves cut side up to a wire rack. Cool for 5 to 10 minutes before serving.

## Steakhouse Baked Potatoes

Servings: 3
Cooking Time: 55 Minutes
**Ingredients:**
* 3 10-ounce russet potatoes
* 2 tablespoons Olive oil
* 1 teaspoon Table salt
**Directions:**
1. Preheat the air fryer to 375°F.
2. Poke holes all over each potato with a fork. Rub the skin of each potato with 2 teaspoons of the olive oil, then sprinkle ¼ teaspoon salt all over each potato.
3. When the machine is at temperature, set the potatoes in the basket in one layer with as much air space between them as possible. Air-fry for 50 minutes, turning once, or until soft to the touch but with crunchy skins. If the machine is at 360°F, you may need to add up to 5 minutes to the cooking time.
4. Use kitchen tongs to gently transfer the baked potatoes to a wire rack. Cool for 5 or 10 minutes before serving.

## Easy Green Bean Casserole

Servings:4
Cooking Time: 20 Minutes
**Ingredients:**
* 1 can condensed cream of mushroom soup
* ¼ cup heavy cream
* 2 cans cut green beans, drained
* 1 teaspoon minced garlic
* ½ teaspoon salt
* ¼ teaspoon ground black pepper
* 1 cup packaged French fried onions
**Directions:**
1. Preheat the air fryer to 320°F.

2. In a 4-quart baking dish, pour soup and cream over green beans and mix to combine.
3. Stir in garlic, salt, and pepper until combined. Top with French fried onions.
4. Place in the air fryer basket and cook 20 minutes until top is lightly brown and dish is heated through. Serve warm.

## Blistered Green Beans

Servings: 3
Cooking Time: 10 Minutes
**Ingredients:**
* ¾ pound Green beans, trimmed on both ends
* 1½ tablespoons Olive oil
* 3 tablespoons Pine nuts
* 1½ tablespoons Balsamic vinegar
* 1½ teaspoons Minced garlic
* ¾ teaspoon Table salt
* ¾ teaspoon Ground black pepper
**Directions:**
1. Preheat the air fryer to 400°F.
2. Toss the green beans and oil in a large bowl until all the green beans are glistening.
3. When the machine is at temperature, pile the green beans into the basket. Air-fry for 10 minutes, tossing often to rearrange the green beans in the basket, or until blistered and tender.
4. Dump the contents of the basket into a serving bowl. Add the pine nuts, vinegar, garlic, salt, and pepper. Toss well to coat and combine. Serve warm or at room temperature.

## Spicy Corn Fritters

Servings: 4
Cooking Time: 22 Minutes
**Ingredients:**
* 1 can yellow corn, drained
* ½ cup all-purpose flour
* ¾ cup shredded pepper jack cheese
* 1 large egg
* ½ teaspoon chili powder
* ¼ teaspoon garlic powder
* ½ teaspoon salt
* ¼ teaspoon ground black pepper
**Directions:**
1. Cut parchment paper to fit the air fryer basket.
2. In a large bowl, mix all ingredients until well combined. Using a ½-cup scoop, separate mixture into four portions.
3. Gently press each into a 4" round and spritz with cooking spray. Place in freezer 10 minutes.
4. Preheat the air fryer to 400°F.
5. Place fritters in the air fryer basket and cook 12 minutes, turning halfway through cooking time, until fritters are brown on the top and edges and firm to the touch. Serve warm.

99

# Asiago Broccoli

Servings: 4
Cooking Time: 14 Minutes
**Ingredients:**
- 1 head broccoli, cut into florets
- 1 tablespoon extra-virgin olive oil
- 1 teaspoon minced garlic
- ¼ teaspoon ground black pepper
- ¼ teaspoon salt
- ¼ cup asiago cheese

**Directions:**
1. Preheat the air fryer to 360°F.
2. In a medium bowl, toss the broccoli florets with the olive oil, garlic, pepper, and salt. Lightly spray the air fryer basket with olive oil spray.
3. Place the broccoli florets into the basket and cook for 7 minutes. Shake the basket and sprinkle the broccoli with cheese. Cook another 7 minutes.
4. Remove from the basket and serve warm.

# Hasselbacks

Servings: 4
Cooking Time: 41 Minutes
**Ingredients:**
- 2 large potatoes
- oil for misting or cooking spray
- salt, pepper, and garlic powder
- 1½ ounces sharp Cheddar cheese, sliced very thin
- ¼ cup chopped green onions
- 2 strips turkey bacon, cooked and crumbled
- light sour cream for serving (optional)

**Directions:**
1. Preheat air fryer to 390°F.
2. Scrub potatoes. Cut thin vertical slices ¼-inch thick crosswise about three-quarters of the way down so that bottom of potato remains intact.
3. Fan potatoes slightly to separate slices. Mist with oil and sprinkle with salt, pepper, and garlic powder to taste. Potatoes will be very stiff, but try to get some of the oil and seasoning between the slices.
4. Place potatoes in air fryer basket and cook for 40 minutes or until centers test done when pierced with a fork.
5. Top potatoes with cheese slices and cook for 30 seconds to 1 minute to melt cheese.
6. Cut each potato in half crosswise, and sprinkle with green onions and crumbled bacon. If you like, add a dollop of sour cream before serving.

# Perfect Broccoli

Servings: 4
Cooking Time: 12 Minutes
**Ingredients:**
- 5 cups 1- to 1½-inch fresh broccoli florets (not frozen)
- Olive oil spray

- ¾ teaspoon Table salt

**Directions:**
1. Preheat the air fryer to 375°F .
2. Put the broccoli florets in a big bowl, coat them generously with olive oil spray, then toss to coat all surfaces, even down into the crannies, spraying them in a couple of times more. Sprinkle the salt on top and toss again.
3. When the machine is at temperature, pour the florets into the basket. Air-fry for 10 minutes, tossing and rearranging the pieces twice so that all the covered or touching bits are eventually exposed to the air currents, until lightly browned but still crunchy.
4. Pour the florets into a serving bowl. Cool for a minute or two, then serve hot.

# Dijon Roast Cabbage

Servings:4
Cooking Time: 10 Minutes
**Ingredients:**
- 1 small head cabbage, cored and sliced into 1"-thick slices
- 2 tablespoons olive oil, divided
- ½ teaspoon salt
- 1 tablespoon Dijon mustard
- 1 teaspoon apple cider vinegar
- 1 teaspoon granular erythritol

**Directions:**
1. Drizzle each cabbage slice with 1 tablespoon olive oil, then sprinkle with salt. Place slices into ungreased air fryer basket, working in batches if needed. Adjust the temperature to 350°F and set the timer for 10 minutes. Cabbage will be tender and edges will begin to brown when done.
2. In a small bowl, whisk remaining olive oil with mustard, vinegar, and erythritol. Drizzle over cabbage in a large serving dish. Serve warm.

# Cheesy Cauliflower Tots

Servings:4
Cooking Time: 12 Minutes Per Batch
**Ingredients:**
- 1 steamer bag riced cauliflower
- ⅓ cup Italian bread crumbs
- ¼ cup all-purpose flour
- 1 large egg
- ¾ cup shredded sharp Cheddar cheese
- ½ teaspoon salt
- ¼ teaspoon ground black pepper

**Directions:**
1. Cook cauliflower according to the package directions. Let cool, then squeeze in a cheesecloth or kitchen towel to drain excess water.
2. Preheat the air fryer to 400°F. Cut parchment paper to fit the air fryer basket.

3. In a large bowl, mix drained cauliflower, bread crumbs, flour, egg, and Cheddar. Sprinkle in salt and pepper, then mix until well combined.
4. Roll 2 tablespoons of mixture into a tot shape. Repeat to use all of the mixture.
5. Place tots on parchment in the air fryer basket, working in batches as necessary. Spritz with cooking spray. Cook 12 minutes, turning tots halfway through cooking time, until golden brown. Serve warm.

# Mouth-watering Provençal Mushrooms

Servings: 4
Cooking Time: 35 Minutes
Ingredients:
- 2 lb mushrooms, quartered
- 2-3 tbsp olive oil
- ½ tsp garlic powder
- 2 tsp herbs de Provence
- 2 tbsp dry white wine

Directions:
1. Preheat air fryer to 320°F. Beat together the olive oil, garlic powder, herbs de Provence, and white wine in a bowl. Add the mushrooms and toss gently to coat. Spoon the mixture onto the frying basket and Bake for 16-18 minutes, stirring twice. Serve hot and enjoy!

# Charred Radicchio Salad

Servings: 4
Cooking Time: 5 Minutes
Ingredients:
- 2 Small 5- to 6-ounce radicchio head(s)
- 3 tablespoons Olive oil
- ½ teaspoon Table salt
- 2 tablespoons Balsamic vinegar
- Up to ¼ teaspoon Red pepper flakes

Directions:
1. Preheat the air fryer to 375°F.
2. Cut the radicchio head(s) into quarters through the stem end. Brush the oil over the heads, particularly getting it between the leaves along the cut sides. Sprinkle the radicchio quarters with the salt.
3. When the machine is at temperature, set the quarters cut sides up in the basket with as much air space between them as possible. They should not touch. Air-fry undisturbed for 5 minutes, watching carefully because they burn quickly, until blackened in bits and soft.
4. Use a nonstick-safe spatula to transfer the quarters to a cutting board. Cool for a minute or two, then cut out the thick stems inside the heads. Discard these tough bits and chop the remaining heads into bite-size bits. Scrape them into a bowl. Add the vinegar and red pepper flakes. Toss well and serve warm.

# Sage Hasselback Potatoes

Servings: 4
Cooking Time: 45 Minutes
Ingredients:
- 1 lb fingerling potatoes
- 1 tbsp olive oil
- 1 tbsp butter
- 1tsp dried sage
- Salt and pepper to taste

Directions:
1. Preheat the air fryer to 400°F. Rinse the potatoes dry, then set them on a work surface and put two chopsticks lengthwise on either side of each so you won't cut all the way through. Make vertical, crosswise cuts in the potato, about ⅛ inch apart. Repeat with the remaining potatoes. Combine the olive oil and butter in a bowl and microwave for 30 seconds or until melted. Stir in the sage, salt, and pepper. Put the potatoes in a large bowl and drizzle with the olive oil mixture. Toss to coat, then put the potatoes in the fryer and Air Fry for 22-27 minutes, rearranging them after 10-12 minutes. Cook until the potatoes are tender. Serve hot and enjoy!

# Sweet Potato Fries

Servings: 3
Cooking Time: 20 Minutes
Ingredients:
- 2 10-ounce sweet potato(es)
- Vegetable oil spray
- To taste Coarse sea salt or kosher salt

Directions:
1. Preheat the air fryer to 400°F.
2. Peel the sweet potato(es), then cut lengthwise into ¼-inch-thick slices. Cut these slices lengthwise into ¼-inch-thick matchsticks. Place these matchsticks in a bowl and coat them with vegetable oil spray. Toss well, spray them again, and toss several times to make sure they're all evenly coated.
3. When the machine is at temperature, pour the sweet potato matchsticks into the basket, spreading them out in as close to an even layer as possible. Air-fry for 20 minutes, tossing and rearranging the matchsticks every 5 minutes, until lightly browned and crisp.
4. Pour the contents of the basket into a bowl, add some salt to taste, and toss well to coat.

# Twice-baked Potatoes With Pancetta

Servings: 5
Cooking Time: 30 Minutes
Ingredients:
- 2 teaspoons canola oil
- 5 large russet potatoes, peeled
- Sea salt and ground black pepper, to taste
- 5 slices pancetta, chopped

- 5 tablespoons Swiss cheese, shredded

**Directions:**

1. Start by preheating your Air Fryer to 360 °F.
2. Drizzle the canola oil all over the potatoes. Place the potatoes in the Air Fryer basket and cook approximately 20 minutes, shaking the basket periodically.
3. Lightly crush the potatoes to split and season them with salt and ground black pepper. Add the pancetta and cheese.
4. Place in the preheated Air Fryer and bake an additional 5 minutes or until cheese has melted. Bon appétit!

# Brussels Sprouts

Servings: 3
Cooking Time: 5 Minutes

**Ingredients:**

- 1 10-ounce package frozen brussels sprouts, thawed and halved
- 2 teaspoons olive oil
- salt and pepper

**Directions:**

1. Toss the brussels sprouts and olive oil together.
2. Place them in the air fryer basket and season to taste with salt and pepper.
3. Cook at 360°F for approximately 5minutes, until the edges begin to brown.

# Perfect Broccolini

Servings: 4
Cooking Time: 15 Minutes

**Ingredients:**

- 1 pound Broccolini
- Olive oil spray
- Coarse sea salt or kosher salt

**Directions:**

1. Preheat the air fryer to 375°F .
2. Place the broccolini on a cutting board. Generously coat it with olive oil spray, turning the vegetables and rearranging them before spraying a couple of times more, to make sure everything's well coated, even the flowery bits in their heads.
3. When the machine is at temperature, pile the broccolini in the basket, spreading it into as close to one layer as you can. Air-fry for 5 minutes, tossing once to get any covered or touching parts exposed to the air currents, until the leaves begin to get brown and even crisp. Watch carefully and use this visual cue to know the moment to stop the cooking.
4. Transfer the broccolini to a platter. Spread out the pieces and sprinkle them with salt to taste.

# Grilled Lime Scallions

Servings:6
Cooking Time: 15 Minutes

**Ingredients:**

- 2 bunches of scallions
- 1 tbsp olive oil

- 2 tsp lime juice
- Salt and pepper to taste
- ¼ tsp Italian seasoning
- 2 tsp lime zest

**Directions:**

1. Preheat air fryer to 370°F. Trim the scallions and cut them in half lengthwise. Place them in a bowl and add olive oil and lime juice. Toss to coat. Place the mix in the frying basket and Air Fry for 7 minutes, tossing once. Transfer to a serving dish and stir in salt, pepper, Italian seasoning and lime zest. Serve immediately.

# Herbed Croutons With Brie Cheese

Servings:1
Cooking Time: 20 Minutes

**Ingredients:**

- 1 tbsp french herbs
- 7 oz brie cheese, chopped
- 2 slices bread, halved

**Directions:**

1. Preheat air fryer to 340°F. In a bowl, mix oil with herbs. Brush the bread slices with oil mixture. Place on a flat surface. Top with brie cheese. Place in air fryer's basket; cook for 7 minutes. Cut into cubes.

# Asparagus Fries

Servings: 4
Cooking Time: 5 Minutes Per Batch

**Ingredients:**

- 12 ounces fresh asparagus spears with tough ends trimmed off
- 2 egg whites
- ¼ cup water
- ¾ cup panko breadcrumbs
- ¼ cup grated Parmesan cheese, plus 2 tablespoons
- ¼ teaspoon salt
- oil for misting or cooking spray

**Directions:**

1. Preheat air fryer to 390°F.
2. In a shallow dish, beat egg whites and water until slightly foamy.
3. In another shallow dish, combine panko, Parmesan, and salt.
4. Dip asparagus spears in egg, then roll in crumbs. Spray with oil or cooking spray.
5. Place a layer of asparagus in air fryer basket, leaving just a little space in between each spear. Stack another layer on top, crosswise. Cook at 390°F for 5 minutes, until crispy and golden brown.
6. Repeat to cook remaining asparagus.

# Pancetta Mushroom & Onion Sautée

Servings:4
Cooking Time: 20 Minutes
**Ingredients:**
- 16 oz white button mushrooms, stems trimmed, halved
- 1 onion, cut into half-moons
- 4 pancetta slices, diced
- 1 clove garlic, minced

**Directions:**
1. Preheat air fryer to 350ºF. Add all ingredients, except for the garlic, to the frying basket and Air Fry for 8 minutes, tossing once. Stir in the garlic and cook for 1 more minute. Serve right away.

# Okra

Servings: 4
Cooking Time: 12 Minutes
**Ingredients:**
- 7–8 ounces fresh okra
- 1 egg
- 1 cup milk
- 1 cup breadcrumbs
- ½ teaspoon salt
- oil for misting or cooking spray

**Directions:**
1. Remove stem ends from okra and cut in ½-inch slices.
2. In a medium bowl, beat together egg and milk. Add okra slices and stir to coat.
3. In a sealable plastic bag or container with lid, mix together the breadcrumbs and salt.
4. Remove okra from egg mixture, letting excess drip off, and transfer into bag with breadcrumbs.
5. Shake okra in crumbs to coat well.
6. Place all of the coated okra into the air fryer basket and mist with oil or cooking spray. Okra doesn't need to cook in a single layer, nor is it necessary to spray all sides at this point. A good spritz on top will do.
7. Cook at 390°F for 5minutes. Shake basket to redistribute and give it another spritz as you shake.
8. Cook 5 more minutes. Shake and spray again. Cook for 2 minutes longer or until golden brown and crispy.

# Roasted Broccoli Salad

Servings:4
Cooking Time: 7 Minutes
**Ingredients:**
- 2 cups fresh broccoli florets, chopped
- 1 tablespoon olive oil
- ¼ teaspoon salt
- ⅛ teaspoon ground black pepper
- ¼ cup lemon juice, divided
- ¼ cup shredded Parmesan cheese
- ¼ cup sliced roasted almonds

**Directions:**
1. In a large bowl, toss broccoli and olive oil together. Sprinkle with salt and pepper, then drizzle with 2 tablespoons lemon juice.
2. Place broccoli into ungreased air fryer basket. Adjust the temperature to 350°F and set the timer for 7 minutes, shaking the basket halfway through cooking. Broccoli will be golden on the edges when done.
3. Place broccoli into a large serving bowl and drizzle with remaining lemon juice. Sprinkle with Parmesan and almonds. Serve warm.

# Flaky Biscuits

Servings:8
Cooking Time: 15 Minutes Per Batch
**Ingredients:**
- ¼ cup salted butter
- 2 cups self-rising flour
- ¼ teaspoon salt
- ⅔ cup whole milk

**Directions:**
1. Preheat the air fryer to 320°F. Cut parchment paper to fit the air fryer basket.
2. Place butter in the freezer 10 minutes. In a large bowl, mix flour and salt.
3. Grate butter into bowl and use a wooden spoon to evenly distribute. Add milk and stir until a soft dough forms.
4. Turn dough onto a lightly floured surface. Gently press and flatten dough until mostly smooth and uniform. Gently roll into an 8" × 10" rectangle. Use a sharp knife dusted in flour to cut dough into eight squares.
5. Place biscuits on parchment paper in the air fryer basket, working in batches as necessary, and cook 15 minutes until golden brown on the top and edges and feel firm to the touch. Let cool 5 minutes before serving.

# Garlic-parmesan French Fries

Servings:4
Cooking Time: 45 Minutes
**Ingredients:**
- 3 large russet potatoes, peeled, trimmed, and sliced into ½" × 4" sticks
- 2 ½ tablespoons olive oil, divided
- 2 teaspoons minced garlic
- ½ teaspoon salt
- ¼ teaspoon ground black pepper
- 1 teaspoon dried parsley
- ¼ cup grated Parmesan cheese

**Directions:**
1. Place potato sticks in a large bowl of cold water and let soak 30 minutes.
2. Preheat the air fryer to 350°F.
3. Drain potatoes and gently pat dry. Place in a large, dry bowl.
4. Pour 2 tablespoons oil over potatoes. Add garlic, salt, and pepper, then toss to fully coat.

5.  Place fries in the air fryer basket and cook 15 minutes, shaking the basket twice during cooking, until fries are golden and crispy on the edges.

6.  Place fries into a clean medium bowl and drizzle with remaining ½ tablespoon oil. Sprinkle parsley and Parmesan over fries and toss to coat. Serve warm.

## Smashed Fried Baby Potatoes

Servings: 3
Cooking Time: 18 Minutes
**Ingredients:**
- 1½ pounds baby red or baby Yukon gold potatoes
- ¼ cup butter, melted
- 1 teaspoon olive oil
- ½ teaspoon paprika
- 1 teaspoon dried parsley
- salt and freshly ground black pepper
- 2 scallions, finely chopped

**Directions:**

1.  Bring a large pot of salted water to a boil. Add the potatoes and boil for 18 minutes or until the potatoes are fork-tender.

2.  Drain the potatoes and transfer them to a cutting board to cool slightly. Spray or brush the bottom of a drinking glass with a little oil. Smash or flatten the potatoes by pressing the glass down on each potato slowly. Try not to completely flatten the potato or smash it so hard that it breaks apart.

3.  Combine the melted butter, olive oil, paprika, and parsley together.

4.  Preheat the air fryer to 400°F.

5.  Spray the bottom of the air fryer basket with oil and transfer one layer of the smashed potatoes into the basket. Brush with some of the butter mixture and season generously with salt and freshly ground black pepper.

6.  Air-fry at 400°F for 10 minutes. Carefully flip the potatoes over and air-fry for an additional 8 minutes until crispy and lightly browned.

7.  Keep the potatoes warm in a 170°F oven or tent with aluminum foil while you cook the second batch. Sprinkle minced scallions over the potatoes and serve warm.

# Chapter 9. Desserts And Sweets

## Strawberry Cups

Servings: 8
Cooking Time: 10 Minutes
**Ingredients:**
- 16 strawberries, halved
- 2 tablespoons coconut oil
- 2 cups chocolate chips, melted

**Directions:**

1.  In a pan that fits your air fryer, mix the strawberries with the oil and the melted chocolate chips, toss gently, put the pan in the air fryer and cook at 340°F for 10 minutes. Divide into cups and serve cold.

## Toasted Coconut Flakes

Servings: 1
Cooking Time: 5 Minutes
**Ingredients:**
- 1 cup unsweetened coconut flakes
- 2 tsp. coconut oil, melted
- ¼ cup granular erythritol
- Salt

**Directions:**

1.  In a large bowl, combine the coconut flakes, oil, granular erythritol, and a pinch of salt, ensuring that the flakes are coated completely.

2.  Place the coconut flakes in your fryer and cook at 300°F for three minutes, giving the basket a good shake a few times throughout the cooking time. Fry until golden and serve.

## Lemon Mousse

Servings:6
Cooking Time:10 Minutes
**Ingredients:**
- 12-ounces cream cheese, softened
- ¼ teaspoon salt
- 1 teaspoon lemon liquid stevia
- 1/3 cup fresh lemon juice
- 1½ cups heavy cream

**Directions:**

1.  Preheat the Air fryer to 345°F and grease a large ramekin lightly.

2.  Mix all the ingredients in a large bowl until well combined.

3.  Pour into the ramekin and transfer into the Air fryer.

4. Cook for about 10 minutes and pour into the serving glasses.
5. Refrigerate to cool for about 3 hours and serve chilled.

## Chocolate Doughnut Holes

Servings:20
Cooking Time: 6 Minutes
**Ingredients:**
- 1 cup blanched finely ground almond flour
- ½ cup low-carb vanilla protein powder
- ½ cup granular erythritol
- ¼ cup unsweetened cocoa powder
- ½ teaspoon baking powder
- 2 large eggs, whisked
- ½ teaspoon vanilla extract

**Directions:**
1. Mix all ingredients in a large bowl until a soft dough forms. Separate and roll dough into twenty balls, about 2 tablespoons each.
2. Cut a piece of parchment to fit your air fryer basket. Working in batches if needed, place doughnut holes into air fryer basket on ungreased parchment. Adjust the temperature to 380°F and set the timer for 6 minutes, flipping doughnut holes halfway through cooking. Doughnut holes will be golden and firm when done. Let cool completely before serving, about 10 minutes.

## Sage Cream

Servings: 4
Cooking Time: 30 Minutes
**Ingredients:**
- 7 cups red currants
- 1 cup swerve
- 1 cup water
- 6 sage leaves

**Directions:**
1. In a pan that fits your air fryer, mix all the ingredients, toss, put the pan in the fryer and cook at 330°F for 30 minutes. Discard sage leaves, divide into cups and serve cold.

## Fried Banana S'mores

Servings: 4
Cooking Time: 6 Minutes
**Ingredients:**
- 4 bananas
- 3 tablespoons mini semi-sweet chocolate chips
- 3 tablespoons mini peanut butter chips
- 3 tablespoons mini marshmallows
- 3 tablespoons graham cracker cereal

**Directions:**
1. Preheat the air fryer to 400°F.
2. Slice into the un-peeled bananas lengthwise along the inside of the curve, but do not slice through the bottom of the peel. Open the banana slightly to form a pocket.
3. Fill each pocket with chocolate chips, peanut butter chips and marshmallows. Poke the graham cracker cereal into the filling.
4. Place the bananas in the air fryer basket, resting them on the side of the basket and each other to keep them upright with the filling facing up. Air-fry for 6 minutes, or until the bananas are soft to the touch, the peels have blackened and the chocolate and marshmallows have melted and toasted.
5. Let them cool for a couple of minutes and then simply serve with a spoon to scoop out the filling.

## Peanut Butter S'mores

Servings:10
Cooking Time: 1 Minute
**Ingredients:**
- 10 Graham crackers (full, double-square cookies as they come out of the package)
- 5 tablespoons Natural-style creamy or crunchy peanut butter
- ½ cup Milk chocolate chips
- 10 Standard-size marshmallows (not minis and not jumbo campfire ones)

**Directions:**
1. Preheat the air fryer to 350°F .
2. Break the graham crackers in half widthwise at the marked place, so the rectangle is now in two squares. Set half of the squares flat side up on your work surface. Spread each with about 1½ teaspoons peanut butter, then set 10 to 12 chocolate chips point side up into the peanut butter on each, pressing gently so the chips stick.
3. Flatten a marshmallow between your clean, dry hands and set it atop the chips. Do the same with the remaining marshmallows on the other coated graham crackers. Do not set the other half of the graham crackers on top of these coated graham crackers.
4. When the machine is at temperature, set the treats graham cracker side down in a single layer in the basket. They may touch, but even a fraction of an inch between them will provide better air flow. Air-fry undisturbed for 45 seconds.
5. Use a nonstick-safe spatula to transfer the topped graham crackers to a wire rack. Set the other graham cracker squares flat side down over the marshmallows. Cool for a couple of minutes before serving.

# Coconut And Berries Cream

Servings: 6
Cooking Time: 30 Minutes
**Ingredients:**
- 12 ounces blackberries
- 6 ounces raspberries
- 12 ounces blueberries
- ¾ cup swerve
- 2 ounces coconut cream

**Directions:**
1. In a bowl, mix all the ingredients and whisk well. Divide this into 6 ramekins, put them in your air fryer and cook at 320°F for 30 minutes. Cool down and serve it.

# Cream Cheese Shortbread Cookies

Servings:12
Cooking Time: 20 Minutes
**Ingredients:**
- ¼ cup coconut oil, melted
- 2 ounces cream cheese, softened
- ½ cup granular erythritol
- 1 large egg, whisked
- 2 cups blanched finely ground almond flour
- 1 teaspoon almond extract

**Directions:**
1. Combine all ingredients in a large bowl to form a firm ball.
2. Place dough on a sheet of plastic wrap and roll into a 12"-long log shape. Roll log in plastic wrap and place in refrigerator 30 minutes to chill.
3. Remove log from plastic and slice into twelve equal cookies. Cut two sheets of parchment paper to fit air fryer basket. Place six cookies on each ungreased sheet. Place one sheet with cookies into air fryer basket. Adjust the temperature to 320°F and set the timer for 10 minutes, turning cookies halfway through cooking. They will be lightly golden when done. Repeat with remaining cookies.
4. Let cool 15 minutes before serving to avoid crumbling.

# Grape Stew

Servings: 4
Cooking Time: 14 Minutes
**Ingredients:**
- 1 pound red grapes
- Juice and zest of 1 lemon
- 26 ounces grape juice

**Directions:**
1. In a pan that fits your air fryer, add all ingredients and toss.
2. Place the pan in the fryer and cook at 320°F for 14 minutes.
3. Divide into cups, refrigerate, and serve cold.

# Fried Cannoli Wontons

Servings: 10
Cooking Time: 8 Minutes
**Ingredients:**
- 8 ounces Neufchâtel cream cheese
- ¼ cup powdered sugar
- 1 teaspoon vanilla extract
- ¼ teaspoon salt
- ¼ cup mini chocolate chips
- 2 tablespoons chopped pecans (optional)
- 20 wonton wrappers
- ¼ cup filtered water

**Directions:**
1. Preheat the air fryer to 370°F.
2. In a large bowl, use a hand mixer to combine the cream cheese with the powdered sugar, vanilla, and salt. Fold in the chocolate chips and pecans. Set aside.
3. Lay the wonton wrappers out on a flat, smooth surface and place a bowl with the filtered water next to them.
4. Use a teaspoon to evenly divide the cream cheese mixture among the 20 wonton wrappers, placing the batter in the center of the wontons.
5. Wet the tip of your index finger, and gently moisten the outer edges of the wrapper. Then fold each wrapper until it creates a secure pocket.
6. Liberally spray the air fryer basket with olive oil mist.
7. Place the wontons into the basket, and cook for 5 to 8 minutes. When the outer edges begin to brown, remove the wontons from the air fryer basket. Repeat cooking with remaining wontons.
8. Serve warm.

# Cocoa Bombs

Servings: 12
Cooking Time: 8 Minutes
**Ingredients:**
- 2 cups macadamia nuts, chopped
- 4 tablespoons coconut oil, melted
- 1 teaspoon vanilla extract
- ¼ cup cocoa powder
- 1/3 cup swerve

**Directions:**
1. In a bowl, mix all the ingredients and whisk well. Shape medium balls out of this mix, place them in your air fryer and cook at 300°F for 8 minutes. Serve cold.

# Fiesta Pastries

Servings:8
Cooking Time:20 Minutes
**Ingredients:**
- ½ of apple, peeled, cored and chopped
- 1 teaspoon fresh orange zest, grated finely
- 7.05-ounce prepared frozen puff pastry, cut into 16 squares
- ½ tablespoon white sugar
- ½ teaspoon ground cinnamon

**Directions:**
1. Preheat the Air fryer to 390°F and grease an Air fryer basket.
2. Mix all ingredients in a bowl except puff pastry.
3. Arrange about 1 teaspoon of this mixture in the center of each square.
4. Fold each square into a triangle and slightly press the edges with a fork.
5. Arrange the pastries in the Air fryer basket and cook for about 10 minutes.
6. Dish out and serve immediately.

# Fried Oreos

Servings: 12
Cooking Time: 6 Minutes Per Batch
**Ingredients:**
- oil for misting or nonstick spray
- 1 cup complete pancake and waffle mix
- 1 teaspoon vanilla extract
- ½ cup water, plus 2 tablespoons
- 12 Oreos or other chocolate sandwich cookies
- 1 tablespoon confectioners' sugar

**Directions:**
1. Spray baking pan with oil or nonstick spray and place in basket.
2. Preheat air fryer to 390°F.
3. In a medium bowl, mix together the pancake mix, vanilla, and water.
4. Dip 4 cookies in batter and place in baking pan.
5. Cook for 6minutes, until browned.
6. Repeat steps 4 and 5 for the remaining cookies.
7. Sift sugar over warm cookies.

# Ricotta Lemon Cake

Servings: 8
Cooking Time: 40 Minutes
**Ingredients:**
- 1 lb ricotta
- 4 eggs
- 1 lemon juice
- 1 lemon zest
- ¼ cup erythritol

**Directions:**
1. Preheat the air fryer to 325°F.

2. Spray air fryer baking dish with cooking spray.
3. In a bowl, beat ricotta cheese until smooth.
4. Whisk in the eggs one by one.
5. Whisk in lemon juice and zest.
6. Pour batter into the prepared baking dish and place into the air fryer.
7. Cook for 40 minutes.
8. Allow to cool completely then slice and serve.

# Kiwi Pastry Bites

Servings: 6
Cooking Time: 45 Minutes
**Ingredients:**
- 3 kiwi fruits, cut into 12 pieces
- 12 wonton wrappers
- ½ cup peanut butter

**Directions:**
1. Lay out wonton wrappers on a flat, clean surface. Place a kiwi piece on each wrapper, then with 1 tsp of peanut butter. Fold each wrapper from one corner to another to create a triangle. Bring the 2 bottom corners together, but do not seal. Gently press out any air, then press the open edges to seal. Preheat air fryer to 370°F. Bake the wontons in the greased frying basket for 15-18 minutes, flipping once halfway through cooking, until golden and crisp. Let cool for a few minutes.

# Delicious Spiced Apples

Servings: 6
Cooking Time: 10 Minutes
**Ingredients:**
- 4 small apples, sliced
- 1 tsp apple pie spice
- 1/2 cup erythritol
- 2 tbsp coconut oil, melted

**Directions:**
1. Add apple slices in a mixing bowl and sprinkle sweetener, apple pie spice, and coconut oil over apple and toss to coat.
2. Transfer apple slices in air fryer dish. Place dish in air fryer basket and cook at 350°F for 10 minutes.
3. Serve and enjoy.

# Chocolate-covered Maple Bacon

Servings: 4
Cooking Time: 25 Minutes
**Ingredients:**
- 8 slices sugar-free bacon
- 1 tbsp. granular erythritol
- 1/3 cup low-carb sugar-free chocolate chips
- 1 tsp. coconut oil
- ½ tsp. maple extract

**Directions:**
1. Place the bacon in the fryer's basket and add the erythritol on top. Cook for six minutes at 350°F and turn the

bacon over. Leave to cook another six minutes or until the bacon is sufficiently crispy.

2. Take the bacon out of the fryer and leave it to cool.

3. Microwave the chocolate chips and coconut oil together for half a minute. Remove from the microwave and mix together before stirring in the maple extract.

4. Set the bacon flat on a piece of parchment paper and pour the mixture over. Allow to harden in the refrigerator for roughly five minutes before serving.

# Pumpkin Pie–spiced Pork Rinds

Servings:4
Cooking Time: 5 Minutes
**Ingredients:**
- 3 ounces plain pork rinds
- 2 tablespoons salted butter, melted
- 1 teaspoon pumpkin pie spice
- ¼ cup confectioners' erythritol

**Directions:**

1. In a large bowl, toss pork rinds in butter. Sprinkle with pumpkin pie spice, then toss to evenly coat.

2. Place pork rinds into ungreased air fryer basket. Adjust the temperature to 400°F and set the timer for 5 minutes. Pork rinds will be golden when done.

3. Transfer rinds to a medium serving bowl and sprinkle with erythritol. Serve immediately.

# Apple Dumplings

Servings: 4
Cooking Time: 10 Minutes
**Ingredients:**
- 4 Small tart apples, preferably McIntosh, peeled and cored
- ¼ cup Granulated white sugar
- 1½ tablespoons Ground cinnamon
- 1 sheet, thawed and cut into four quarters A 17.25-ounce box frozen puff pastry (vegetarian, if a concern)

**Directions:**

1. Set the apples stem side up on a microwave-safe plate, preferably a glass pie plate. Microwave on high for 3 minutes, or until somewhat tender when poked with the point of a knife. Cool to room temperature, about 30 minutes.

2. Preheat the air fryer to 400°F.

3. Combine the sugar and cinnamon in a small bowl. Roll the apples in this mixture, coating them completely on their outsides. Also sprinkle this cinnamon sugar into each hole where the core was.

4. Roll the puff pastry squares into 6 x 6-inch squares. Slice the corners off each rolled square so that it's sort of like a circle. Place an apple in the center of one of these squares and fold it up and all around the apple, sealing it at the top by pressing the pastry together. The apple must be completely sealed in the pastry. Repeat for the remaining apples.

5. Set the pastry-covered apples in the basket with at least ½ inch between them. Air-fry undisturbed for 10 minutes, or until puffed and golden brown.

6. Use a nonstick-safe spatula, and maybe a flatware tablespoon for balance, to transfer the apples to a wire rack. Cool for at least 5 minutes or up to 15 minutes before serving warm.

# Banana And Rice Pudding

Servings: 6
Cooking Time: 20 Minutes
**Ingredients:**
- 1 cup brown rice
- 3 cups milk
- 2 bananas, peeled and mashed
- ½ cup maple syrup
- 1 teaspoon vanilla extract

**Directions:**

1. Place all the ingredients in a pan that fits your air fryer; stir well.

2. Put the pan in the fryer and cook at 360°F for 20 minutes.

3. Stir the pudding, divide into cups, refrigerate, and serve cold.

# Lemon Iced Donut Balls

Servings: 6
Cooking Time: 25 Minutes
**Ingredients:**
- 1 can jumbo biscuit dough
- 2 tsp lemon juice
- ½ cup icing sugar, sifted

**Directions:**

1. Preheat air fryer to 360°F. Divide the biscuit dough into 16 equal portions. Roll the dough into balls of 1½ inches thickness. Place the donut holes in the greased frying basket and Air Fry for 8 minutes, flipping once. Mix the icing sugar and lemon juice until smooth. Spread the icing over the top of the donuts. Leave to set a bit. Serve.

# Almond Shortbread Cookies

Servings:8
Cooking Time: 1 Hour 10 Minutes
**Ingredients:**
- ½ cup salted butter, softened
- ¼ cup granulated sugar
- 1 teaspoon almond extract
- 1 teaspoon vanilla extract
- 2 cups all-purpose flour

**Directions:**

1. In a large bowl, cream butter, sugar, and extracts. Gradually add flour, mixing until well combined.

2. Roll dough into a 12" x 2" log and wrap in plastic. Chill in refrigerator at least 1 hour.

3. Preheat the air fryer to 300°F.

4. Slice dough into ¼"-thick cookies. Place in the air fryer basket 2" apart, working in batches as needed, and cook 10 minutes until the edges start to brown. Let cool completely before serving.

## Tortilla Fried Pies

Servings: 12
Cooking Time: 5 Minutes
**Ingredients:**
- 12 small flour tortillas
- ½ cup fig preserves
- ¼ cup sliced almonds
- 2 tablespoons shredded, unsweetened coconut
- oil for misting or cooking spray

**Directions:**
1. Wrap refrigerated tortillas in damp paper towels and heat in microwave 30 seconds to warm.
2. Working with one tortilla at a time, place 2 teaspoons fig preserves, 1 teaspoon sliced almonds, and ½ teaspoon coconut in the center of each.
3. Moisten outer edges of tortilla all around.
4. Fold one side of tortilla over filling to make a half-moon shape and press down lightly on center. Using the tines of a fork, press down firmly on edges of tortilla to seal in filling.
5. Mist both sides with oil or cooking spray.
6. Place hand pies in air fryer basket close but not overlapping. It's fine to lean some against the sides and corners of the basket. You may need to cook in 2 batches.
7. Cook at 390°F for 5 minutes or until lightly browned. Serve hot.
8. Refrigerate any leftover pies in a closed container. To serve later, toss them back in the air fryer basket and cook for 2 or 3 minutes to reheat.

## Cream Cups

Servings: 6
Cooking Time: 10 Minutes
**Ingredients:**
- 2 tablespoons butter, melted
- 8 ounces cream cheese, soft
- 3 tablespoons coconut, shredded and unsweetened
- 3 eggs
- 4 tablespoons swerve

**Directions:**
1. In a bowl, mix all the ingredients and whisk really well. Divide into small ramekins, put them in the fryer and cook at 320°F and bake for 10 minutes. Serve cold.

## Apple Pie

Servings: 7
Cooking Time: 25 Minutes
**Ingredients:**
- 2 large apples
- ½ cup flour
- 2 tbsp. unsalted butter

- 1 tbsp. sugar
- ½ tsp. cinnamon

**Directions:**
1. Pre-heat the Air Fryer to 360°F
2. In a large bowl, combine the flour and butter. Pour in the sugar, continuing to mix.
3. Add in a few tablespoons of water and combine everything to create a smooth dough.
4. Grease the insides of a few small pastry tins with butter. Divide the dough between each tin and lay each portion flat inside.
5. Peel, core and dice up the apples. Put the diced apples on top of the pastry and top with a sprinkling of sugar and cinnamon.
6. Place the pastry tins in your Air Fryer and cook for 15 - 17 minutes.
7. Serve.

## Fried Snickers Bars

Servings: 8
Cooking Time: 4 Minutes
**Ingredients:**
- ⅓ cup All-purpose flour
- 1 Large egg white(s), beaten until foamy
- 1½ cups Vanilla wafer cookie crumbs
- 8 Fun-size Snickers bars, frozen
- Vegetable oil spray

**Directions:**
1. Preheat the air fryer to 400°F.
2. Set up and fill three shallow soup plates or small pie plates on your counter: one for the flour, one for the beaten egg white(s), and one for the cookie crumbs.
3. Unwrap the frozen candy bars. Dip one in the flour, turning it to coat on all sides. Gently shake off any excess, then set it in the beaten egg white(s). Turn it to coat all sides, even the ends, then let any excess egg white slip back into the rest. Set the candy bar in the cookie crumbs. Turn to coat on all sides, even the ends. Dip the candy bar back in the egg white(s) a second time, then into the cookie crumbs a second time, making sure you have an even coating all around. Coat the covered candy bar all over with vegetable oil spray. Set aside so you can dip and coat the remaining candy bars.
4. Set the coated candy bars in the basket with as much air space between them as possible. Air-fry undisturbed for 4 minutes, or until golden brown.
5. Remove the basket from the machine and let the candy bars cool in the basket for 10 minutes. Use a nonstick-safe spatula to transfer them to a wire rack and cool for 5 minutes more before chowing down.

# Pumpkin Pie

Servings:6
Cooking Time: 2 Hours 25 Minutes
**Ingredients:**
- 1 can pumpkin pie mix
- 1 large egg
- 1 teaspoon vanilla extract
- ⅓ cup sweetened condensed milk
- 1 premade graham cracker piecrust

**Directions:**
1. Preheat the air fryer to 325°F.
2. In a large bowl, whisk together pumpkin pie mix, egg, vanilla, and sweetened condensed milk until well combined. Pour mixture into piecrust.
3. Place in the air fryer basket and cook 25 minutes until pie is brown, firm, and a toothpick inserted into the center comes out clean.
4. Chill in the refrigerator until set, at least 2 hours, before serving.

# Cherry Cheesecake Rolls

Servings: 6
Cooking Time: 30 Minutes
**Ingredients:**
- 1 can crescent rolls
- 4 oz cream cheese
- 1 tbsp cherry preserves
- 1/3 cup sliced fresh cherries
- Cooking spray

**Directions:**
1. Roll out the dough into a large rectangle on a flat work surface. Cut the dough into 12 rectangles by cutting 3 cuts across and 2 cuts down. In a microwave-safe bowl, soften cream cheese for 15 seconds. Stir together with cherry preserves. Mound 2 tsp of the cherries-cheese mix on each piece of dough. Carefully spread the mixture but not on the edges. Top with 2 tsp of cherries each. Roll each triangle to make a cylinder.
2. Preheat air fryer to 350°F. Place the first batch of the rolls in the greased air fryer. Spray the rolls with cooking oil and Bake for 8 minutes. Let cool in the air fryer for 2-3 minutes before removing. Serve.

# Chocolate Lava Cakes

Servings:2
Cooking Time: 15 Minutes
**Ingredients:**
- 2 large eggs, whisked
- ¼ cup blanched finely ground almond flour
- ½ teaspoon vanilla extract
- 2 ounces low-carb chocolate chips, melted

**Directions:**
1. In a medium bowl, mix eggs with flour and vanilla. Fold in chocolate until fully combined.

2. Pour batter into two 4" ramekins greased with cooking spray. Place ramekins into air fryer basket. Adjust the temperature to 320°F and set the timer for 15 minutes. Cakes will be set at the edges and firm in the center when done. Let cool 5 minutes before serving.

# Roasted Pumpkin Seeds & Cinnamon

Servings: 2
Cooking Time: 35 Minutes
**Ingredients:**
- 1 cup pumpkin raw seeds
- 1 tbsp. ground cinnamon
- 2 tbsp. sugar
- 1 cup water
- 1 tbsp. olive oil

**Directions:**
1. In a frying pan, combine the pumpkin seeds, cinnamon and water.
2. Boil the mixture over a high heat for 2 - 3 minutes.
3. Pour out the water and place the seeds on a clean kitchen towel, allowing them to dry for 20 - 30 minutes.
4. In a bowl, mix together the sugar, dried seeds, a pinch of cinnamon and one tablespoon of olive oil.
5. Pre-heat the Air Fryer to 340°F.
6. Place the seed mixture in the fryer basket and allow to cook for 15 minutes, shaking the basket periodically throughout.

# S'mores Pockets

Servings: 6
Cooking Time: 5 Minutes
**Ingredients:**
- 12 sheets phyllo dough, thawed
- 1½ cups butter, melted
- ¾ cup graham cracker crumbs
- 1 Giant Hershey's milk chocolate bar
- 12 marshmallows, cut in half

**Directions:**
1. Place one sheet of the phyllo on a large cutting board. Keep the rest of the phyllo sheets covered with a slightly damp, clean kitchen towel. Brush the phyllo sheet generously with some melted butter. Place a second phyllo sheet on top of the first and brush it with more butter. Repeat with one more phyllo sheet until you have a stack of 3 phyllo sheets with butter brushed between the layers. Cover the phyllo sheets with one quarter of the graham cracker crumbs leaving a 1-inch border on one of the short ends of the rectangle. Cut the phyllo sheets lengthwise into 3 strips.
2. Take 2 of the strips and crisscross them to form a cross with the empty borders at the top and to the left. Place 2 of the chocolate rectangles in the center of the cross. Place 4 of the marshmallow halves on top of the chocolate. Now fold the pocket together by folding the bottom phyllo strip up

over the chocolate and marshmallows. Then fold the right side over, then the top strip down and finally the left side over. Brush all the edges generously with melted butter to seal shut. Repeat with the next three sheets of phyllo, until all the sheets have been used. You will be able to make 2 pockets with every second batch because you will have an extra graham cracker crumb strip from the previous set of sheets.

3. Preheat the air fryer to 350°F.

4. Transfer 3 pockets at a time to the air fryer basket. Air-fry at 350°F for 4 to 5 minutes, until the phyllo dough is light brown in color. Flip the pockets over halfway through the cooking process. Repeat with the remaining 3 pockets.

5. Serve warm.

# Easy Churros

Servings: 12
Cooking Time: 10 Minutes
**Ingredients:**
- ½ cup Water
- 4 tablespoons (¼ cup/½ stick) Butter
- ¼ teaspoon Table salt
- ½ cup All-purpose flour
- 2 Large egg(s)
- ¼ cup Granulated white sugar
- 2 teaspoons Ground cinnamon

**Directions:**
1. Bring the water, butter, and salt to a boil in a small saucepan set over high heat, stirring occasionally.

2. When the butter has fully melted, reduce the heat to medium and stir in the flour to form a dough. Continue cooking, stirring constantly, to dry out the dough until it coats the bottom and sides of the pan with a film, even a crust. Remove the pan from the heat, scrape the dough into a bowl, and cool for 15 minutes.

3. Using an electric hand mixer at medium speed, beat in the egg, or eggs one at a time, until the dough is smooth and firm enough to hold its shape.

4. Mix the sugar and cinnamon in a small bowl. Scoop up 1 tablespoon of the dough and roll it in the sugar mixture to form a small, coated tube about ½ inch in diameter and 2 inches long. Set it aside and make 5 more tubes for the small batch or 11 more for the large one.

5. Set the tubes on a plate and freeze for 20 minutes. Meanwhile, Preheat the air fryer to 375°F .

6. Set 3 frozen tubes in the basket for a small batch or 6 for a large one with as much air space between them as possible. Air-fry undisturbed for 10 minutes, or until puffed, brown, and set.

7. Use kitchen tongs to transfer the churros to a wire rack to cool for at least 5 minutes. Meanwhile, air-fry and cool the second batch of churros in the same way.

# Roasted Pecan Clusters

Servings:8

Cooking Time: 8 Minutes
**Ingredients:**
- 3 ounces whole shelled pecans
- 1 tablespoon salted butter, melted
- 2 teaspoons confectioners' erythritol
- ½ teaspoon ground cinnamon
- ½ cup low-carb chocolate chips

**Directions:**
1. In a medium bowl, toss pecans with butter, then sprinkle with erythritol and cinnamon.

2. Place pecans into ungreased air fryer basket. Adjust the temperature to 350°F and set the timer for 8 minutes, shaking the basket two times during cooking. They will feel soft initially but get crunchy as they cool.

3. Line a large baking sheet with parchment paper.

4. Place chocolate in a medium microwave-safe bowl. Microwave on high, heating in 20-second increments and stirring until melted. Place 1 teaspoon chocolate in a rounded mound on ungreased parchment-lined baking sheet, then press 1 pecan into top, repeating with remaining chocolate and pecans.

5. Place baking sheet into refrigerator to cool at least 30 minutes. Once cooled, store clusters in a large sealed container in refrigerator up to 5 days.

# Glazed Donuts

Servings: 2 – 4
Cooking Time: 25 Minutes
**Ingredients:**
- 1 can [8 oz.] refrigerated croissant dough
- Cooking spray
- 1 can [16 oz.] vanilla frosting

**Directions:**
1. Cut the croissant dough into 1-inch-round slices. Make a hole in the center of each one to create a donut.

2. Put the donuts in the Air Fryer basket, taking care not to overlap any, and spritz with cooking spray. You may need to cook everything in multiple batches.

3. Cook at 400°F for 2 minutes. Turn the donuts over and cook for another 3 minutes.

4. Place the rolls on a paper plate.

5. Microwave a half-cup of frosting for 30 seconds and pour a drizzling of the frosting over the donuts before serving.

# Party S´mores

Servings: 6
Cooking Time: 15 Minutes
**Ingredients:**
- 2 dark chocolate bars, cut into 12 pieces
- 12 buttermilk biscuits
- 12 marshmallows

**Directions:**
1. Preheat air fryer to 350°F. Place 6 biscuits in the air fryer. Top each square with a piece of dark chocolate. Bake

for 2 minutes. Add a marshmallow to each piece of chocolate. Cook for another minute. Remove and top with another piece of biscuit. Serve warm.

## Monkey Bread

Servings:6
Cooking Time: 20 Minutes
**Ingredients:**
- 1 can refrigerated biscuit dough
- ½ cup granulated sugar
- 1 tablespoon ground cinnamon
- ¼ cup salted butter, melted
- ¼ cup brown sugar
- Cooking spray

**Directions:**
1. Preheat the air fryer to 325°F. Spray a 6" round cake pan with cooking spray. Separate biscuits and cut each into four pieces.
2. In a large bowl, stir granulated sugar with cinnamon. Toss biscuit pieces in the cinnamon and sugar mixture until well coated. Place each biscuit piece in prepared pan.
3. In a medium bowl, stir together butter and brown sugar. Pour mixture evenly over the biscuit pieces.
4. Place pan in the air fryer basket and cook 20 minutes until brown. Let cool 10 minutes before flipping bread out of the pan and serving.

## Banana Chips With Chocolate Glaze

Servings: 2
Cooking Time: 20 Minutes
**Ingredients:**
- 2 banana, cut into slices
- 1/4 teaspoon lemon zest
- 1 tablespoon agave syrup
- 1 tablespoon cocoa powder
- 1 tablespoon coconut oil, melted

**Directions:**
1. Toss the bananas with the lemon zest and agave syrup. Transfer your bananas to the parchment-lined cooking basket.
2. Bake in the preheated Air Fryer at 370°F for 12 minutes, turning them over halfway through the cooking time.
3. In the meantime, melt the coconut oil in your microwave; add the cocoa powder and whisk to combine well.
4. Serve the baked banana chips. Enjoy!

## Orange Marmalade

Servings: 4
Cooking Time: 20 Minutes
**Ingredients:**
- 4 oranges, peeled and chopped
- 3 cups sugar
- 1½ cups water

**Directions:**

1. In a pan that fits your air fryer, mix the oranges with the sugar and the water; stir.
2. Place the pan in the fryer and cook at 340°F for 20 minutes.
3. Stir well, divide into cups, refrigerate, and serve cold.

## Chocolate Brownie

Servings: 4
Cooking Time: 16 Minutes
**Ingredients:**
- 1 cup bananas, overripe
- 1 scoop protein powder
- 2 tbsp unsweetened cocoa powder
- 1/2 cup almond butter, melted

**Directions:**
1. Preheat the air fryer to 325°F.
2. Spray air fryer baking pan with cooking spray.
3. Add all ingredients into the blender and blend until smooth.
4. Pour batter into the prepared pan and place in the air fryer basket.
5. Cook brownie for 16 minutes.
6. Serve and enjoy.

## Baked Apple

Servings: 6
Cooking Time: 20 Minutes
**Ingredients:**
- 3 small Honey Crisp or other baking apples
- 3 tablespoons maple syrup
- 3 tablespoons chopped pecans
- 1 tablespoon firm butter, cut into 6 pieces

**Directions:**
1. Put ½ cup water in the drawer of the air fryer.
2. Wash apples well and dry them.
3. Split apples in half. Remove core and a little of the flesh to make a cavity for the pecans.
4. Place apple halves in air fryer basket, cut side up.
5. Spoon 1½ teaspoons pecans into each cavity.
6. Spoon ½ tablespoon maple syrup over pecans in each apple.
7. Top each apple with ½ teaspoon butter.
8. Cook at 360°F for 20 minutes, until apples are tender.

## Fried Pineapple Chunks

Servings: 3
Cooking Time: 10 Minutes
**Ingredients:**
- 3 tablespoons Cornstarch
- 1 Large egg white, beaten until foamy
- 1 cup Ground vanilla wafer cookies (not low-fat cookies)
- ¼ teaspoon Ground dried ginger
- 18 Fresh 1-inch chunks peeled and cored pineapple

**Directions:**
1. Preheat the air fryer to 400°F.

2. Put the cornstarch in a medium or large bowl. Put the beaten egg white in a small bowl. Pour the cookie crumbs and ground dried ginger into a large zip-closed plastic bag, shaking it a bit to combine them.

3. Dump the pineapple chunks into the bowl with the cornstarch. Toss and stir until well coated. Use your cleaned fingers or a large fork like a shovel to pick up a few pineapple chunks, shake off any excess cornstarch, and put them in the bowl with the egg white. Stir gently, then pick them up and let any excess egg white slip back into the rest. Put them in the bag with the crumb mixture. Repeat the cornstarch-then-egg process until all the pineapple chunks are in the bag. Seal the bag and shake gently, turning the bag this way and that, to coat the pieces well.

4. Set the coated pineapple chunks in the basket with as much air space between them as possible. Even a fraction of an inch will work, but they should not touch. Air-fry undisturbed for 10 minutes, or until golden brown and crisp.

5. Gently dump the contents of the basket onto a wire rack. Cool for at least 5 minutes or up to 15 minutes before serving.

## Cinnamon-sugar Pretzel Bites

Servings:4
Cooking Time: 1 Hour 10 Minutes
**Ingredients:**
- 1 cup all-purpose flour
- 1 teaspoon quick-rise yeast
- 2 tablespoons granulated sugar, divided
- ¼ teaspoon salt
- 1 tablespoon olive oil
- ⅓ cup warm water
- 2 teaspoons baking soda
- 1 teaspoon ground cinnamon
- Cooking spray

**Directions:**
1. In a large bowl, mix flour, yeast, 2 teaspoons sugar, and salt until combined.
2. Pour in oil and water and stir until a dough begins to form and pull away from the edges of the bowl. Remove dough from the bowl and transfer to a lightly floured surface. Knead 10 minutes until dough is mostly smooth.
3. Spritz dough with cooking spray and place into a large clean bowl. Cover with plastic wrap and let rise 1 hour.
4. Preheat the air fryer to 400°F.
5. Press dough into a 6" × 4" rectangle. Cut dough into twenty-four even pieces.
6. Fill a medium saucepan over medium-high heat halfway with water and bring to a boil. Add baking soda and let it boil 1 minute, then add pretzel bites. You may need to work in batches. Cook 45 seconds, then remove from water and drain. They will be puffy but should have mostly maintained their shape.
7. Spritz pretzel bites with cooking spray. Place in the air fryer basket and cook 5 minutes until golden brown.

8. In a small bowl, mix remaining sugar and cinnamon. When pretzel bites are done cooking, immediately toss in cinnamon and sugar mixture and serve.

## Easy Mug Brownie

Servings: 1
Cooking Time: 10 Minutes
**Ingredients:**
- 1 scoop chocolate protein powder
- 1 tbsp cocoa powder
- 1/2 tsp baking powder
- 1/4 cup unsweetened almond milk

**Directions:**
1. Add baking powder, protein powder, and cocoa powder in a mug and mix well.
2. Add milk in a mug and stir well.
3. Place the mug in the air fryer and cook at 390°F for 10 minutes.
4. Serve and enjoy.

## Dark Chocolate Peanut Butter S'mores

Servings: 4
Cooking Time: 6 Minutes
**Ingredients:**
- 4 graham cracker sheets
- 4 marshmallows
- 4 teaspoons chunky peanut butter
- 4 ounces dark chocolate
- ½ teaspoon ground cinnamon

**Directions:**
1. Preheat the air fryer to 390°F. Break the graham crackers in half so you have 8 pieces.
2. Place 4 pieces of graham cracker on the bottom of the air fryer. Top each with one of the marshmallows and bake for 6 or 7 minutes, or until the marshmallows have a golden brown center.
3. While cooking, slather each of the remaining graham crackers with 1 teaspoon peanut butter.
4. When baking completes, carefully remove each of the graham crackers, add 1 ounce of dark chocolate on top of the marshmallow, and lightly sprinkle with cinnamon. Top with the remaining peanut butter graham cracker to make the sandwich. Serve immediately.

## Coconut Rice Cake

Servings: 8
Cooking Time: 30 Minutes
**Ingredients:**
- 1 cup all-natural coconut water
- 1 cup unsweetened coconut milk
- 1 teaspoon almond extract
- ¼ teaspoon salt
- 4 tablespoons honey

- cooking spray
- ¾ cup raw jasmine rice
- 2 cups sliced or cubed fruit

**Directions:**

1. In a medium bowl, mix together the coconut water, coconut milk, almond extract, salt, and honey.
2. Spray air fryer baking pan with cooking spray and add the rice.
3. Pour liquid mixture over rice.
4. Cook at 360°F for 15minutes. Stir and cook for 15 minutes longer or until rice grains are tender.
5. Allow cake to cool slightly. Run a dull knife around edge of cake, inside the pan. Turn the cake out onto a platter and garnish with fruit.

## Cinnamon Pretzels

Servings:6
Cooking Time: 10 Minutes
**Ingredients:**
- 1½ cups shredded mozzarella cheese
- 1 cup blanched finely ground almond flour
- 2 tablespoons salted butter, melted, divided
- ¼ cup granular erythritol, divided
- 1 teaspoon ground cinnamon

**Directions:**

1. Place mozzarella, flour, 1 tablespoon butter, and 2 tablespoons erythritol in a large microwave-safe bowl. Microwave on high 45 seconds, then stir with a fork until a smooth dough ball forms.
2. Separate dough into six equal sections. Gently roll each section into a 12" rope, then fold into a pretzel shape.
3. Place pretzels into ungreased air fryer basket. Adjust the temperature to 370°F and set the timer for 8 minutes, turning pretzels halfway through cooking.
4. In a small bowl, combine remaining butter, remaining erythritol, and cinnamon. Brush ½ mixture on both sides of pretzels.
5. Place pretzels back into air fryer and cook an additional 2 minutes at 370°F.
6. Transfer pretzels to a large plate. Brush on both sides with remaining butter mixture, then let cool 5 minutes before serving.

## Shortbread Fingers

Servings: 10
Cooking Time: 20 Minutes
**Ingredients:**
- 1 ½ cups butter
- 1 cup flour
- ¾ cup sugar
- Cooking spray

**Directions:**

1. Pre-heat your Air Fryer to 350°F.
2. In a bowl. combine the flour and sugar.

3. Cut each stick of butter into small chunks. Add the chunks into the flour and the sugar.
4. Blend the butter into the mixture to combine everything well.
5. Use your hands to knead the mixture, forming a smooth consistency.
6. Shape the mixture into 10 equal-sized finger shapes, marking them with the tines of a fork for decoration if desired.
7. Lightly spritz the Air Fryer basket with the cooking spray. Place the cookies inside, spacing them out well.
8. Bake the cookies for 12 minutes.
9. Let cool slightly before serving. Alternatively, you can store the cookies in an airtight container for up to 3 days.

## Ricotta Stuffed Apples

Servings: 4
Cooking Time: 25 Minutes
**Ingredients:**
- ½ cup cheddar cheese
- ¼ cup raisins
- 2 apples
- ½ tsp ground cinnamon

**Directions:**

1. Preheat air fryer to 350°F. Combine cheddar cheese and raisins in a bowl and set aside. Chop apples lengthwise and discard the core and stem. Sprinkle each half with cinnamon and stuff each half with 1/4 of the cheddar mixture. Bake for 7 minutes, turn, and Bake for 13 minutes more until the apples are soft. Serve immediately.

## Pecan Snowball Cookies

Servings:12
Cooking Time: 24 Minutes
**Ingredients:**
- 1 cup chopped pecans
- ½ cup salted butter, melted
- ½ cup coconut flour
- ¾ cup confectioners' erythritol, divided
- 1 teaspoon vanilla extract

**Directions:**

1. In a food processor, blend together pecans, butter, flour, ½ cup erythritol, and vanilla 1 minute until a dough forms.
2. Form dough into twelve individual cookie balls, about 1 tablespoon each.
3. Cut three pieces of parchment to fit air fryer basket. Place four cookies on each ungreased parchment and place one piece parchment with cookies into air fryer basket. Adjust air fryer temperature to 325°F and set the timer for 8 minutes. Repeat cooking with remaining batches.
4. When the timer goes off, allow cookies to cool 5 minutes on a large serving plate until cool enough to handle. While still warm, dust cookies with remaining erythritol. Allow to cool completely, about 15 minutes, before serving.

# Delicious Vanilla Custard

Servings: 2
Cooking Time: 20 Minutes
**Ingredients:**
- 5 eggs
- 2 tbsp swerve
- 1 tsp vanilla
- ½ cup unsweetened almond milk
- ½ cup cream cheese

**Directions:**
1. Add eggs in a bowl and beat using a hand mixer.
2. Add cream cheese, sweetener, vanilla, and almond milk and beat for 2 minutes more.
3. Spray two ramekins with cooking spray.
4. Pour batter into the prepared ramekins.
5. Preheat the air fryer to 350°F.
6. Place ramekins into the air fryer and cook for 20 minutes.
7. Serve and enjoy.

# Lemon Berries Stew

Servings: 4
Cooking Time: 20 Minutes
**Ingredients:**
- 1 pound strawberries, halved
- 4 tablespoons stevia
- 1 tablespoon lemon juice
- 1 and ½ cups water

**Directions:**
1. In a pan that fits your air fryer, mix all the ingredients, toss, put it in the fryer and cook at 340°F for 20 minutes. Divide the stew into cups and serve cold.

# Hearty Banana Pastry

Servings:2
Cooking Time: 15 Minutes
**Ingredients:**
- 3 tbsp honey
- 2 puff pastry sheets, cut into thin strips
- fresh berries to serve

**Directions:**
1. Preheat your air fryer up to 340°F.
2. Place the banana slices into the cooking basket. Cover with the pastry strips and top with honey. Cook for 10 minutes. Serve with fresh berries.

# Brown Sugar Cookies

Servings:9
Cooking Time: 27 Minutes
**Ingredients:**
- 4 tablespoons salted butter, melted
- ⅓ cup granular brown erythritol
- 1 large egg
- ½ teaspoon vanilla extract

- 1 cup blanched finely ground almond flour
- ½ teaspoon baking powder

**Directions:**
1. In a large bowl, whisk together butter, erythritol, egg, and vanilla. Add flour and baking powder, and stir until combined.
2. Separate dough into nine pieces and roll into balls, about 2 tablespoons each.
3. Cut three pieces of parchment paper to fit your air fryer basket and place three cookies on each ungreased piece. Place one piece of parchment into air fryer basket. Adjust the temperature to 300°F and set the timer for 9 minutes. Edges of cookies will be browned when done. Repeat with remaining cookies. Serve warm.

# Cranberries Pudding

Servings: 6
Cooking Time: 20 Minutes
**Ingredients:**
- 1 cup cauliflower rice
- 2 cups almond milk
- ½ cup cranberries
- 1 teaspoon vanilla extract

**Directions:**
1. In a pan that fits your air fryer, mix all the ingredients, whisk a bit, put the pan in the fryer and cook at 360°F for 20 minutes. Stir the pudding, divide into bowls and serve cold.

# Coconut Macaroons

Servings: 12
Cooking Time: 8 Minutes
**Ingredients:**
- 1⅓ cups shredded, sweetened coconut
- 4½ teaspoons flour
- 2 tablespoons sugar
- 1 egg white
- ½ teaspoon almond extract

**Directions:**
1. Preheat air fryer to 330°F.
2. Mix all ingredients together.
3. Shape coconut mixture into 12 balls.
4. Place all 12 macaroons in air fryer basket. They won't expand, so you can place them close together, but they shouldn't touch.
5. Cook at 330°F for 8 minutes, until golden.

# Fruit Turnovers

Servings: 6
Cooking Time: 25 Minutes
**Ingredients:**
- 1 sheet puff pastry dough
- 6 tsp peach preserves
- 3 kiwi, sliced
- 1 large egg, beaten

- 1 tbsp icing sugar

**Directions:**

1. Prepare puff pastry by cutting it into 6 rectangles. Roll out the pastry with a rolling pin into 5-inch squares. On your workspace, position one square so that it looks like a diamond with points to the top and bottom. Spoon 1 tsp of the preserves on the bottom half and spread it, leaving a ½-inch border from the edge. Place half of one kiwi on top of the preserves. Brush the clean edges with the egg, then fold the top corner over the filling to make a triangle. Crimp with a fork to seal the pastry. Brush the top of the pastry with egg. Preheat air fryer to 350°F. Put the pastries in the greased frying basket. Air Fry for 10 minutes, flipping once until golden and puffy. Remove from the fryer, let cool and dush with icing sugar. Serve.

# Brownies

Servings: 8
Cooking Time: 20 Minutes
**Ingredients:**

- ½ cup all-purpose flour
- 1 cup granulated sugar
- ¼ cup cocoa powder
- ½ teaspoon baking powder
- 6 tablespoons salted butter, melted
- 1 large egg
- ½ cup semisweet chocolate chips

**Directions:**

1. Preheat the air fryer to 350°F. Generously grease two 6" round cake pans.
2. In a large bowl, combine flour, sugar, cocoa powder, and baking powder.
3. Add butter, egg, and chocolate chips to dry ingredients. Stir until well combined.
4. Divide batter between prepared pans. Place in the air fryer basket and cook 20 minutes until a toothpick inserted into the center comes out clean. Cool 5 minutes before serving.

# Easy Keto Danish

Servings:6
Cooking Time: 12 Minutes
**Ingredients:**

- 1½ cups shredded mozzarella cheese
- ½ cup blanched finely ground almond flour
- 3 ounces cream cheese, divided
- ¼ cup confectioners' erythritol
- 1 tablespoon lemon juice

**Directions:**

1. Place mozzarella, flour, and 1 ounce cream cheese in a large microwave-safe bowl. Microwave on high 45 seconds, then stir with a fork until a soft dough forms.
2. Separate dough into six equal sections and press each in a single layer into an ungreased 4" × 4" square nonstick baking dish to form six even squares that touch.

3. In a small bowl, mix remaining cream cheese, erythritol, and lemon juice. Place 1 tablespoon mixture in center of each piece of dough in baking dish. Fold all four corners of each dough piece halfway to center to reach cream cheese mixture.
4. Place dish into air fryer. Adjust the temperature to 320°F and set the timer for 12 minutes. The center and edges will be browned when done. Let cool 10 minutes before serving.

# Apple Pie Crumble

Servings:4
Cooking Time:25 Minutes
**Ingredients:**

- 1 can apple pie
- ¼ cup butter, softened
- 9 tablespoons self-rising flour
- 7 tablespoons caster sugar
- Pinch of salt

**Directions:**

1. Preheat the Air fryer to 320°F and grease a baking dish.
2. Mix all the ingredients in a bowl until a crumbly mixture is formed.
3. Arrange the apple pie in the baking dish and top with the mixture.
4. Transfer the baking dish into the Air fryer basket and cook for about 25 minutes.
5. Dish out in a platter and serve.

# Pumpkin Cake

Servings:8
Cooking Time: 25 Minutes
**Ingredients:**

- 4 tablespoons salted butter, melted
- ½ cup granular brown erythritol
- ¼ cup pure pumpkin puree
- 1 cup blanched finely ground almond flour
- ½ teaspoon baking powder
- ⅛ teaspoon salt
- 1 teaspoon pumpkin pie spice

**Directions:**

1. Mix all ingredients in a large bowl. Pour batter into an ungreased 6" round nonstick baking dish.
2. Place dish into air fryer basket. Adjust the temperature to 300°F and set the timer for 25 minutes. The top will be dark brown, and a toothpick inserted in the center should come out clean when done. Let cool 30 minutes before serving.

# Moon Pie

Servings:4
Cooking Time: 10 Minutes
**Ingredients:**
- 8 large marshmallows
- 8 squares each of dark, milk and white chocolate

**Directions:**
1. Arrange the cracker halves on a cutting board. Put 2 marshmallows onto half of the graham cracker halves. Place 2 squares of chocolate onto the cracker with the marshmallows. Put the remaining crackers on top to create 4 sandwiches. Wrap each one in the baking paper so it resembles a parcel. Cook in the fryer for 5 minutes at 340°F.

# INDEX

Sweet And Spicy Pork Ribs 62

Sweet Chili Peanuts 22

Sweet Nutty Chicken Breasts 46

Sweet Pepper Nachos 89

Sweet Potato Chips 19

Sweet Potato Fries 101

Sweet Potato–wrapped Shrimp 75

Sweet Roasted Carrots 88

Sweet Roasted Pumpkin Rounds 93

Sweet-and-salty Pretzels 28

Swordfish With Capers And Tomatoes 70

## T

Taj Tofu 39

Tandoori Cauliflower 97

Tangy Mustard Wings 46

Teriyaki Chicken Legs 51

Teriyaki Salmon 75

Thick-crust Pepperoni Pizza 17

Thyme Lentil Patties 86

Thyme Scallops 74

Thyme Sweet Potato Chips 21

Toasted Coconut Flakes 104

Toasted Ravioli 84

Tomato & Garlic Roasted Potatoes 16

Tomatoes Frittata 33

Tortilla Chips 16

Tortilla Fried Pies 109

Tortilla Pizza Margherita 90

Tri-color Frittata 30

Tuna And Arugula Salad 34

Tuna-stuffed Tomatoes 70

Turkey-hummus Wraps 47

Turmeric Crispy Chickpeas 89

Tuscan Stuffed Chicken 41

Twice-baked Broccoli-cheddar Potatoes 87

Twice-baked Potatoes With Pancetta 101

## V

Vegetable Nuggets 81

Very Berry Breakfast Puffs 33

## W

Wasabi-coated Pork Loin Chops 58

White Wheat Walnut Bread 38

Whole-grain Cornbread 35

Wilted Brussels Sprout Slaw 92

Wine Infused Mushrooms 82

## Y

Yeast Rolls 95

Yellow Squash And Zucchinis Dish 95

Yummy Shredded Chicken 52

Yummy Stuffed Chicken Breast 41

## Z

Zesty Mahi Mahi 78

Zucchini And Spring Onions Cakes 33

Zucchini Fries 97

Zucchini Gratin 81

Printed in Great Britain
by Amazon

84348392R20070